厦门知识产权
典型案例研析

Studies on Amoy Classic IP Cases

厦门市思明区人民法院
厦门大学知识产权研究院   主编

Amoy Siming District People's Court
Intellectual Property Research Institute of XMU   Edited

知识产权出版社
全国百佳图书出版单位

图书在版编目（CIP）数据

厦门知识产权典型案例研析／厦门市思明区人民法院，厦门大学知识产权研究院主编.—北京：知识产权出版社，2018.1
  ISBN 978-7-5130-5238-2

Ⅰ.①厦… Ⅱ.①厦…②厦… Ⅲ.①知识产权—审判—案例—厦门 Ⅳ.①D927.574.340.5

中国版本图书馆CIP数据核字（2017）第261218号

责任编辑：邓 莹　　　　　　　责任校对：谷 洋
责任出版：刘译文　　　　　　　封面设计：SUN 工作室

厦门知识产权典型案例研析
Xiamen Zhishichanquan Dianxing Anli Yanxi

厦门市思明区人民法院
　　　　　　　　　　　　　主编
厦门大学知识产权研究院

出版发行：知识产权出版社 有限责任公司	网　　址：http://www.ipph.cn
社　　址：北京市海淀区气象路50号院	邮　　编：100081
责编电话：010-82000860 转 8346	责编邮箱：dengying@cnipr.com
发行电话：010-82000860 转 8101/8102	发行传真：010-82000893/82005070/82000270
印　　刷：北京科信印刷有限公司	经　　销：新华书店及相关专业书店
开　　本：720mm×960mm　1/16	印　　张：13.5
版　　次：2018年1月第1版	印　　次：2018年1月第1次印刷
字　　数：235千字	定　　价：45.00元
ISBN 978-7-5130-5238-2	

出版权专有　侵权必究
如有印装质量问题，本社负责调换。

《厦门知识产权典型案例研析》
编委会

主　编：傅远平　林秀芹
副主编：刘德芬　朱　冬
参　编：李缘缘　倪宗泽　曾争志
　　　　林　鸿　曹宇君　李雅光
　　　　刘　禹　田双莉　王灵烨
　　　　赵　涛　张伟昌

Studies on Amoy Classic IP Cases

Editorial Board

Chief Editors

Fu Yuanping   Lin Xiuqin

Deputy Chief Editors

Liu Defen   Zhu Dong

Contributors

Li Yuanyuan	Ni Zongze	Zeng Zhengzhi
Lin Hong	Cao Yujun	Li Yaguang
Liu Yu	Tian Shuangli	Wang Lingye
Zhao Tao	Zhang Weichang	

序　一

实践是理论之源。2017年5月5日，习近平总书记在中国政法大学考察时提出，"法学学科是实践性很强的学科，法学教育要处理好知识教学和实践教学的关系"。"国家知识产权培训（福建）基地思明法院实践中心暨厦门大学知识产权研究院理论与实践创新基地"就是"打破高校和社会之间的体制壁垒"，融会贯通知识教学和实践教学的典范样本。早在2010年，厦门市思明区人民法院与厦门大学知识产权研究院共同成立的这一基地，让法官走进校园，走上讲台，总结审判经验，分享办案心得，"将优质司法实践资源引入高校"；也让法学专业的大学生们获得了走进法院，接触实务，学以致用，感受审判的畅通渠道，为将来走向社会运用所学提供了难得宝贵机会。

案例是法院案件审判工作的最终成果，是法官智慧的结晶，司法文书以及由此凝炼而成的案例，集中体现了司法机关对于法律的理解和对于情理法碰撞冲突的综合把握。优秀的案例不仅能够体现法律的具体实践过程、指导审判，更能够起到宣传法制、教育公众的重要作用。作为福建省案件数最多的法院，思明法院的法官们每年都要审理数百个案件，但并不是每一个案件都具有典型性。本书是思明法院与厦门大学知识产权研究院共同努力，从思明法院知识产权庭历年审理的几千个案件中精心挑选出的具有参考、启发、规范作用的典型案例，全面涵盖知识产权民事、刑事、行政各种类型。这些案件有的是某类案件中最具有代表性的判决，有的是刚出现的新类型案件，有的反映某一行业发展中遇到的趋势性法律问题，充分、集中地展现了思明法院知识产权庭成立8年来的审判成果，也充分展现了厦门大学知识产权研究院对于经典案例的深入研究和理论思考。

经济全球化、科技发展等因素决定了知识产权保护全球化、国际化的趋势，我国处于经济高速发展、法制不断完善的进程当中，本书采用中英文双语的编纂方式，也向全球充分展示我国在知识产权法制保护进程中所做出的努力和实践，这更是一种全新的的尝试。

时值思明法院建院60周年之际，思明法院历来具有重视调研、文以载道的光荣传统，案例、调研、信息等工作长期名列国内基层法院前列，是最高院《人民法院案例选》先进组织单位和福建省唯一连续3年蝉联全国法院年度学术讨论会"组织工作先进奖"的基层法院。希望本书的出版能给广大的法律学习与从业者们带来更多的思考，从而深化对法律的理解、研究、应用。

是为序。

厦门市思明区人民法院党组书记、院长

傅远平

2017年11月12日

序 二

纵观时下之国际社会，国家间强弱变局之关键，竞争力高低失衡之所在，为创新。党的十九大报告中指出，要加快建设创新型国家。创新是引领发展的第一动力，是建设现代化经济体系的战略支撑。要倡导创新文化，强化知识产权的创造、保护、运用。其中知识产权内容之开发、维持和延续，很大程度上依赖知识产权法律制度的完善与运行。

夫法律之行止于纸书制度之说者，实难契现实问题之本，而利社会经济之进步。法律之维治理社会，当脱离制度文本之形，于运行之中定争止纷，此理与"纸上得来终觉浅，绝知此事要躬行"之谓，存异曲同工之妙。窃以为知识产权法之行，亦当如此。知识产权法不应束之高阁于文本纸卷之中，或限阈激烈仅存法理论争之内。知识产权法律制度，如欲有效调整知识产权有关社会关系，便需将规则之规定应用于社会问题之上。二者紧密结合，方能平社会之争端，促创新之发展。此规则与问题之结合过程，司法审判典型案例之典文指引，尤为应秉之要。

知识产权之客体，种类繁多。特别近年来，随着社会经济文化和科学技术飞速发展，知识产权之内容大为丰富、传播方式也更为多样。在知识产权之创造、保护、运用过程中，可涉争端样态攀升、复杂性增大。知识产权保护对象之多样性与知识产权案件之技术专业性等特征，导致知识产权纠纷之实体与程序法律适用，较之传统民事诉讼纠纷，更为复杂和困难。然内涉复杂性与困难性之知识产权纠纷案件，在案件审判经验之上，仍有相通之法律机理指导、仍存相似之法律规则适用。对知识产权典型案例之掇选、编排，可作为法院审判相同或相似案件时之参考和当事人诉讼时佐证说理之初步材料。

厦门市思明区人民法院,基于多年一线知识产权审判实践和审判经验,对其中典型案例进行筛择萃取,携手厦门大学知识产权研究院共同剖析精研,形成本书。本书精要反映厦门市思明区人民法院在处理相关知识产权案件之审判思路,展示了我国知识产权司法保护之实践与风范。书中收录10个厦门市思明区人民法院审理的具有典型意义之知识产权一审民事、行政和刑事案件,涉及著作权、商标权以及其他不正当竞争等多种类型知识产权案件。本书以案成篇,每篇典型案例皆为承办案件法官亲自撰写,由其心血凝结而成。结构分为案情简介、裁判结果、争议焦点、案例评析与典型意义五大部分。案情简介扼要介绍当事人的诉讼主张,裁判结果展示法院对案件的态度和立场,争议焦点整理案件的核心争议,案例评析表明法院的审理思路和裁判理由,典型意义体现案件之可能社会影响与借鉴意义。

本书将厦门市思明区人民法院在审理案件时之司法原则与司法裁量,较为完整和精要的展示给读者,是社会公众了解厦门市思明区人民法院知识产权审判工作和司法保护水平的优良窗口。知识产权司法、行政执法以及理论研究之同仁志士,亦可从中了解厦门市思明区人民法院知识产权立法精神和法律规则之理解与运用,对知识产权问题之研究与实践,也将大有裨益。

鉴于本书收录之案例篇幅与数量有限,其中难免存在周延不尽之处。谨以此书求教于广大法官、学者以及其他致力于知识产权法律制度与实践的各位先进,恳请赐教和共同精进。

厦门大学知识产权研究院院长

林秀芹

2017 年 12 月 15 日

目 录

赵某某诉富安邦、南方饭店著作权侵权纠纷案研析 ……………………（1）
华晟公司诉关西公司著作权侵权纠纷案研析………………………（10）
兴茂公司诉誉海公司、东本公司侵害商标权及不正当竞争纠纷案
  研析……………………………………………………………………（21）
厦门宝岛眼镜诉福州宝岛眼镜不正当竞争纠纷案研析………………（30）
银据公司诉集恩图造公司等不正当竞争纠纷案研析…………………（39）
王某某与厦门工商局、宇电公司行政处罚决定案研析………………（47）
萧某某假冒注册商标罪案研析…………………………………………（56）
张某某假冒注册商标罪案研析…………………………………………（67）
林某某、王某某等 8 人销售假冒注册商标的商品罪案研析…………（73）
叶某、张某某销售假冒注册商标的商品罪案研析……………………（82）

Catalogue

Study on Zhao Moumou vs. Fu'an bang Co. & South Hotel Copyright
　Infringement Dispute ·· (91)
Study on Huasheng Co. vs. Kansai Co. Copyright Infringement Dispute
　·· (102)
Study on Xingmao Co. vs. Yuhai Co. & Dongben Co. Trademark
　Infringement & Unfair Competition Dispute ······················ (116)
Study on Amoy Baodao vs. Fuzhou Baodao Unfair Competition Dispute
　·· (127)
Study on Yinju Co. vs. Joint Co., et al Unfair Competition Dispute ······ (138)
Study on Wang Moumou vs. Amoy Municipal Administration for Industry
　and Commerce & Yudian Co. Administrative Penalty Dispute ········ (150)
Study on Xiao Moumou Crime of Counterfeiting Registered Trademark
　·· (163)
Study on Zhang Moumou Crime of Counterfeiting Registered Trademark
　·· (173)
Study on Lin Moumou et al. Crime of Selling Counterfeit Registered
　Trademark Goods ·· (180)
Study on Ye Mou, Zhang Moumou Crime of Selling Counterfeit
　Registered Trademark Goods ······································· (191)

赵某某诉富安邦、南方饭店著作权侵权纠纷案研析

一、案情简介

原告赵某某诉称，1992年原告经朝华出版社出版了自己的美术作品《京剧脸谱》（2003年1月再版时名为《中国京剧脸谱画册》）。画册中的568幅京剧脸谱、21幅京剧人物画都是原告独立创作。被告富安邦公司系被告南方饭店公司主楼屋顶上悬挂的广告的发布者、使用者，被告富安邦公司擅自使用了原告《中国京剧脸谱画册》中"程普"等12幅京剧脸谱美术作品。被告富安邦公司在使用原告作品时，没有注明作者姓名，也未支付报酬，原告提起诉讼，请求法院判令二被告立即停止侵权行为；在《厦门日报》上向原告公开赔礼道歉；连带赔偿经济损失共计人民币18万元整，以及制止侵权行为的合理费用人民币2 000元。

被告富安邦公司辩称，首先，京剧脸谱是中国传统的民间艺术，是艺术家们长久传承下来的。原告不享有讼争京剧脸谱的著作权，其著作权依据仅是汇编的画册。其次，原告没有证据证明被告广告牌上的京剧脸谱出自原告画册。被告委托他人制作该广告布，使用的京剧脸谱是广告制作人从广告制作大全中取得，与原告的画册没有直接关系。再次，讼争京剧脸谱很常见，被告不知上述脸谱有著作权，被告侵权不具有主观故意。最后，被告发布该脸谱广告的时间很短，2010年6月27日已将讼争广告布覆盖，且在7月27日改用其他广告布。使用该广告期间被告并未因此获利，也没有造成原告实际损失。

二、裁判结果

厦门市思明区人民法院经审理认为,原告赵某某享有《中国京剧脸谱画册》中京剧脸谱美术作品的著作权,其权利应受法律保护。被告富安邦公司未经原告许可擅自使用原告的京剧脸谱美术作品进行广告宣传,其行为侵犯了原告的著作权,应当承担停止侵权、赔偿损失的民事责任。关于赔礼道歉的适用,法院认为被告使用原告作品的行为并未对原告的精神、名誉造成损害,故原告要求赔礼道歉缺乏事实依据,应予驳回。

三、争议焦点

本案的争议焦点有:
(1) 原告是否对讼争脸谱图片享有著作权?
(2) 被告是否侵犯了原告的著作权?

四、案例评析

赵某某是中国著名京剧人物画家。涉案作品《中国京剧脸谱画册》一书于2003年再版,书中部分脸谱被很多企业广泛使用,赵某某认为自己的著作权受到侵犯,于是开始了持久而大规模的系列维权之举。赵某某已在北京、上海、重庆、山西、内蒙古、浙江、河北、湖南、福建等地区提起了几十起诉讼,被告包括不限于网站、工艺品生产商、销售商、大型商场、广告公司、酒店、食品公司以及艺术饰品公司,等等。在这一系列案件当中,原告均主张其绘制的脸谱具有独创性,被告使用脸谱的行为侵犯了原告的著作权,请求法院判决被告停止侵权、赔偿损失。

(一) 原告是否对讼争脸谱图片享有著作权

原告主张被告侵犯其著作权的前提是原告享有有效的著作权。这主要包括以下几层意思:第一,原告是其主张的画册里的京剧脸谱原始权利人或者合法继受权利人;第二,涉案京剧脸谱构成著作权法上的作品;第三,原告基于京剧脸谱所享有的权利尚未由其放弃或者进入公共领域。其中第二点最为关键。根据我国《著作权法实施条例》第2条规定,作品是指文学、艺术和科学领域内具有独创性并能以某种有形形式复制的智力成果。对于京剧脸谱来说，其文学艺术性、可复制性是显而易见的，因此涉案京剧脸谱具有独创性与否是判断其是否构成著作权法上"作品"之决定性因素。

所谓独创性，"独"是指作品应当是行为人独立创作，而非复制抄袭他人智力成果；"创"是指应当达到最低限度的创新高度。对于"创"的程度，英美法系版权法与大陆法系著作权法有不同的要求。总的来说，英美法系对于独创性的认定标准比较低。例如，英国在1916年的University of London Press v. University Tutorial Press Ltd. 案中确立了"独立完成+足够的创作投入"标准，该标准被公认为是一种经典解释并沿用至今；美国最高法院在1991年的Feist Publications, Inc., v. Rural Telephone Service Co. 案中指出，独创性中"创造性的要求是极低的，即使是一点点也足够了"。❶ 与英美法系的版权法相比，大陆法系的著作权法将作品更多地视为作者人格的延伸和精神的反映，并非普通的财产。相应地，大陆法系要求作品应当体现作者特定的人格，"那些运用普通人的能力就能做到的东西，那些几乎每个人都可以做成的东西，即使这些东西是新的，也不能作为作品受到保护"。❷

我国立法文件、司法解释并未对独创性进行规定，但无论是实践界还是理论界，对于"独"的理解并无争议，有争议的是在于"创"的高度的把握，对此我国司法实践中各法院的裁判尺度并不统一，给法律遵守及法律适用带来了不确定性。

对于"创"的要求，至关重要的是确定判断主体与具体的高度，简而言之就是由谁来判断一部"作品"的创新性，是由法官还是相关领域的专家，抑或是其他主体？同时，这种创造性到底应当达到何种程度，是否不同的作品类型都适用同一套评价标准，还是根据具体的作品类型，确定不同的标准？

对于第一个问题，总的来说主要有四种观点。其一是作品独创性由法

---

❶ Feist Publications, Inc., v. Rural Telephone Service Co., 499 U.S. 340 (1991).

❷ ［德］M. 雷炳德：《著作权法》，张恩民译，法律出版社2004年版，第117页。

院判断，这是最常见的观点。其二是由专业人员判断。其主张设置专业机构评判独创性。因为大多数情况下独创性是一个事实问题，法官难以独立完成，需要由所属领域的专家和从业人员组成的类似于司法鉴定机构的作品独创性评判组织，根据不同类型的作品进行判定。这样，法院无须再把过多精力放在其并不擅长的查验作品形成机制和创作方式等事实问题的调查上，而可以专注于侵权与否的法律判断。❶ 其三是由法院判断，但是可以听取专家意见。我国著作权法所保护的作品种类繁多，作品独创性程度的判断需要运用多种学科知识和技能，法官并不是无所不晓的全能人员。而且，由于现行著作权法对"独创性"并没有完整详细的表述和标准要求，即使某领域的专家来判断该领域作品独创性程度问题也并非易事。❷ 其四是法院和专业人员都不宜判定，因为"由只受过法律训练的人来判断作品的价值是危险的，不能以民众的口味低为由否定一幅画的版权保护"。❸ 同时，让专业委员会判定作品品质，同样是复活了文艺审查制度。❹ "独创性"不仅是一个法律判断，还涉及艺术方面的判断。因此，一般而言，独创性的判断应当以法官的判断为主，诉讼当事人为了主张自己的权利或者进行不侵权抗辩，可以聘请专家证人或者委托司法鉴定，对独创性之有无进行论证，但证据是否采纳决定权应当把握在法官手中。

对于第二个问题，即如何确定创新性的高度，在无相关规范性文件统一规定的情形下，很大程度上取决于法官的自由裁量，但判决的基点应当维持社会公共利益与创作者权益之间的平衡，在裁判案件之时，法官必须思考两个问题：第一，判决能够在多大的程度上激励创造者并在多大的程度上使公众获得利益；第二，在多大的程度上垄断权的确认会损害公众。

对于京剧脸谱是否具有独创性，司法实践中有肯定说和否定说两种截然不同的意见。例如，在"重庆美多食品有限公司与赵某某、重庆市家乐福商业有限公司著作权侵权纠纷案"中，重庆市高级人民法院明确指出：

---

❶ 赵锐："作品独创性标准的反思与认知"，载《知识产权》2011年第9期。
❷ 刘辉："作品独创性程度三分法理论评析"，载《知识产权》2011年第4期。
❸ Bleistein v. Donaldson Lithographing Co., 188 U.S. 239（1903）。
❹ 刘文杰："微博平台上的著作权"，载《法学研究》2012年第6期。

"被上诉人赵某某在其所著《中国京剧脸谱画册》一书中,以我国民间传统京剧脸谱艺术为创作素材,在对民间传统京剧脸谱艺术理解的基础上,运用其掌握的绘画技巧,以正面画法绘制的 568 个京剧人物的脸谱,有别于此前他人绘画的脸谱,是具有独创性的美术作品,赵某某依法享有著作权"。❶ 但也有个别法院持否定说。例如,长沙市中级人民法院则认为原告画册中的脸谱不具有独创性,"即使原告脸谱的勾画线条、笔画与传统脸谱有所不同,但京剧脸谱主要是通过谱式和色彩向观众传递信息,离开了已经成型的脸谱谱式和色彩,细微的笔画改动也就失去了单独存在的意义。人们在台下欣赏京剧时,能清晰地看见演员的表演、听到演员的唱功,但一般很难分辨脸谱的细微不同。除非原告对脸谱勾画线条、笔画的改动导致其使用与传统脸谱不同的谱式和色彩来表现人物特点,否则这种改动就不足以使其产生创作性……由于京剧脸谱属于传统文化的范畴,对其类似作品的独创性应提出更高的要求,原告未举证证明相关脸谱相对于传统脸谱的创造性及显著不同,不能因原告绘制、出版了《中国京剧脸谱画册》一书而认定原告对书中脸谱的谱式图形本身享有著作权"。❷

之所以会出现以上的分歧,根本原因在于各地法院对于独创性的标准并不统一。这种分歧在面对基于民间文学艺术而创作的"作品"时,表现得更为突出。在对京剧脸谱独创性进行认定时,首先应当区分民间文学艺术素材与民间文学艺术作品,用著作权法上的语言来说就是要先过滤掉已经流入公共领域的那一部分,在此基础上,再对脸谱剩余部分的描绘,进行独创性分析,判断其是否由原告独立创作,是否达到了一定的创新高度。

京剧脸谱是我国的传统民间艺术,具有 300 多年的历史。京剧脸谱不是凭空臆造的,而是历代的戏曲艺术家在长期的艺术实践中,对生活现象的观察、体验、综合,对剧中角色不断分析,逐步形成的一整套完整的艺术手法。京剧脸谱通过各种颜色在演员面部进行夸张的勾画,运用不同的颜色、图案反映人物性格、身份、地位等。京剧表演中各种人物的脸谱都有自己特定的谱式和色彩规律,例如红色表示忠诚、白色表示奸诈、年长

---

❶ (2011) 渝高法民终字第 188 号。
❷ (2006) 长中民三初字第 0399 号。

者眼睛下弯、年轻的眼睛上挑、包公的额头上有一个月亮等。任何人在勾画某一具体的京剧人物的脸谱时，都必然要遵循这些特定的谱式、色彩和图案。但是，京剧脸谱艺术的表达方式并不是唯一的，京剧脸谱在长期的发展中已形成多种流派的勾脸方法，例如郝派、裘派等，这些流派在勾脸的技法上各自有其特点。此外，勾脸不能完全按谱照搬，还要根据演员自己的脸型、表演特色等进行调整，这样才能生动地体现戏曲人物的外貌、情感和性格特征，使脸谱与表演充分融合起来。因此，同一人物的脸谱只要能体现人物的某些代表性的特征，在勾脸的方法上并不要求完全一致。当戏曲表演中的脸谱被艺术家以美术作品的形式表现出来时，其中体现了作者的创作风格和特点，线条、笔锋、构成图案的分布位置等勾法上的不同，则反映出不同勾画者的独创性。

思明区人民法院认可脸谱在一定条件下可以构成独立的作品，享有著作权保护。首先，我国《著作权法》第11条规定，如无相反证明，在作品上署名的公民、法人或者其他组织为作者。本案中，《中国京剧脸谱画册》中注明原告赵某某为该画册的编绘者，故其为该画册中京剧脸谱美术作品的作者，其对该作品享有的著作权应受我国著作权法的保护。其次，虽然京剧表演中各种人物的脸谱有相对特定的谱式、色彩和图案，但在勾画具体脸谱时，不同的勾画者会采用不同的勾法。不同的线条、笔锋、构成图案的分布位置和比例反映出不同勾画者的独创性。本案原告运用自己的绘画技巧结合其对京剧脸谱艺术的理解，以美术作品的形式对每一个特定戏剧人物的脸谱进行再创作，并将这些脸谱编排起来。这些作品体现了作者的创造性劳动，并不是将已有的脸谱简单的收集汇编在一起，故本案讼争作品具有独创性，作者赵某某享有讼争京剧脸谱美术作品的著作权。

（二）被告是否侵犯了原告著作权

在涉案画册已经具有独创性的前提下，需要进一步判断被告使用京剧脸谱的行为是否构成侵权。在司法实践中，判定著作权侵权的基本规则是"接触+实质性相似"，即如果被控作品与权利人的作品实质性相似，同时作品权利人又有证据表明被告在此前具备了接触该作品的条件，那么就应当由被告来证明其所使用的作品的合法来源，否则即应承担侵权赔偿责任。

具体来讲，所谓"接触"，是指被控侵权作品的创作者以前曾研究、复制对方独立创作的作品或者有研究、复制对方作品的机会，即创作成果不是源自于创作者本人，这实际上是对被告存在抄袭等侵权行为的进一步佐证。从法理上讲，"接触"应当是一种客观的现象，对"接触"的认定，应当主要从接触的主体、接触行为本身以及接触人的心态等方面入手。接触的主体可以是任何人，没有特定的限制；接触的行为可以是合法的（如通过合同转让、雇佣工作等），也可以是非法的（如盗窃、胁迫、欺诈等）；行为人接触时的心态可以是以侵权为目的而故意实施的，也可以是无意接触而事后产生侵权意图。

"接触"主要通过以下两种方式证明：一是以直接证据予以证明，例如被告曾阅读过、见到过、购买过原告的作品或者被告曾在原告处工作等方式接触过原告的作品；二是通过间接证据予以证明，比如原告作品在被告作品之前就已经通过发行、展览、表演、放映、广播等方式公诸于众，原告之前已经对其作品办理注册或者登记，而注册或登记档案可供公众查阅。在具体司法实践中，对于行为人是否有机会接触或者已经实际接触，法官通常采纳高度盖然性标准，即按照《最高人民法院关于适用〈中华人民共和国民事诉讼法〉的解释》第108条的规定，"对负有举证证明责任的当事人提供的证据，人民法院经审查并结合相关事实，确信待证事实的存在具有高度可能性的，应当认定该事实存在"。

"实质性相似"，则是指侵权作品中体现创作者个性的部分与原作的独创性部分实质性相似，系一种把他人作品据为己有，仅将个别部分略作变动的情形。它所比较的对象是原告作品中拥有独创性的那一部分，过滤掉了思想、公共领域的表达后剩下的那些表达，它是"抽象—过滤—比对"三步法中的"比对"的结果。与"三步法"采用的抽象观察法不同，司法实践中，还有一种与"抽象观察法"不同的"整体观察法"，后者是从"整体概念和感觉"出发，将多种创作要素（包括不受保护的作品要素）作为一个整体，以识别讼争作品是否构成"实质性相似"。[1] 通常认为，在

---

[1] Roth Greeting Cards v. United Card Co., 429 F. 2d 1106 (9th Cir. 1970).

"实质性相似"的分析中,应该以"抽象观察法"为主,以"整体观察法"为辅,即仅在前者无法适用或适用结果明显不合理的情况下才能适用后者。在这里还要指出的是,作品相似达到何种实质性程度方可作为侵权行为予以认定,也是一个值得思考的问题。在司法实践中,大量引用他人作品或者引用该作品的精髓部分,都会构成"实质性使用"。❶

具体到本案,在"接触"的认定上,思明法院采纳的高度盖然性标准,即原被告作品"基本相同",且原告作品在被告作品之前就发行公之于众,被告有充分的可能接触到该作品,被告为反驳负有举证证明责任的原告所主张事实,并没有提供相应的证据,因此,对于其主张的"使用的脸谱不是来源于原告作品"法院没有支持。针对被告所使用的作品是否与原告作品构成实质性相似,法院并没有采用"抽象观察法",即按照"抽象—过滤—比对"三步法进行认定,而是直接从整体观察的角度,从"整体概念和感觉"出发,将多种创作要素(包括不受保护的作品要素)作为一个整体进行考察,思明法院认为:"经比较,被告富安邦公司广告牌上使用的11幅京剧脸谱与原告赵某某《中国京剧脸谱画册》的京剧脸谱作品仅有个别细微差别,其线条、构图、比例、色彩及表现风格上均基本相同。"最终认定被告构成著作权侵权。

五、典型意义

本案属于京剧脸谱系列侵权案件中的典型一例。近年来,京剧走遍世界各地,成为介绍、传播中国传统艺术文化的重要媒介,被誉为中国的"国粹"。2010年11月16日,京剧又被列入"人类非物质文化遗产代表作名录"。京剧所蕴藏和承载的文化内涵和精神价值,能够为民族魂魄的振作、民族精神的弘扬、民族价值观念的再造、民族文化的复兴提供营养和资源,对构建具有中国特色的社会主义与和谐的人类社会有着重要的现实意义。因此,如何保护传统文化已经成为我国面临的重大课题。

本案判决的典型意义在于,明确了将京剧脸谱艺术作为一种创作素材,

---

❶ 吴汉东:"试论'实质性相似+接触'的侵权认定规则",载《法学》2015年第8期。

凝结了作者创作性劳动的京剧脸谱艺术作品应该受到法律的保护。创作者通过运用自己的绘画技巧结合对京剧脸谱艺术的理解以美术作品的形式表现出来，并区别于其他已有的作品，这是利用京剧脸谱艺术这一民间艺术进行的再创作，体现的是一种智力创造性劳动，具有著作权法所要求的独创性。对脸谱作品确认著作权并加以保护不但不会限制京剧脸谱艺术的继承和发展，反而有利于鼓励京剧艺术家的艺术创作，有利于京剧脸谱艺术的繁荣发展，有利于类似的传统文化遗产的保护。

（曾争志　赵　涛）

华晟公司诉关西公司著作权侵权纠纷案研析

一、案情简介

原告福州时代华晟版权代理有限公司（以下简称"华晟公司"）系专业的版权运营公司，经授权获得包括《当爱还没说出口》等58部涉案音乐电视作品在内的100部音乐电视作品在厦门地区的放映权专有使用权，有权利同使用者商谈使用条件并发放使用许可，征集使用情况，以作品权利人的身份向使用者收取使用费，并以原告的名义对侵权行为提起诉讼。被告厦门关西娱乐有限公司（以下简称"关西公司"）在其经营场所提供的卡拉OK点唱系统中收录《当爱还没说出口》等58部涉案音乐电视作品。并且，被告未经原告许可，在其卡拉OK点唱系统营业性播放上述涉案音乐电视作品。

原告认为，被告的上述行为侵犯其所享有的作品放映权，应当承担停止侵权、赔偿损失的法律责任。故原告诉至法院，请求判令被告立即停止侵权、赔偿原告经济损失人民币58 000元及制止侵权的合理费用人民币9 000元，并承担本案的全部诉讼费用。

被告主要从以下几个方面进行抗辩：第一，原告无权代理音乐作品著作权人进行诉讼要求赔偿；第二，原告持有的著作权授权协议存在瑕疵；第三，其使用的歌曲系统是运营商提供的，其增加或删除均由运营商操作，其没有侵权的故意；第四，原告诉求的金额也不合理。

二、裁判结果

厦门市思明区人民法院经审理认为，原告根据著作权转让合同取得了涉案作品在厦门地区的放映权,依法可以作为本案适格原告提起诉讼。被告关西公司疏于审查对涉案作品的权利,在其经营的KTV公开放映原告作品,构成对原告作品放映权的侵权,依法应承担相应的民事责任。因原告未具体证明其所受损失,也没有证明被告所获利益,法院根据被告侵权的主观过错程度、侵权时间以及作品的知名度等情节综合考量酌定赔偿数额。原告本可以向被告提出侵权警告来解决纷争,却以成本更高的诉讼方式,原告维权手段不尽合理,对由此造成的维权费用包括公证费用、律师费用等应承担部分责任。最后判令被告立即停止侵权,并赔偿原告经济损失及合理费用共计人民币 32 000 元。

三、争议焦点

本案的争议焦点有:
(1) 被告的行为是否构成侵害放映权?
(2) 被告是否可以主张合理来源抗辩?
(3) 原告的维权开支是否合理?

四、案例评析

(一) 被告的行为是否构成侵犯放映权

KTV公司主要经营产品是MTV,每家KTV的点播系统里都有数万件MTV。KTV经营者主要通过以下三种渠道获得MTV:一是从一些无权运营商手中购买所得;二是自己从网上下载,通过技术人员装进点播系统;三是加入中国音像著作权集体管理协会(以下简称"音著协"),每年缴纳版权会费,从音著协统一曲库中获得。一般而言,前两种途径涉嫌侵犯MTV著作权,但具体侵犯了何人何种著作权,则需要根据具体情形进行分析。

首先,播放客体不同,决定行为性质不同。目前,市场中大部分MTV都体现了制作者独创性的劳动:画面的选择、编排和创意与词曲的意境相互配合,借助光影营造歌曲的情调、氛围,运用色彩表现音乐的情感,运用运动造型形成对视觉的强烈冲击等,凝聚了编剧、导演、摄影、演员、剪辑、合成等的独创性劳动,并且唱片公司为此付出了大量的人力、物力和精力,满足著作权法上的独创性之要求,并以类似摄制电影的方法摄制而成。因此,可以将这部分 MTV 当作以类似摄制电影方法创作的作品进行保护。根据我国《著作权法》及《著作权实施条例》的规定,电影作品和以类似摄制电影的方法创作的作品的著作权由制片者享有,因此,作为作品的 MTV 制片者是著作权人,拥有《著作权法》第 10 条规定的各项权利,包括复制权、放映权、信息网络传播权等。电影作品和以类似摄制电影的方法创作的作品中的剧本、音乐等可以单独使用的作品的作者有权单独行使其著作权。但是在司法实践中,仍然有小部分 MTV 不具备作品之构成要件,此类 MTV 背景画面和歌曲之间并无有机的配合,只是机械地将自然风光、人物或他人的现场表演通过摄像设备予以存储,其功能重点是记录和复制,同时,即使为了保证声音和画面的质量,在摄像过程中进行了适应性的机位调整,或者在后期制作中通过简单的剪辑和处理而形成的 MTV,由于其尚达不到作品独创性的要求,目前这类 MTV 只能被认定为录像制品。根据我国《著作权法》的规定,录像制作者即录像制品的首次制作人,享有著作邻接权,有权许可他人复制、发行、出租、通过信息网络向公众传播,但是并无放映权。因此,在判断行为人具体侵犯了何人的何种权利,应当首先判断其播放的客体是音乐电视"作品"还是"录像制品",再判断原告是否享有诉讼资格,作品重点在于判断其是否是 MTV 作品的制片者,或者得到了制片者许可,以及 MTV 中的剧本、音乐等可以单独使用的作品的作者及其被许可人,对于录音录像制品则判断原告是否是该制品的首次制作人及其被许可人,最后再根据被告行为的具体态样,确定被告行为落入何种专有权利的控制范围。

其次,点歌系统不同,行为性质亦可能不同。目前市场上的 KTV 点歌系统主要包括单机版点歌系统与 VOD 点歌系统。前者是指没有网络支持,而是通过一台独立的电脑或其他终端完成点歌和放歌过程的系统。在单机版点歌系统下,MTV 的传播主要还是传统的单向行为,并不涉及交互传播的问题,因为每个包厢都有一套独立的 KTV 点播设备和相应类似服务器的设备,KTV 经营者将 MTV 收录在相应的技术设备中,该点歌系统仅是再现已存在于该设备中的 MTV 作品（制品）的设备，并不存在网络传输的问题；VOD 点歌系统又被称为网络版点歌系统，是指以用户为主的双向交互式系统，利用计算机网络，在服务器上存放歌曲，通过各种有盘包房电脑、无盘包房电脑、有盘机顶盒、无盘机顶盒等终端设备来完成点歌和放歌的系统。用户可以在自己选定的时间和地点获得作品。使用 VOD 点歌系统虽然也往往导致作品被播放、放映等，但与传统的单向传播还是有着本质的区别，它是随着网络技术的发展产生的一种交互式或按需传播行为。目前，市面上至少 80% 以上的 KTV 是提供 VOD 点歌系统为消费者提供歌曲伴唱服务。在单机版点歌系统环境中，KTV 经营者有可能侵犯作品的复制权、放映权、获得报酬的权利，以及录音录像制品复制权、获得报酬的权利；而在 VOD 点歌系统环境中，KTV 经营者则可能会侵犯作品、录音录像制品的信息网络传播权、放映权。

值得进一步讨论的是，被告的播放行为通常会同时涉及复制、传播两个环节，复制的目的往往在于后续的传播，相应的，也就可能同时侵犯了复制权和信息网络传播权、放映权，那么原告是否可以既主张复制权，又主张信息网络传播权？放映权与信息网络传播权之间又有何联系及区别呢？

关于第一个问题，司法实践中存在不同的处理方式。当原告既主张复制权，又主张放映权或者信息网络传播权时，法院一般对著作权人复制权受到侵犯予以支持，同时会认定被告还侵犯了放映权或者信息网络传播权。但也有一些法院并不认为复制权受到侵犯，例如，在"华谊公司诉北京白云索思好景互联网上网服务有限责任公司著作权侵权纠纷案"中，北京市西城区人民法院即认为，"原告华谊兄弟公司主张被告白云索思好景公司的行为侵犯了其享有的复制权、放映权，是由于其对著作权相关法律概念认识有误造成……被告白云索思好景公司未经权利人许可，将电影作品通过局域网传播给社会公众，使公众在其个人选定的时间、地点获取该影视作品的行为，应认定为对权利人信息网络传播权的侵犯"。❶

无论是采取单机版点歌系统还是 VOD 点歌系统，通常都会将音乐作品

---

❶ "华谊公司诉北京白云索思好景互联网上网服务有限责任公司著作权侵权纠纷案"，北京市西城区人民法院（2008）西民初字第 2431 号民事判决书。

上传至独立包间的终端设备上，并形成作品的非临时性复制件，因此，KTV 经营者构成侵犯复制权本不应当存在任何争议，值得讨论的是，在某项行为已经构成信息网络传播权侵权的前提下是否还有必要对复制权进行单独苛责的问题。此种情形属于民法中的请求权竞合，当事人可以同时或者分别主张信息网络传播权和复制权侵权。但是由于侵害复制权的责任范围小于侵害信息网络传播权，因此当行为人只是主张其复制权受到侵害时，其获得的法律保护是有限的，基于程序法上的当事人处分原则及不告不理原则，法院不宜再对侵害信息网络传播权进行认定。

具体而言，KTV 经营者进行复制的目的是为进行传播，若其仅仅从事复制行为，而没有任何的传播行为，其对于著作权的侵害程度显然是相当低的。相应地，单纯侵犯复制权之责任范围也应当限于恢复原状，即《著作权法》第 47 条规定的"停止侵害""消除影响"，权利人主张损害赔偿通常而言难以得到支持。而侵犯信息网络传播权比起侵犯复制权从危害程度来看严重得多，不仅形成非临时性的复制件，还对复制件进行传播，干扰了正版 KTV 作品（制品）的市场及正常利用，损害了权利人的合法利益，因此权利人不但有权要求其停止侵害、消除影响，还可以要求侵权人承担赔偿损失的责任。此外，根据《信息网络传播权保护条例》的规定，侵犯信息网络传播权的责任形态包括停止侵害、消除影响、赔礼道歉、赔偿损失。单纯侵害复制权触及的是恢复原状责任之承担，并不会涉及损害赔偿的问题，因此，若权利人主张损害赔偿，其请求权基础只能是信息网络传播权保护规范，不能是复制权保护规范。但是权利人若只是主张停止侵害、消除影响，其既可以基于复制权受到侵犯也可以基于信息网络传播权受到侵犯而提起诉讼。

关于第二个问题，即放映权与信息网络传播权的区别。根据我国《著作权法》第 10 条的规定，放映权是指通过放映机、幻灯机等技术设备公开再现美术、摄影、电影和以类似摄制电影的方法创作的作品等的权利。信息网络传播权，即以有线或者无线方式向公众提供作品，使公众可以在其个人选定的时间和地点获得作品的权利。通过定义可以发现，放映权和信息网络传播权最大的区别在于它们所规制的作品传播形式不一样，放映权主要规制通过"放映机、幻灯机等技术设备"公开再现作品,而信息网络传播权则是规制通过以"有线或者无线"的形式,交互式地提供展现作品。权利区别的背后体现的是作品传播技术的更新换代。具体到KTV侵权诉讼,如果经营者采取的是单机版点歌系统(每个包房拥有一套独立的点播设备),即使消费者可以在"选定的时间""选定的地点"点播作品,由于其采取的并不是"有线或者无线"的方式传播,该行为也不构成信息网络传播,而是属于通过技术设备公开再现作品,受放映权之规制。但是,当KTV经营者采用的是将音乐电视作品上传至局域网,并通过服务器与各包间的终端设备连接起来,不特定的第三人可以在其选定的时间、地点点播音乐电视作品,则同时满足交互式传播和"以有限或者无线"、向公众提供三个要求,因此,KTV经营者之行为构成侵犯信息网络传播权。但是可能有人认为,不管是通过有线或者无线,也不管有没有采取交互式传播,说通过信息网络传播作品属于通过"技术设备公开再现作品"在逻辑上至少是过得去的,换言之,即使不存在信息网络传播权对信息网络这种传播形式进行规制,其也可以被纳入放映权的专有范围予以调整,因为"等技术设备"可以被解释为包括信息网络设备。我国的信息网络传播权的定义直接来自于《世界知识产权组织版权条约》(WCT)第8条的表述,❶ 之所以专门针对网络形式的交互式传播设置"信息网络传播权",是因为传统的传播权都是建立在单向的、被动的传播方式的基础之上,"而WCT第八条所要达到的主要目的,就是使各国著作权立法将'交互式'传播行为也纳入著作权人'专有权利'的控制范围"。❷ 因此,在《著作权法》已经就这种特别的传播方式作出具体规定时,就不能弃特殊规定而适用其他更为一般的条款。

在本案中,思明法院肯定了涉案音乐电视的作品属性,并结合本案案情最终认定被告提供KTV服务的行为侵犯了原告对涉案作品的放映权。

(二)被告是否可以主张合理来源抗辩

在诉讼中,KTV经营者提出抗辩通常是:音乐电视点播系统是由供应

---

❶ 胡康生主编:《中华人民共和国著作权法释义》,法律出版社2002年版,第56页。
❷ 王迁:《网络环境中的著作权保护研究》,法律出版社2011年版,第114页。

商提供，歌曲亦是点播系统供应商安装的，其有合法的来源。

销售者合法来源抗辩制度，又称销售者善意侵权制度，其法理基础在于传统民法中保护善意第三人的理论，从公平正义的角度出发，法律需要对善意和恶意的行为人之间作出区分，使具有不同主观态度的行为人承担不同的民事责任。如果行为人出于善意，并付出了相应的对价，根据公平原则，该善意行为人的权利应当得到合理保护。从效率的角度来看，如果苛求销售者对供应商提供的产品进行细致入微的调查，以确保自己将要销售的产品绝对不侵权，将增加交易成本，降低交易的积极性，不利于社会经济的发展。但是销售者仅仅只是善意，而不能提出侵权商品的合法来源以供权利人去追究始作俑者，还是应当承担相关的法律责任，因为从立法考虑的价值位阶来看，此种情形下，对权利人损失进行弥补之正义优先于交易的效率予以考量。

我国法律体系中，合法来源抗辩制度主要体现在《专利法》第70条、《商标法》第60条，但是我国《著作权法》没有明确规定销售者是否可以主张合法来源抗辩。我国《著作权法》第53条规定，"复制品的出版者、制作者不能证明其出版、制作有合法授权的，复制品的发行者或者电影作品或者以类似摄制电影的方法创作的作品、计算机软件、录音录像制品的复制品的出租者不能证明其发行、出租的复制品有合法来源的，应当承担法律责任"。该条款仅规定了出版者、制作者在不能证明合法授权或者发行者、出租者不能证明合法来源的情况下要依法承担法律责任，但并未明确提及销售者、服务提供商能否主张合法来源抗辩。为解决这一问题，最高人民法院先后出台《关于审理著作权民事纠纷案件适用法律若干问题的解释》和《关于做好涉及网吧著作权纠纷案件审判工作的通知》，但是对侵权商品的销售者能否直接主张合法来源抗辩问题仍然未予明确。我国《著作权法》在"合法来源"抗辩条款上虽未明确列明销售商这一诉讼主体，但作为著作权侵权纠纷诉讼中销售商理应具有"合法来源"抗辩的权利。理由如下：首先，这是著作权意义上"发行者"的内涵本身所应有之义。著作权意义上的发行者，通常是指以出售或者赠与方式向公众提供作品原件或者复制件的自然人、法人。对包含有著作权商品的销售行为本身是属于著作权意义上发行作品的一种较为常见的方式，也就是说销售行为本身是包含在发行行为中的。其次，这是我国知识产权立法体系整体平衡、内在法律体系一致性之需要。我国《专利法》和《商标法》均明确赋予销售商在特定条件下的免赔责任，即销售者只要证实其所销售商品系合法取得并能说明提供者，且不知道销售商品侵权之事实的可以免除赔偿责任。作为三大知识产权法律之一的《著作权法》赋予著作权侵权案件中销售商合法来源抗辩权，也是整个知识产权立法体系平衡的需要。最后，这是实现社会公平正义的需要。销售商毕竟不是侵权的源头，不赋予著作权产品的销售商以合法来源抗辩，等于将其置于与侵权产品制作者相同的境地。这对销售商来说是不公平的。过重的法律注意义务将使发行者、出租者在交易中谨小慎微，甚至为了避免侵权风险而不愿意发行、销售产品，这将不利于商品的流通，最终将影响到文化作品的传播和我国文化产业的建设和发展。

关于销售商合法来源抗辩成立条件，我国《商标法》和《专利权法》都明确规定销售者如果能够证明合法来源的，则不承担赔偿责任。但在《著作权法》上采取了另一种表述方式，即如不能证明合法来源的，则应承担法律责任。这两种表述，虽然看似近似，但从法律逻辑学的严格意义上讲是不完全相同的。从现有著作权法的规定上能够推断出来的结论是：如果销售商不承担法律责任，那么其前提是能够证明合法来源抗辩的，但是不能够得出：能够举证合法来源，就可以不承担民事责任。这是因为在行为人能够证明发行或出租的作品有合法来源的情况下，其也有可能明知发行或出租的作品为盗版作品，这种情况下依然享受免责的待遇对著作权人是不公平的，也无法起到打击盗版保护市场交易的作用。故证明合法来源仅是其销售商不承担法律责任的一个必要条件，而非充分条件。当然，合法来源也不等同于合法授权。只要销售者所销售的复制品是其通过正当的、合法的交易渠道从上家供应商取得的，这种客观存在的交易关系就应受法律保护。同时，根据TRIPs协议对经营者"提供来源"义务要求，即"告知权利持有人有关参与生产和分配侵权产品或服务的第三者的身份，以及他们的分配渠道"，以便于权利人能更直接地行使权利，制止侵权于源头。

除了合法来源外，作为销售商合法来源抗辩事由成立的另一要件就是其主观心态方面。销售商的主观心态可分为以下三种类型：一是销售者知道其销售的商品是侵犯著作权的；二是销售者应当知道其销售的商品是侵犯著作权的，但销售者实际不知道的；三是销售者不知道、也不应当知道其销售的商品是侵犯著作权的。如果销售者承认知道自己销售的是侵权产品，这就是属于第一种情况，销售者自然就不能免除其赔偿责任。第二种情况属于过失，即为推定知道的情况。第三种情况属于"不知道"的情况是不言而喻的。有争议的是第二种情况应否纳入"不知道"的范围。在知识产权侵权行为中，停止侵害责任适用无过错原则，而对于承担赔偿责任则适用过错推定原则。在司法实践中，侵权商品的销售者通常会以"不知道"作为抗辩的理由，所以我们需要对其是否应当知道进行判断。由于第二种情况属于过错中的过失，销售者作为市场经营主体，在进货时应当尽到合理的注意义务，当其在进货时未尽到合理的注意义务时，即视为其应当知道而不知道，不能直接免除销售者的赔偿责任。

综上所述，销售商或者服务提供者进行合法来源抗辩事由最终成立必须同时具备两个要件：一是具有合法来源，二是在主观上无过失。本案中，思明法院在判决书中明确指出："被告并未提供相应的证据证明其放映的涉案音乐电视作品有合法来源，本院不予采纳。被告在并未取得著作权人的许可和授权的情况下，采取营利的方式直接使用涉案音乐电视作品，侵犯了著作权人的合法权利，被告在主观上明显存有过错。"从判决中可以看出法院对过错的认定采取的是客观标准，即通过被告表示于外的行为去推测行为人的主观内容，被告未经许可营利性使用涉案音乐电视作品，本身即能推定其主观上具有一定的过错。

（三）原告的维权开支是否合理

我国《著作权法》第49条规定，侵犯著作权的损害赔偿数额还应当包括权利人为制止侵权行为所支付的合理开支。根据上述规定，行为人请求法院判决被告全额支付为了制止侵权所支付的合理费用的前提是其维权行为本身应当在法律允许的合理边界之内。该规定的法理基础是民法中的不真正义务理论。不真正义务又称间接义务，它是指法律关系相对人虽不得请求义务人履行，义务人违反亦不会发生损害赔偿责任，而仅使负担此义务者遭受权利减损或丧失后果的义务，简而言之就是权利人对自己利益的维护照顾义务。因为对不真正义务的违反，从本质上说是权利人对自己利益的疏忽或者放弃，相对方没有过错，因而不可归责于相对方。不真正义务的主要特征是权利人通常不得请求履行，违反它也不会发生损害赔偿责任，仅使负担该义务的一方遭受权利减损或丧失。例如，当事人一方因另一方违反合同受到损害的，这时就应当及时采取措施，防止损失扩大，就是不真正义务。不真正义务的理论根据是诚实信用原则。在合同关系中，如果一方违约造成另一方损失，非违约方面对损失扩大而坐视不管，待以后向违约方请求损害赔偿，这显然会造成资源的巨大浪费，更是一种滥用自己权利的非诚信行为。在侵权损害赔偿诉讼中，被侵权人维权时采取明显过当的行为或者维权费用高昂且不符合通常事理，却期待能从侵权人处获得赔偿，这显然与诚实信用原则相悖，对于这部分超出合理范围的费用，相对方并没有过错，权利人应当自行负责。

在本案中，原告公司于2011年1月12日注册，于2011年1月14日得到涉案作品的授权，2011年1月17日申请公证取证，在没有向被告提出相应的侵权警告后直接提起诉讼。从原告准备诉讼和提起诉讼的过程以及原告获得涉案作品的授权期限、权利类型、权利行使的地域等方面综合分析不难看出，原告公司的设立就是为了进行涉案作品的诉讼，而诉讼的目的并非仅仅为了制止侵权，而是意图通过诉讼谋取非正常的经济利益。原告在得到授权3天后就公证取证，说明原告明知被告曲库中存在其管理的作品，但原告并未提出侵权警告，而是直接公证取证并起诉。在发出侵权警告就可能制止侵权行为的情况下，原告直接采用了成本更高的诉讼维权方式，显然不尽合理，这是原告权利的滥用，对由此造成的维权成本的扩大，原告存在相应的过错，而被告并无过错，因此对于扩大的这部分维权开支，理应由原告自行承担。

五、典型意义

本案属于KTV系列侵权案件中的典型一例，被评为"2012年厦门市法院十大精品案例"。

KTV公司主要经营产品是音乐电视作品,每家KTV的点播系统里都有数万件音乐电视作品。从目前的情况来看,我国KTV行业的著作权侵权现象较为严重。这主要是由于著作权人和KTV公司不可能一对一地产生授权与被授权关系造成的。因此在涉及KTV著作权侵权系列案件的审理中,音集协作为行业组织的作用应该得到充分的考虑。尤其是在侵权过错的认定上,对于那些加入音集协,接受行业组织统一管理,并按规定缴纳版权会费,从音集协统一曲库中获得音乐电视作品的KTV公司,应当认定其不构成侵犯著作权。

本案判决的典型意义在于可以促使厦门市各大KTV公司积极加入音集协,接受行业组织统一管理,积极履行尊重和保护知识产权的义务,对净化KTV行业市场环境起到重大的促进作用。著作权人、KTV公司都能从中获益,同时也让类似侵权大量减少,取得良好的法律效果。在本案司法判决以外,思明法院又针对KTV等娱乐行业公司的侵权现状,向厦门市娱乐行业协会发出司法建议书,建议行业自律,亦取得良好社会效果。

此外,思明法院在本案中针对原告公司维权方式不当导致维权费用不合理增加的现象进行了专门分析,并判决原告公司自行承担部分不合理的维权费用,给今后类似案件的判决提供了借鉴。

(曾争志 赵 涛)

兴茂公司诉誉海公司、东本公司侵害商标权及不正当竞争纠纷案研析

一、案情简介

厦门"鼓浪屿"是福建省厦门市著名的风景区，每年有大量海内外游客到这里游玩。"鼓浪屿"原本是厦门市的一个行政区，后鼓浪屿区并入思明区，不再是县一级的行政区划。

"鼓浪屿"闻名遐迩，其馅饼产品也行销海内外。很多商家在生产销售馅饼时，在包装盒印刷有"鼓浪屿""鼓浪屿特产""鼓浪屿风味""鼓浪屿馅饼"等各种各样的标语。这样一来，可以利用"鼓浪屿"这一地名增强产品的竞争力。而事实上，"鼓浪屿"是厦门市兴茂贸易公司（以下简称"兴茂公司"）拥有的合法商标，并且早在20世纪80年代就被用在该公司生产的馅饼上。兴茂公司认为商家对"鼓浪屿"的使用构成对其商标权的侵犯，并由此提起诉讼，起诉被告厦门市誉海食品有限公司（以下简称"誉海公司"）使用的两个馅饼包装侵犯了原告的商标权。

事情起源于1983年，"鼓浪屿"注册商标原权利人鼓浪屿食品厂开始在其生产的厦门馅饼等食品上使用"鼓浪屿"商标。经多年广泛宣传和销售，"鼓浪屿"馅饼及糕点在业界获得较高的声誉，"鼓浪屿"馅饼也获得国家级、省级的众多荣誉称号。案外人曾某某于2010年6月18日受让了上述"鼓浪屿"商标，后授权兴茂公司独占使用，以及独立行使商标权权益及与此相关的反不正当竞争的维权行动。2013年4月，原告兴茂公司在被告厦门市东本贸易有限公司（以下简称"东本公司"）的门店发现，誉

海公司在其生产的馅饼包装盒上突出使用"鼓浪屿馅饼"等文字,而且产品包装盒规格大小与原告的包装盒一致;包装盒的内外装潢包括款式及图案的颜色、造型等与原告高度近似,以致当原告与誉海公司的包装盒分开摆放时,一般消费者难以区分。而誉海公司将产品描述为"鼓浪屿馅饼按照传统工艺和独家配方精工细作而成",则是企图通过虚假宣传让消费者误以为其企业及产品就是正宗的"鼓浪屿馅饼",具有显见的侵权恶意。因誉海公司常年销售侵权产品,给原告造成巨大经济损失。因此,原告认为,被告的行为侵害了其注册商标专用权且构成不正当竞争,故请求法院判令被告立即停止在其生产、销售的产品上使用含有"鼓浪屿"字样并与原告的"鼓浪屿馅饼"包装盒的装潢近似的包装盒,立即销毁所有侵犯原告注册商标专用权及进行不正当竞争的产品包装盒,并赔偿侵权行为给原告造成的经济损失人民币20万元,要求被告在《厦门日报》刊登致歉声明,公开向原告赔礼道歉。

二、裁判结果[1]

厦门市思明区人民法院经审理认为,原告合法拥有"鼓浪屿"商标的注册商标专用权,并且可以自己的名义提起诉讼。被告誉海公司生产、销售的包装盒(见图1)带有原告商标"鼓浪屿"字样的馅饼,侵犯了原告注册商标专用权,依法应当停止侵权并赔偿损失。誉海公司使用的带有"鼓浪屿特产"字样的馅饼包装盒(见图2)及包装盒扉页中"鼓浪屿馅饼"的字样,对"鼓浪屿"的使用属于地名的合法使用,不构成侵权。被告东本公司已经证明其所销售的馅饼的合法来源,故无需承担责任。最终法院判令厦门市誉海食品有限公司立即停止在其生产、销售的产品上使用带有"鼓浪屿"字样包装盒(见图1),并赔偿原告厦门兴茂贸易有限公司经济损失及合理费用人民币80 000元。此外,由于被告使用原告享有独占使用权的注册商标并未涉及人身权范畴,因此原告提出的赔礼道歉主张不予支持。

---

[1] 类似的关于"鼓浪屿"馅饼的商标侵权及不正当竞争纠纷,另参见厦门市中级人民法院于2017年7月31日作出的(2015)厦民初字第1473号判决,福建省高级人民法院于2017年12月18日作出的(2017)闽民终899号判决。

图 1   图 2

三、争议焦点

本案争议焦点为：

（1）兴茂公司是否为适格原告？

（2）被告誉海公司在其馅饼包装盒上使用"鼓浪屿"字样是否侵犯原告商标权？

（3）被告誉海公司的馅饼包装盒是否构成不正当竞争？

四、案例评析

（一）兴茂公司是否为适格原告

根据《最高人民法院关于审理商标民事纠纷案件适用法律若干问题的解释》第 4 条的规定，在发生注册商标专用权被侵害时，独占使用许可合同的被许可人可以向人民法院提起诉讼。

"鼓浪屿"商标在厦门馅饼等食品上的注册和使用有着悠久的历史。早在 1983 年，"鼓浪屿"注册商标原权利人鼓浪屿食品厂开始在其生产的厦门馅饼等食品上使用"鼓浪屿"商标。后企业改制，"鼓浪屿"商标所有人变更为案外人曾某某。曾某某于 2005 年取得商标局核准的第 3847042 号"鼓浪屿（艺术体）"商标，核定使用的商品为馅饼（点心）、馅饼、肉馅饼、蛋糕、饼干（曲奇）、面包、果馅饼、糖点（酥皮糕点）、粽子、月饼；又于 2011 年取得商标局核准的第 1571341 号"鼓浪屿"商标，核定使用的商品为糖、糖果、饼干、糕点、饺子、米果、冰淇淋、鱼皮花生、酥糖、南糖。2013年4月1日，曾某某将上述两个商标授权兴茂公司独占使用，以及独立进行商标权权益及与此相关的反不正当竞争的维权行动。许可使用期限自2013年4月1日至2014年3月31日。因此，原告合法取得上述"鼓浪屿"商标的独占使用权，并可以自己的名义独立提起诉讼，因此原告兴茂公司具有诉讼主体资格。

（二）被告誉海公司在其馅饼包装盒上使用"鼓浪屿"字样是否侵犯原告商标权

"鼓浪屿"是一种地名商标。地名商标，顾名思义，是以"地名"为限制条件的，以某一地名为内容申请的商品标志。地名商标由于"地名"的限制，使其具有了一定的特殊性。第一，商标的基本属性之一是显著性，地名商标并不具有很强的显著性，因为除了商标本身的功能，还兼具有地名的功能属性。第二，地名本为公众所使用的词汇，正是由于地名商标的显著性不强，国家对于将地名注册为商标的行为进行适当的限制。我国《商标法》第10条第2款规定："县级以上行政区划的地名或者公众知晓的外国地名，不得作为商标。但是，地名具有其他含义或者作为集体商标、证明商标组成部分的除外；已经注册的使用地名的商标继续有效。"❶

我国将地名作为商标注册的原则有：第一，地名作为集体商标、证明商标可以受到商标法保护。此时作为集体商标和证明商标而受保护的地名是地理标志。第二，县级以上行政区划和公众知晓的外国地名在两种情况下可以获得商标法律保护，即该地名已经获得商标注册或者该地名具有其他含义。第三，县级以上行政区划和公众知晓的外国地名以外的地名可以作为商标获得注册，但是不能引起公众的误解或者具有不良影响。❷

---

❶ 所谓县级以上行政区划，包括县级的县、自治县、县级市、市辖区；地级的市、自治州、地区、盟；省级的省、直辖市、自治区；两个特别行政区即香港、澳门；台湾地区。县级以上行政区划的地名以我国民政部编辑出版的《中华人民共和国行政区划简册》为准。县级以上行政区划地名，包括全称、简称以及县级以上的省、自治区、直辖市、省会城市、计划单列市、著名的旅游城市的拼音形式。下列三种情形，地名可以作为商标：一是地名具有其他含义。所谓地名具有其他含义，是指地名作为词汇具有确定含义且该含义强于作为地名的含义，不会误导公众。二是地名作为集体商标、证明商标的组成部分。三是已经注册的使用地名的商标，依法继续有效。

❷ 杜颖："地名商标的可注册性及其合理使用——从'百家湖'案谈起"，载《法学》2007年第11期。

地名商标与地理标志不同，地理标志是指对某商品的质量、声誉或者其他特殊特性与其原产地域相关联进行标识，方便消费者识别该商品原产地。地名商标具有商标权的一般内容，为商标所有权人专有，地理标志则不具有独占性和排他性；地名商标以其财产性权利属性在经过合法注册之后可以依法转让或者许可他人使用，而地理标志并不为个人所专有，也无法随意转让。

鼓浪屿之前是厦门的一个区，属于县级以上的地名，由于行政区划改革，2003年鼓浪屿区并入思明区，鼓浪屿不再是一个县级行政区划。"鼓浪屿"作为地名商标在鼓浪屿的行政区划改变之后具有了合法性。这一"禁止事项"取消后，"鼓浪屿"作为地名是可以被注册为商标的，正是因为这样，很多商家看到商机，为了借用鼓浪屿的名气，在各种商品上抢注"鼓浪屿"商标，甚至在卫浴上也出现了"鼓浪屿"商标。

商标在商品交易活动中具有标识商品质量等特征信息的作用，可以有效加强买卖双方的信息交流，如果没有合理的商标保护制度，消费者在购买过程中很难与卖家享有信息对称。因此，商标不仅凝含了商誉，也能使消费者将商品或服务与其提供者正确联系在一起。同样的，商标法不仅要维护商标权人凝聚在商标中的商誉，也要保护消费者正确识别商品来源的权利不受干扰，避免造成混淆。为此，我国《商标法》第57条规定，（1）未经商标注册人的许可，在同一种商品上使用与其注册商标相同的商标的；（2）未经商标注册人的许可，在同一种商品上使用与其注册商标近似的商标，或者在类似商品上使用与其注册商标相同或者近似的商标，容易导致混淆的，均属于侵犯注册商标专用权的行为。

可见，可能导致消费者对商品或服务来源产生混淆，是构成商标侵权的必要条件，对可能造成商标混淆的行为进行了立法上的禁止，可以有效保护消费者的利益。

最高人民法院《关于审理商标民事纠纷案件适用法律若干问题的解释》第9条将"易使相关公众对商品的来源产生误认或者认为其来源与原告注册商标的商品有特定的联系"作为判断"商标近似"的标准，而第11条则将"相关公众一般认为其存在特定联系，容易造成混淆"作为"商品类似"的标准之一。可见，判断是否构成混淆，需要站在相关公众的角度，判断所涉及商标是否足以影响消费者判断商品或者服务来源。

回到本案对于馅饼包装盒上使用"鼓浪屿"字样是否侵犯原告商标权的认定。在"鼓浪屿"不再作为县级行政区划名称之后，根据商标法其可以被注册为合法商标。但是，"鼓浪屿"同时是一个地名，这意味着，作为地名，普通的企业完全可以利用"鼓浪屿"三个字表明其产地，以作为产品来源。这样一来，就会出现一个问题，到底什么情况下可以使用鼓浪屿，什么情况下不可以使用鼓浪屿呢？一般来说，既然鼓浪屿已经成为合理商标，为了保护正常的鼓浪屿商标，其他企业不可以侵犯"鼓浪屿"商标的正常使用，因此，要以地名正常使用"鼓浪屿"三个字，就需要在不对"鼓浪屿"三个字作突出使用的情况下进行使用，例如，使用"鼓浪屿特产""鼓浪屿风味"，在不突出使用的情况下，并不构成对"鼓浪屿"商标的侵权，属于正当使用。

第一，在包装盒上突出使用"鼓浪屿"字样构成商标侵权。

根据《商标法实施条例》第49条的规定，对通用名称、地名的使用应当是"正当使用"。虽然"鼓浪屿"是十分著名的地名，"馅饼"也是食品行业的通用名称，但在图1中，"鼓浪屿"和"馅饼"在盒盖正面呈现为分开、各自独立的两行，可见被告并非将"鼓浪屿馅饼"作为不可分割的整体使用，而是特别突出"鼓浪屿"三个字。另外，"鼓浪屿"三个字用在盒盖正面正中间的位置，所用字体亦是整个盒盖正面所有文字中最大的，反之被告拟注册的"臻食轩"商标则位于比较不显眼的左上角且字体较小，因此从整体上看，"鼓浪屿"三个字在馅饼盒外包装中处于居中、显眼的位置，消费者购买时最先注意到的是"鼓浪屿"三字而非被告的"臻食轩"商标。被告在馅饼盒上显著、突出地使用了原告享有独占使用权的商标"鼓浪屿"，极易使相关公众就产品的来源与原告产品产生混淆和误认，因此，这种使用并不属于《商标法实施条例》所规定的对于地名的正当使用。

第二，在包装盒上不突出使用"鼓浪屿"字样不构成商标侵权。

在图2包装盒中，盒盖正中间的位置标明"馅饼"，并在"馅饼"二字左侧以较小字体写明"鼓浪屿特产"，"鼓浪屿"与"特产"形成一个整体。原告虽是注册商标"鼓浪屿"的独占使用权人，但同时鼓浪屿也是一个耳熟能详的地名，根据《商标法实施条例》第49条的规定，原告并不能禁止其他人合理使用作为地名的"鼓浪屿"。原告经合法途径取得的注册商标是"鼓浪屿"，在馅饼是厦门特产或鼓浪屿特产并无定论的情况下，被告在外包装盒上标明自己的商标"臻食轩"，同时使用"鼓浪屿特产"的字样，而没有将"鼓浪屿"三个字单独突出使用，并不会导致消费者购买时将被告的产品误认为是原告的"鼓浪屿"牌馅饼，因此，被告在包装上标明"鼓浪屿特产"的做法并无不妥，属于《商标法实施条例》中规定的正当使用。

第三，被告誉海公司在产品盒盖扉页中使用"鼓浪屿馅饼"字样不构成构成商标侵权。

"馅饼"作为厦门地区比较著名的食品，其生产、销售、材料来源范围并未局限于鼓浪屿地区，无证据表明馅饼与鼓浪屿有某种特定的联系，亦无证据证明经过长期使用或宣传，"鼓浪屿馅饼"已经成为商品通用名称或知名商品特有的名称。被告誉海公司的地址曾位于鼓浪屿，后才迁出，故其在盒盖扉页中将产品表述为"鼓浪屿馅饼"，可以认为是将"鼓浪屿"作为一个地名使用。另外，"鼓浪屿馅饼"的表述位于盒盖扉页且未将"鼓浪屿"三个字独立突出使用，并不会造成消费者购买时的混淆和误解。因此，被告誉海公司在扉页中使用"鼓浪屿"字样并不构成侵权。

（三）被告誉海公司的馅饼外包装盒是否构成不正当竞争

不正当竞争是指经营者以及其他有关市场参与者采取违反公平、诚实信用等公认的商业道德的手段去争取交易机会或者破坏他人的竞争优势，损害消费者和其他经营者的合法权益，扰乱社会经济秩序的行为。

法律鼓励正当竞争，禁止不正当竞争。我国《反不正当竞争法》第5条规定："擅自使用知名商品特有的名称、包装、装潢，或者使用与知名商品近似的名称、包装、装潢，造成和他人的知名商品相混淆，使购买者误认为是该知名商品"的，属于以不正当手段从事市场交易，损害竞争对手的行为。《最高人民法院关于审理不正当竞争民事案件应用法律若干问题的解释》对于知名商品特有名称、包装、装潢权纠纷中知名商品的认定、特有名称的认定、侵权的认定等作出详细规定。该解释第 4 条第 3 款规定："认定知名商品特有名称、包装、装潢相同或者近似，可以参照商标相同或者近似的判断原则和方法。"知名商品特有名称、包装、装潢使用权已经为我国法律所认可，受反不正当竞争法保护，该权利相同或近似的认定参照商标相同或近似的判断原则。

知名商品特有的名称、包装、装潢之所以受反不正当竞争法保护，是因为它们具有识别商品来源的作用，成为区别商品来源的标识，如果不加以保护，既不利于维护使用人正当竞争取得的市场成果，也不利于防止市场混淆和保护消费者。

本案所涉及商品特有的包装、装潢，是指不为相关商品所通用，具有区别商品来源的显著特征的包装、装潢。《反不正当竞争法》第 5 条规定的"知名商品特有的包装、装潢"中所谓的"特有"，应当是指包装、装潢的区别性，即具有识别商品来源的意义。

第一，原告所使用的由牛皮纸制作、"翻盖式"的包装盒并非原告一家独有，厦门其他馅饼品牌也均在馅饼产品上使用牛皮纸材质、"翻盖式"的包装盒，原告提供的证据不足以证明其使用的材质、装潢、"翻盖式"设计属于其特有。

第二，原告被告双方的包装盒存在多处不同：（1）原告盒盖正面中间有比较突出的建筑图案，被告盒盖正面是文字以及红色印章；（2）原告盒盖正面四角的花朵图案形状设计与原告不同，比被告的装饰花朵更大、延伸部分更多；（3）原告盒盖上部中间位置有带飘带延伸的图案，并标明艺术字体的"鼓浪屿馅饼"，被告盒盖上部正中间同样位置并无图案；（4）原告外包装四个侧边的颜色是红色、被告四个侧边的颜色是棕色；（5）原告盒盖可折叠延伸部分标明艺术体的"鼓浪屿"商标及花朵图案，被告同一个位置标明的是"臻食轩"商标。

综上所述，原告并未提交证据证明涉案的产品包装、装潢系其特有，且原被告的包装盒存在诸多不同，被告的馅饼包装盒并未构成对原告的不正当竞争。

五、典型意义

本案的意义在于划定了地名商标保护的范围和侵权行为的界限。地名和商标的重合是司法实践中经常遇到的问题。鼓浪屿原来是厦门的一个区，属于县级以上的地名，由于行政区划改革，2003年鼓浪屿区并入思明区，鼓浪屿不再是一个县级行政区划。在这一"禁止事项"取消后，鼓浪屿作为一个全国知名风景区，迅速被抢注商标。

直观来看，鼓浪屿既是商标也是地名，如果一味保护商标，则会影响作为地名的正常使用，如果一味保护地名，则不能合理正确地保护商标。这就使"鼓浪屿"在被使用时，更多遭受了地名使用和商标权之间的冲突。这种具有注册商标和地名双重意义的商标，如何在审判中平衡商标所有人和大众对于地名的使用是最大的难点。

本案判决涉及的馅饼包装，其中一种是将"鼓浪屿"突出使用，另一种是将"鼓浪屿"与馅饼合在一起使用，最终法院认定对"鼓浪屿"三个字突出使用构成对"鼓浪屿"商标侵权，而"鼓浪屿"与"特产"合在一起使用，则是对"鼓浪屿"地名的合理使用，不构成商标侵权。本判决将作为商标和作为地名的"鼓浪屿"进行巧妙地区分，"鼓浪屿"三个字在包装、宣传中该如何使用能起到很好的指导，其他地名商标也可以在实际使用中参照。

（李缘缘　张伟昌）

厦门宝岛眼镜诉福州宝岛眼镜不正当竞争纠纷案研析

一、案情简介

原告厦门宝岛眼镜有限公司（以下简称"厦门宝岛"）诉称，原告成立于1997年，经过长期经营发展，已经建立良好的商业信誉，原告的企业名称经过长期使用，在消费者中具有较高的知名度，"宝岛眼镜"字号深入人心。近期，原告在厦门市思明区禾祥西路266号之三发现一家名称为"宝岛眼镜公司——中国第619店"的眼镜销售商铺，即被告福州宝岛眼镜有限公司（以下简称"福州宝岛"）厦门第十三营业部，但其并非原告的连锁店。被告福州宝岛厦门第十三营业部在其所经营店铺的招牌中使用"宝岛眼镜公司"字样，在其销售的眼镜盒、眼镜布上标有宝岛眼镜（连锁）公司，其开具的配镜单显示为"宝岛眼镜公司（全国连锁店）"，并加盖"宝岛眼镜公司——中国第619店"收款专用章，被告福州宝岛厦门第十三营业部的上述行为系擅自使用原告企业字号，误导消费者，系不正当竞争行为。被告福州宝岛厦门第十三营业部为被告福州宝岛公司的分支机构，被告福州宝岛公司应对福州宝岛厦门第十三营业部的行为承担连带责任。

被告福州宝岛辩称，原告的要求属行政诉讼受案范围，本案是侵犯企业名称权属于民事受案范围，法院应驳回原告的要求；被告福州宝岛为依法登记设立的企业，其企业名称权依法应当受到保护；被告福州宝岛公司在社会上享有较高声誉，被告福州宝岛厦门第十三营业部系合法使用被告福州宝岛公司的企业字号，不构成不正当竞争行为。

二、裁判结果

厦门市思明区人民法院经审理认为，原审被告福州宝岛厦门第十三营业部在其店面牌匾上使用"宝岛眼镜公司——中国第619店"，并在其商品、商品包装上使用其"宝岛眼镜公司（全国连锁店）"字样及使用上述简化名称在厦门市进行商业宣传的行为，足以使相关公众对其企业名称及商品的来源产生混淆，侵犯了原审原告企业名称权，属于不正当竞争，应当承担规范使用、赔偿损失的民事责任。鉴于原审被告福州宝岛厦门第十三营业部系原审被告福州宝岛公司的分公司，本案的民事赔偿责任由被告福州宝岛公司承担。据此，判决被告福州宝岛眼镜有限公司厦门第十三经营部规范使用其企业名称，停止在其店铺、商品（包括搭赠的商品）、商品包装上简化使用"宝岛眼镜公司""宝岛眼镜（连锁）公司"字样及停止在厦门市以上述简化企业名称进行商业宣传；被告福州宝岛眼镜有限公司赔偿原告厦门宝岛经济损失人民币10 000元。

三、争议焦点

本案的争议焦点有：

（1）原告的诉讼请求是否属于民事诉讼受理范围？
（2）被告的行为是否侵犯了原告的企业名称权？
（3）原告要求的损害赔偿金额是否合理？

四、案件评析

（一）原告的诉讼请求是否属于民事诉讼受理范围

原告以被告擅自使用原告企业名称误导消费者构成不正当竞争为由，请求判令被告立即停止使用原告企业字号及利用原告字号进行商业宣传并赔偿其损失。本案审理对象为被告行为是否侵犯原告企业名称权，被告是否构成不正当竞争及是否应当承担民事赔偿责任。原告要求属于民事诉讼受理范围，故被告关于本案要求属于行政诉讼受理范围的答辩意见，法院不予支持。

（二）被告的行为是否侵犯了原告的企业名称权

企业名称是在市场上表彰法人主体的重要商业标志，也是商品生产经营者经营特色和商誉的重要载体。企业名称的使用能够为其所有者带来一定的经济利益，企业从事经营活动，提供优良的商品和服务，培育并树立良好的企业形象，所形成的良好商业信誉，最终都归纳承载在其名称上，消费者通过企业名称对企业进行辨认与识别，因此更是企业进行市场竞争的重要手段。

1. 企业名称的保护途径

在我国现行法律体系下，企业名称保护主要有以下几种途径。

第一，《企业名称登记管理规定》上的保护。企业名称权包括使用权与禁止权两个方面。企业名称使用权为企业合法使用该名称的权利；而企业名称禁止权为排除他人不正当使用相同或类似企业名称之权利。《企业名称登记管理规定》的规范，也分为两方面：一是事前的对企业取得名称使用作出规范，确立使用特定企业名称的条件，确保依法登记的名称之间不至于互相冲突，依法登记进而依法保护。二是对企业名称专用权的保护，对于侵害他人企业名称的行为设有罚则。

第二，商标法上的保护。尽管商标法保护的核心是商标，但是也有间接保护企业名称权的效果。这是因为企业名称与商标有其相似性。在形式上，任何能够将自然人、法人或者其他组织的商品与他人的商品区别开的可视性标志，包括文字、图形、字母、数字符、三维标志和颜色组合，以及上述要素的组合，均可以作为商标申请注册，但在仅有文字商标的情形下，商标与商号形式上是近似的。而在功能上，商标的作用是对于产品或服务标记，用以区分不同产品或服务，避免混淆，可以作为消费者对产品或服务体验的归纳对象，有承载商誉功能。企业名称则是一个企业的标记，用以区分不同企业，同样可以作为消费者对产品或服务体验的归纳对象，亦有承载商誉功能。两者有着类似的功能性，也因其功能类似，在例如产品生产商将商号突出标示于产品、说明书、广告及宣传册、包装物以及营业场所等地；或是服务提供商在其服务商标并没有一个物质性的载体的情况下,商标与商号已很难区分。因此,虽然商标法保护的范围是商标,然而商标的功能与形式一定程度上与企业名称有重合的情况下,可以说商标法也有间接保护企业名称的功能与形式的效果。

第三,反不正当竞争法上的保护。使用他人企业名称,造成攀附他人商誉,混淆消费者造成错误等造成不正当竞争的行为,可以为反不正当竞争法所规范。例如,《反不正当竞争法》第 5 条第(3)项明确禁止擅自使用他人的企业名称或者姓名,引人误认为是他人的商品的行为。

第四,民法上的保护。民法意义上的人分为自然人与法人,其中法人亦享有名称权,而名称权是侵权责任法保障的民事权利之一,是以民法理论上也保障企业名称,只是实际操作上不如其他法律便利并且不是核心的保障范围,但理论上也具备一定的保障功能。

2. 造成混淆的类型

是否构成侵犯企业名称权的关键在于被告的行为是否可能导致消费者混淆。企业名称、商标皆有承载商誉、区分彼此的功能,此功能的不彰即造成消费者的混淆。在实践中,使用他人企业名称造成消费者混淆可能存在以下三种情形。

其一,企业名称的商号间互相混淆的可能。我国《企业名称登记管理规定》第 7 条规定,企业名称应当由字号(或者商号)、行业或者经营特点、组织形式,并且应当冠以企业所在地行政区划名称。企业名称经核准登记注册后方可使用,在规定的范围内享有专用权。是以可能发生如本案案情,在不同行政区两个均经合法登记的企业名称中的字号完全相同的情况。

其二,商号与商标间混淆的可能。商标权与商号权的冲突,是指使用相同或相似的文字的商标与商号分属不同的权利人,而使消费者对商品或服务的来源产生混淆,使其误认为两者为同一人,或者两者之间存在某种特定联系,从而误购商品接受服务。而商号与商标间冲突的可能,来自于两者的相似性与不同体系性。商标与企业名称又有不同体系性,商标与商号两者准据法与范围、主管机关都不同。我国商标法规定相同种类的商品或者服务中不能注册相同或者相近似的商标。这种排它性是在全国范围内,为了防止近似商标的出现。而商号是依照《企业名称登记管理规定》所保护的。商号虽也有唯一性的要求，但它的唯一性不是在全国范围内，而在于注册的工商行政管理部门所辖区域。只要在该辖区内相同行业中没有相同或相近似的商号即可，具有明显的区域性。是以不同体系与范围，可能同时依法成立，却有类似功能与形式，则可能造成商标权与商号权的冲突，即前述使用相同或相似的文字的商标与商号分属不同的权利人，而使消费者对商品或服务的来源产生混淆，使其误认为两者为同一人，或者两者之间存在某种特定联系，从而误购商品接受服务。

其三，商标间互相混淆的可能。此为传统上商标法的核心课题，保护明确且本案无此情形前已述及，故不多加赘述。

3. 本案中的特殊情形

本案被告福州宝岛成立于1992年，依照《企业名称登记管理规定》取得的企业名称为"福州宝岛眼镜有限公司"。本案原告厦门宝岛成立于1997年，依照《企业名称登记管理规定》取得的企业名称为"厦门宝岛眼镜有限公司"。双方皆按照《企业名称登记管理规定》合法取得企业名称。其商号与组织形式皆相同，唯一的区分是企业名称中的行政区划不同。

本案属于企业名称中字号相互冲突的类型，在不同行政区内两个均经合法登记的企业名称中的字号完全相同的情况，在寻求企业名称的保护上，有其特殊性。企业名称中的行业、组织形式、行政区域等具有通用性，不是区别企业的主要标志。字号是企业名称的核心和最重要的区分标志，公众也往往通过字号来记忆和区分不同的企业。但是本案双方关键的字号完全相同，而其分别仅是有共通性的行政区划。造成形式上有区别，登记完全合法，但是在实质上易生混淆。本案中，双方当事人都是按照《企业名称登记管理规定》，对其企业名称进行核准登记注册，因此在规定的范围内享有专用权。既已承认福州宝岛的企业名称使用权，则出现新的难题，两个依法取得的权力相互冲突如何解决？

本案被告福州宝岛特许位于厦门的福州宝岛厦门第十三营业部加盟，造成自己企业名称使用权与厦门宝岛企业名称专用权的冲突，盖福州宝岛合法地使用自己的企业名称，却因为双方企业名称除了行政区划以外皆相同，外观相似。又因特许加盟在厦门营业而与厦门宝岛企业名称可能有混淆可能，造成厦门宝岛公司企业名称专用权有受侵害之虞。

思明法院经审理认为，法律对于企业名称及其简称的登记、使用有严格要求。被告福州宝岛厦门第十三营业部于2010年在厦门成立，其在店面牌匾上未使用登记注册的企业名称，而使用"宝岛眼镜公司中国第619店"，并在其商品、商品包装上使用"宝岛眼镜（连锁）公司"字样。其简化使用企业名称的行为未报登记主管机关备案，不属于对企业名称的规范使用。对于企业名称与在先权利冲突的民事纠纷，应遵循诚实信用、维护公平竞争和保护在先合法权利人利益的原则予以处理。通常情况下，企业名称中的行业、组织形式、行政区域等具有通用性，不是区别企业的主要标志。字号是企业名称的核心和最重要的区分标志，公众也往往通过字号来记忆和区分不同的企业。但本案的特殊之处在于，"厦门宝岛眼镜有限公司"与"福州宝岛眼镜有限公司"两个企业名称中的字号、行业、组织形式完全相同，唯一的区别在于行政区划。在使用过程中，企业名称中的行政区划成为区别两家企业的唯一标志。原告1997年在厦门成立后，通过长期经营发展，企业名称和字号"宝岛眼镜"在消费者中已具有较高的知名度。虽然被告福州宝岛公司成立于1992年，但被告福州宝岛厦门第十三营业部于2010年才在厦门成立。在厦门已经存在一家较为有名的"宝岛眼镜"的前提下，作为后来成立的被告福州宝岛厦门第十三营业部，省略其总公司与原告企业名称中唯一的区别标志，即企业名称中的行政区划"福州"，简化使用"宝岛眼镜公司中国第619店""宝岛眼镜（连锁）公司"的做法虽不属擅自使用原告企业名称，但已足以使消费者难以区分两家企业，误认为被告福州宝岛厦门第十三营业部与原告之间存在特定关联关系，造成混淆。因此，应当确认被告福州宝岛厦门第十三营业部的行为属于不正当竞争，侵犯了原告的企业名称权。

4. 寻求其他企业名称保护途径的可能

本案侵权型态上有其特殊性，不以类推适用难以归类到《反不正当竞争法》中进行保护，前已述及。

实则在前述企业名称保护的途径之外，也许可以寻求有间接保护作用的《商标法》上的保护。按照《最高人民法院关于审理商标民事纠纷案件适用法律若干问题的解释》第1条第（1）项的规定，"将与他人注册商标相同或者相近似的文字作为企业的字号在相同或者类似商品上突出使用，容易使相关公众产生误认的"，属于商标法规定的给他人注册商标专用权造成其他损害的行为。

在本案中，厦门宝岛眼镜公司有数个宝岛眼镜商标的使用权，虽为图形商标，但实则是文字为搭配图形，其中文字部分也用图形方式表现，并不减损其中文字的含义。

厦门宝岛眼镜公司也可以主张，福州宝岛眼镜公司企业名称与厦门宝岛眼镜公司有权使用的商标中图形所显示的文字意义相近似，实际上已经造成混淆，使相关公众误认，给注册商标专用权造成损害。注册商标的保护不限于相同，而包括相近似，较《反不正当竞争法》有弹性，本案侵权态样可以比较完整的被涵摄。根据《商标法》第53条，效果上可以有民事与行政上的救济选择，途径上可能较《反不正当竞争法》的保护路径更广而更有利原告。

惟本案中碍于侵权态样特殊性，两个均经合法登记的企业名称中的字号完全相同；不属假冒他人的注册商标；商标与企业名称本身又难谓知名商品；法院认定双方有区别而不属于擅自使用原告企业名称；也未在商品上伪造冒用标志。造成在《反不正当竞争法》的体系中难以直接归类。但当事人诉讼上主张侧重《反不正当竞争法》的当事人主义限制，法院仍依《反不正当竞争法》裁判。

在当事人主义的限制下，不能以似乎较为便利的《商标法》解决途径处理。承审法院在实体正义与程序正义的两难下，仍然找到了顾及两边的作法，程序上顾及程序正义，实体上促进知识产权的良性发展，取缔对商标或企业名称的侵权能促进企业良性发展。确保商标所区别的商品或服务的竞争成果不受人榨取。商标上承载着公司的商誉，往往也反映着商誉的价值。通过取缔商标侵权行为以降低侵权人的边际收益，从而达到遏制侵权发生的目的，同时提高商誉价值的边际贡献，提供企业良性发展的诱因，促进经济发展,可谓用心良苦。

(三)原告要求的损害赔偿金额是否合理

厦门市思明区人民法院认为,原告要求被告赔偿经济损失及制止侵权支付合理费用10万元,但是原告未能提供相应的证据证明其实际损失以及被告福州宝岛厦门第十三营业部的获利情况,厦门市思明区人民法院将综合考虑被告侵权行为的性质、后果以及被告的主观过错程度等因素,对原告请求的赔偿数额依法酌情予以确定。

五、典型意义

不同企业之间的企业名称权发生冲突是一种典型的知识产权争议。企业名称中通常最重要最有标志性的部分是字号,商家一般也是通过使用、宣传自己的字号来达到让消费者辨认、记忆、认同其企业的目的。

本案中被告使用自己合法登记的企业名称中的字号仍然构成侵权。本案中最关键的问题是:两个均经合法登记的企业名称中的字号完全相同的情况下,如何判断其使用的正当性。企业成立时间、地点、知名度、品牌影响区域等都是法官要考虑的因素。本案最重要的考虑因素是特定区域在先权利与字号使用的实际后果。被告福州宝岛眼镜有限公司尽管经过合法登记,甚至早于原告厦门宝岛眼镜有限公司成立。但其成立在福州。在厦门这个特定区域内,原告先成立且经过的十年的发展与宣传已享有较高知名度。宝岛眼镜在这个特定区域的消费者心中,已有很明确的企业指向和认同,故原告已经在厦门享有了"宝岛眼镜"的在先权利。被告福州宝岛眼镜有限公司2010年在厦门成立被告福州宝岛眼镜有限公司厦门第十三经营部,该经营部省略总公司与原告公司企业名称中唯一的区别标志,在其店铺与商品上简化使用"宝岛眼镜公司""宝岛眼镜(连锁)公司"字样的做法虽然不属于原告所称的擅自使用他人企业名称,但已足以让消费者误认为该经营部与原告之间存在特定关联关系,与原告的在先权利发生冲突并在实际上造成混淆。因此被告的行为被认定为不正当竞争,侵犯了原告的企业名称权。因被告的企业名称经合法登记,故本案根据事实情况只判决象征性赔偿。

取缔对商标或企业名称的侵权能促进企业良性发展。确保商标所区别的商品或者服务的竞争成果不受他人榨取。商标承载着公司的商誉，往往也反映着商誉的价值。取缔商标侵权以降低侵权人的边际利益，降低侵权动机，同时提高商誉价值的边际贡献，提供企业良性发展的诱因，促进经济发展。

（曾争志　曹宇君）

银据公司诉集恩图造公司等不正当竞争纠纷案研析

一、案情简介

原告厦门银据空间地理信息有限公司（以下简称"银据公司"）认为被告李某、被告陈某某和被告厦门集恩图造信息科技股份有限公司（以下简称"集恩图造公司"）侵犯其商业秘密，构成不正当竞争，请求法院判令三被告立即停止利用非法获取的商业秘密、赔礼道歉并赔偿原告损失人民币1元。

被告集恩图造公司、被告李某、被告陈某某共同辩称：涉案的日本客户信息通过日本的相关网站就可以搜集、查询到，没有任何秘密可言，客户不是原告独占的；关于离职后能否从事与原告相同或相近的行业，厦门市劳动仲裁委员会裁决认定被告李某和被告陈某某并无违约行为，原告未履行相关的支付义务，最终裁决驳回原告诉求。据此，被告并不存在侵犯商业秘密的不正当竞争行为。

二、裁判结果

厦门市思明区人民法院对双方提供的证据进行查明，认为被告李某、被告陈某某尚未从原告银据信息公司辞职即成立与原告业务相似的新公司，被告李某到被告集恩图造公司后，仍与在原告工作时的客户保持业务联系，侵犯原告的商业秘密，为被告集恩图造公司谋取利益，因此，被告李某、被告陈某某、被告集恩图造公司的行为属于不正当竞争行为，依法应立即停止侵权。被告李某、被告陈某某是被告集恩图造公司的员工，在职期间从事的行为利益归于被告集恩图造公司，属于职务行为，判令由被告集恩图造公司赔偿原告损失人民币1元。因本案不涉及人身权，驳回原告赔礼道歉的请求。

三、争议焦点

本案的争议焦点有：
(1) 被告的行为是否侵犯原告的商业秘密？
(2) 被告李某、陈某某是否存在违反竞业限制的行为？

四、案例评析

（一）被告的行为是否侵犯原告的商业秘密

商业秘密是指不为公众所知悉、能为权利人带来经济利益、具有实用性并经权利人采取保密措施的技术信息和经营信息。从该定义可知，商业秘密应具备秘密性、具备经济价值且采取一定的保密措施。由于商业秘密本身具有巨大的经济价值，同时商业秘密又具有"一旦泄露，永远泄露"的特性，所以商业秘密一旦流失，将可能会给其权利人带来无法弥补的伤害。我国立法对商业秘密的保护主要体现在《反不正当竞争法》中，除此之外还有《民事诉讼法》在程序上的保护、《合同法》的保护、《劳动合同法》的保护、《刑法》的保护以及一系列行政法规的保护。本案主要涉及的是《反不正当竞争法》中对商业秘密的保护问题。

认定侵犯商业秘密行为的前提是认定该行为侵犯的对象是否为商业秘密，即商业秘密的认定。首先，需要判断该信息是否"不为公众所知悉"。《最高人民法院关于审理不正当竞争民事案件应用法律若干问题的解释》中规定，有关信息所属领域的相关人员普遍不知悉和不容易获得该信息的，即为"不为公众所知悉"，同时，若该信息为其所属技术或者经济领域的人的一般常识或者行业惯例，或者该信息仅涉及产品的尺寸、结构、材料、部件的简单组合等内容，或者进入市场后相关公众通过观察产品即可直接获得，或者该信息已经在公开出版物或者其他媒体上公开披露，或者该信息已通过公开的报告会、展览等方式公开，或者该信息从其他公开渠道可以获得，或者该信息无须付出一定的代价而容易获得则不属于"不为公众所知悉"的范畴。其次，经济价值的判断，有关信息具有现实的或者潜在的商业价值，能为权利人带来竞争优势的即为"能为权利人带来经济利益、具有实用性"。最后，保密措施的判断，根据所涉信息载体的特性、权利人保密的意愿、保密措施的可识别程度、他人通过正当方式获得的难易程度等因素来判断权利人为防止信息泄露是否采取了与其商业价值等具体情况相适应的合理保护措施。对此，相关司法解释还列举了一些合理保密措施立法例，若权利人在限定涉密信息的知悉范围，只对必须知悉的相关人员告知其内容，或者对于涉密信息载体采取加锁等防范措施，或者在涉密信息的载体上标有保密标志，或者对于涉密信息采用密码或者代码等，或者签订保密协议，或者对于涉密的机器、厂房、车间等场所限制来访者或者提出保密要求，或者确保信息秘密的其他合理措施，且在正常情况下足以防止涉密信息泄露则应当认定权利人采取了保密措施。

  本案所涉及的是商业秘密中的客户名单。客户名单，一般是指客户的名称、地址、联系方式以及交易的习惯、意向、内容等构成的区别于相关公知信息的特殊客户信息，包括汇集众多客户的客户名册，以及保持长期稳定交易关系的特定客户。在本案中，银据信息公司早在 2005 年 9 月就与朝日航洋会社订立关于地理数据测量的合作协议，至今一直保持合作关系。有关朝日航洋会社的信息是否构成商业秘密，应从商业秘密的三方面进行判断。首先，有关朝日航洋会社的一般信息，比如公司的地址、联系方式等，可以通过网络检索即可获得，该部分信息属于公众知悉部分。但是除此之外，朝日航洋会社与银据信息公司特定的联系方式、交易习惯、交易内容等是"不为公众所知悉"，满足秘密性要件。其次，对于银据信息公司来说，朝日航洋会社是其重要的客户，与其有着许多经济来往，当然该信息具有重要的经济价值，满足"能为权利人带来经济利益、具有实用性"。最后，银据信息公司通过制定公司保密制度、与员工签订保密条款、要求辞职员工签署保密承诺等措施积极防止泄露相关信息，满足"采取保密措施"的要件。所以，与朝日航洋会社有关的客户信息、交易内容等信息应当认定为商业秘密。

商业秘密认定之后，就需要判断相关行为是否构成侵犯商业秘密的行为。本案中，被告的行为主要涉及违反约定或者违反权利人有关保守商业秘密的要求，披露、使用或者允许他人使用其所掌握的商业秘密。银据信息公司早在 2005 年 9 月就与朝日航洋会社订立关于地理数据测量的合作协议，该协议由李某代表公司与朝日航洋会社订立，此后一系列的往来李某也都参与其中，对银据信息公司与朝日航洋会社之间的合作关系、往来情况、交易内容和要求十分熟悉和了解。之后李某创办集恩图造公司，与银据信息公司从事类似业务，并与朝日航洋会社进行业务上的联系。根据相关司法解释的规定，如果客户基于对职工个人的信赖而与职工所在单位进行市场交易，该职工离职后，能够证明客户自愿选择与自己或者其新单位进行市场交易的，应当认定没有采用不正当手段，但职工与原单位另有约定的除外。李某与银据信息公司签有保密协议，并且其与朝日航洋会社进行业务上的联系也并非是出于客户自身的意愿。从银据信息公司提供的证据来看，李某与朝日航洋会社进行联系时使用的邮箱等一系列表明身份的标志都会让对方产生仍旧与银据信息公司进行业务联系的错误判断，起到误导的作用。因此，该行为构成侵犯商业秘密的行为。

在认定本案中被告行为构成违反商业秘密的行为之后，还涉及赔偿责任的问题。在本案中，原告银据信息公司请求被告支付 1 元的赔偿金，但是并没有提供相关证据来支撑其诉讼请求，法院的判决理由也没有对该问题进行说明。根据相关司法解释的规定，侵犯商业秘密行为的损害赔偿额可以参照确定侵犯专利权的损害赔偿额的方法；因侵权行为导致商业秘密已为公众所知悉的，应当根据该项商业秘密的商业价值确定损害赔偿额。商业秘密的商业价值，根据其研究开发成本、实施该项商业秘密的收益、可得利益、可保持竞争优势的时间等因素确定。所以本案中，对侵犯商业秘密的赔偿金额还有待商榷。

最后，侵犯商业秘密行为判决停止侵害的民事责任时，停止侵害的时间一般持续到该项商业秘密已为公众知悉时为止，但是如果判决停止侵害的时间明显不合理的，可以在依法保护权利人该项商业秘密竞争优势的情况下，判决侵权人在一定期限或者范围内停止使用该项商业秘密。本案中所涉及的客户信息主要是一些与客户联系的特定方式、交易内容以及交易习惯，等等，该种类型的商业秘密与技术类的商业秘密不同，只要科技在进步，一些作为商业秘密的技术就可能被公开，客户信息类的商业秘密除非存在故意泄密的情形，否则不会轻易为公众所指。此外，这些客户信息中涉及的交易内容和交易习惯多少带有一些像李某这类作为原公司相关客户信息取得和维护的人员的习惯。假设某个领域中的需求商较少，而供货商的需求客户也几乎雷同，只是每个供货商相应需求商的联系方式不同，交易习惯不同而已，那么判定停止侵害的时间持续到该项商业秘密已为公众知悉时为止就明显不合理，建议此种情况下停止侵害的时间以竞业限制的期限为准。但是在本案中，由于市场上的需求商较多，且涉案的客户信息只涉及一家公司，所以应当判定被告停止侵害商业秘密直到该项商业秘密已为公众知悉时为止。

（二）被告李某、陈某某是否存在违反竞业限制的行为

竞业限制又称为竞业禁止，是指对与权利人有特定关系的人的特定竞争行为的禁止，即权利人有权要求与其具有特定民事法律关系的特定人不为针对自己的竞争性行为。竞业限制所禁止的客体是特定行为，即与权利人构成竞业的行为；所禁止的主体限于特定人，即与权利人具有特定民事法律关系的义务人。在竞业限制法律关系中，权利人享有请求权，可请求义务人不为竞业行为；义务人承担的是一种不作为的义务。竞业限制按其法律效力的来源可以分为法定竞业限制和约定竞业限制。前者是指特定人的竞业禁止义务直接来自于法律的禁止性规定；后者则源于当事人之间的协议。根据契约自由原则，当事人可以自由作出竞业禁止的约定，使一方或双方负或互负不竞业义务。竞业限制按其义务主体可以分为在职雇员的竞业限制和离职雇员的竞业限制。在职雇员的竞业限制主要为法定竞业限制，雇主也可以与雇员通过协议的方式约定在职雇员的不竞业义务。离职雇员的竞业限制则属约定的竞业限制，即离职雇员承担的应是一种明示的不竞业义务，其产生依据应是合法有效的竞业禁止协议，雇主单方制定的不竞业规章不能作为离职职工竞业禁止明示或默示义务的产生依据。

有关法定竞业限制的规定，我国立法并未集中规定，而是散见于各单行立法之中。例如，《公司法》第148条规定，董事、高级管理人员不得未经股东会或者股东大会同意，利用职务便利为自己或者他人谋取属于公司的商业机会，自营或者为他人经营与所任职公司同类的业务；《合伙企业法》第32条规定，合伙人不得自营或者同他人合作经营与本合伙企业相竞争的业务；《中外合资经营企业法实施条例》第37条规定，总经理或者副总经理不得兼任其他经济组织的总经理或者副总经理，不得参与其他经济组织对本企业的商业竞争；等等。学者认为应对了解或知悉商业秘密的在职劳动者或雇员强制课以不竞业义务，理由是劳动者或雇员与董事、经理人一样对所在公司、企业负有忠实义务，如果允许这些劳动者从事竞业活动，他们极易在竞业活动中有意或无意地泄露或使用其所在用人单位的商业秘密，削弱它们的竞争优势，损害其经济利益，造成不正当竞争，使自己获得不正当利益。虽然对商业秘密有法定的保护手段，但那些手段存在对权利人极为不利的因素，因而不能因商业秘密已有独立的法律保护手段而否认掌握商业秘密的劳动者负不竞业义务。❶ 此观点不能成立，对于在职的了解或知悉商业秘密的劳动者的竞业问题，不仅可以用商业秘密的手段来解决，还可以用合同违约的手段解决。一般用人单位都会在劳动合同中约定职工在职期间的竞业问题，如果职工违约将承担相应的违约责任。这两种手段足以保护用人单位的利益，故无须再将其纳入法定的竞业限制中。

我国《劳动合同法》中所规定的竞业禁止仅指离职雇员的竞业禁止即约定竞业禁止，是指劳动者在与用人单位解除或者终止劳动合同后，不得到与本单位生产或者经营同类产品、从事同类业务的有竞争关系的其他用人单位，或者自己开业生产或者经营同类产品、从事同类业务。首先，竞业禁止的主体仅限于用人单位的高级管理人员、高级技术人员和其他负有保密义务的人员，除此之外，对公司的一般员工不得适用竞业禁止条款。其次，竞业禁止的范围、地域、期限由用人单位与劳动者约定，竞业限制的约定不得违反法律、法规的规定。再次，用人单位在竞业限制期限内要

---

❶ 桂菊平："竞业禁止若干法律问题研究"，载《法商研究》2001年第1期。

按月给予劳动者经济补偿，劳动者若违反竞业限制约定的，应当按照约定向用人单位支付违约金。《最高人民法院关于审理劳动争议案件适用法律若干问题的解释（四）》对此有更细致的规定：一是关于竞业限制协议的解除，对于用人单位而言，在竞业限制期限内，可以随时请求解除竞业限制协议，在此情况下，劳动者可以请求用人单位额外支付劳动者三个月的竞业限制经济补偿；对劳动者而言，只有在用人单位严重违约的情况下才能解除竞业限制协议。二是关于违约责任，对用人单位而言，若当事人在劳动合同或者保密协议中约定了竞业限制和经济补偿，劳动合同解除或者终止后，因用人单位的原因导致三个月未支付经济补偿，劳动者可以请求解除竞业限制约定；对劳动者而言，违反竞业限制约定的，向用人单位支付违约金后，若用人单位要求其按照约定继续履行竞业限制义务的，劳动者应当继续履行。三是关于未约定经济补偿金时的计算问题，未约定竞业限制补偿金的情况下，劳动者履行了竞业限制义务，可以要求用人单位按照劳动者在劳动合同解除或者终止前十二个月平均工资的30%按月支付经济补偿的，若该月平均工资的30%低于劳动合同履行地最低工资标准的，按照劳动合同履行地最低工资标准支付。最后，竞业限制的期限不得超过2年。

具体到本案，银据信息公司的经营范围为：地理信息系统工程、全球定位系统建设；数字化空间信息处理，数据加工生产，数字化城市工程建设；计算机软件开发、销售；计算机网络工程建设；文档资料扫描加工、数字化加工、档案扫描；软件出口及数据服务外包；销售（不含商场零售和超市零售）家用电器、计算机及零配件、通信设备、基础软件、应用软件；集恩图造公司的经营范围为：计算机网络工程、智能化系统工程的设计及施工、计算机软硬件的研发及销售、经营各类商品和技术的进出口等。银据信息公司和集恩图造公司的经营范围存在重合部分，两者存在竞争关系。陈某某与银据信息公司签订《聘用合同书》，期限自2008年8月1日至2011年8月1日止，担任银据信息公司主任，并于2010年9月7日从公司离职。李某与银据信息公司签订《聘用合同书》，期限自2010年5月1日至2012年5月1日止，担任银据信息公司副总经理，并于2010年7月

16 日从公司离职。2010 年 6 月 8 日，集恩图造公司成立，陈某某任公司法定代表人，李某担任公司董事长兼总经理，此时，两人还未从原公司离职。李某作为原公司高管，违反了《公司法》第 148 条的规定，即法定竞业限制，并且李某和陈某某与银据信息公司签订的劳动合同中也约定了在职期间的竞业限制，两人的行为违反合同约定，应承担违约责任。《劳动合同法》和《最高人民法院关于审理劳动争议案件适用法律若干问题的解释（四）》规定当事人在劳动合同或者保密协议中约定了竞业限制，在解除或者终止劳动合同后必须给予劳动者经济补偿，劳动者才有履行竞业限制的义务。两人离职之后，李某是公司的高管人员，陈某某是负有保密义务的人员，两人均符合承担竞业限制义务的主体要求，且从事的是与原公司具有竞争关系的工作，构成竞业行为，陈某某与原公司约定的竞业补贴被包含在薪酬之中，李某离职后的竞业禁止协议中也未约定经济补偿金。陈某某和李某只有在离职后三个月未收到银据信息公司支付的经济补偿款后才能向法院提出不履行竞业限制协议，在此之前仍应履行竞业限制协议。若银据信息公司支付了经济补偿金，则可以要求两人继续履行竞业禁止义务。当然，本案中原告银据信息公司也未提出竞业限制相关的诉讼请求。

五、典型意义

企业客户信息是企业赖以生存的重要资源，一些企业保密意识比较淡薄，未与员工签订保密协议，对客户信息也未采取相应的保密措施，使很多外贸、技术企业员工在跳槽之后随意使用原单位的客户信息搞不正当竞争、拉拢业务。本案的恶意竞争涉及企业高管跳槽另开公司，利用原有客户资源开展业务的情形，最终法院判定构成不正当竞争。

该案对现今较为普遍的员工违反竞业禁止义务，侵害"原东家"的情况具有重要的警示意义。

（李缘缘　李雅光）

王某某与厦门工商局、宇电公司行政处罚决定案研析

一、案情简介

原告王某某与第三人厦门宇电自动化科技有限公司（以下简称"宇电公司"）签订劳动合同，双方约定王某某的工作岗位为总经理助理，劳动合同期限从2007年11月1日起至2010年11月30日止。2007年12月10日，双方签订《保守商业秘密协议书》，约定王某某在宇电公司工作期间，不得对外泄露宇电公司内部的任何"科研资料、生产技术资料、客户资料、供应商资料以及企业新产品信息、发展计划等"，宇电公司每月给王某某加发基本工资的10%作为保密补贴。2010年9月16日，双方签订《劳动合同解除书面协议》，双方解除劳动关系，并约定原告王某某"无论在职或离职后，均不得对外泄露宇电公司内部的任何科研资料、生产技术资料、客户资料、供应商资料及企业发展规划等，违者应赔偿宇电公司由此而遭受的一切损失"。2010年9月21日，原告王某某从宇电公司离职。

厦门艾克特自动化科技有限公司（以下简称"艾克特公司"）成立于2011年5月16日，法定代表人为原告王某某。2012年5月8日，第三人宇电公司向被告厦门市工商行政管理局（以下简称"厦门工商局"）举报称，艾克特公司及王某某、张某某、林某某涉嫌侵犯宇电公司AI产品的程序软件、供应商资料、客户资料等商业秘密。根据福建中证司法鉴定中心〔2012〕数检字第10号电子数据鉴定意见，送检的宇电公司和艾克特公司的人工智能温控器/调节器的主控芯片中的机器代码一致，且经反汇编后的

汇编代码也一致,两者为同一来源。专家组不认可王某某通过反向工程破解宇电公司主芯片与存储芯片的主张,亦否认了王某某陈述的校正过程。被告厦门市工商局据此作出厦工商处〔2012〕151号行政处罚决定,认定王某某违反与宇电公司保守商业秘密的约定要求,允许艾克特公司使用其所掌握的宇电公司商业秘密,构成侵犯他人商业秘密的违法事实。责令当事人王某某停止侵权行为,处罚款人民币15万元。

原告王某某不服被告厦门工商局的行政处罚决定,向福建省厦门市思明区人民法院提起行政诉讼,法院依法通知宇电公司作为第三人参加诉讼。

二、裁判结果

厦门市思明区人民法院经审理认为,宇电公司对其重要技术信息,已经采取相应的保密措施。经鉴定,艾克特公司产品与宇电公司产品构成"实质相同"。原告王某某辞职之前任第三人宇电公司总经理助理,具备"接触"宇电公司技术信息的便利条件。原告主张自己是通过反向工程获得涉案产品,但根据原告陈述,其是委托他人破解涉案芯片程序,支付费用后购买获得。原告所称的"购买"芯片程序的行为并不属于法律规定的"反向工程",且原告没有充分证据证明其获得涉案芯片的来源是真实、有效、合法的购买行为。另外,专家组亦否认了王某某所称的校正过程。最终法院认定被告对原告王某某的行政处罚,认定事实清楚,证据充分,适用法律正确,程序合法,驳回原告诉讼请求。

三、争议焦点

本案的争议焦点主要有:
(1) AI系列智能仪表的芯片程序是否是商业秘密?
(2) 王某某的行为是否构成侵犯商业秘密?

四、案例评析

(一) AI系列智能仪表的芯片程序是否是商业秘密

根据我国《反不正当竞争法》第10条第3款的规定,商业秘密是指

"不为公众所知悉、能为权利人带来经济利益、具有实用性并经权利人采取保密措施的技术信息和经营信息"。因此，认定第三人宇电公司 AI 系列智能仪表的芯片程序是否是商业秘密需从以下几个方面入手。

1. 不为公众所知悉

根据《最高人民法院关于审理不正当竞争民事案件应用法律若干问题的解释》第 9 条第 1 款的规定，"不为公众所知悉"被解释为"有关信息不为其所属领域的相关人员普遍知悉和容易获得"。保密性是商业秘密区别于专利技术、公知技术最显著的特征。因为商业秘密以秘密状态维持其经济价值，一旦被公开，其经济价值就完全或者部分失去。按照 TRIPs 协议的规定，确定秘密性的通常标准一般为不为公众所知悉或没有进入公知领域。商业秘密不为公众所知悉，是因为从技术水准上讲，它经过发明、发现者的相当程度的个人努力，具有与公知知识与信息不同的内容，不易为公众掌握，具有独特性。❶

思明区人民法院认为，原告王某某在诉讼阶段向本院提交证据用以说明"可高精度等级、编程输入技术、模块化技术、AIBUS 通讯协议、改进后的 PID 调节算法独立控制技术、三相三线触发器"等技术都是公众所知悉，从而证明宇电公司涉案技术已为公众知悉。但是这些证据原告在被告实施行政行为过程中并未提出，不能作为行政执法过程中的证据。而在本案的诉讼过程中，这些证据除了公证书以外，其他证据在形式上均为复印件或者网络打印件，不符合法定证据形式，更重要的是上述证据与本案涉案的 AI 系列智能仪表产品的核心芯片程序的"公开性"没有直接的关联性。相关专家也在开庭时指出，这些资料只是通用的技术原理和一般的指导性叙述，并不涉及具体技术参数等技术核心。综上所述，原告王某某主张 AI 系列智能仪表产品芯片程序已为公众所知悉的证据不足。

思明区人民法院的上述分析充分考虑到"通用的技术原理和一般的指导性叙述"与"具体技术参数"的区别，从而正确认定本案中 AI 系列智能仪表产品的核心芯片程序的"不为公众所知悉"特性，值得肯定。例如，

---

❶ "浙江省宁波经济技术开发区江海软件有限公司与赵某某等侵犯商业秘密纠纷上诉案"，(2009) 浙甬知终字第 3 号民事判决书。

广东省高级人民法院就涉案技术图纸信息是否"不为公众所知悉"进行分析时也曾认为,"虽然涉案技术图纸所涉及的产品已经进入公共市场且鸿宝厂等进行过相关宣传,但是对于涉案技术图纸信息来说,进入公共市场的只是技术图纸对应的产品的外观、整体大小、整机功能、特点等浅显、外在的特征描述而非具体的技术部位的设计要求、技术参数。涉案技术图包括的产品种类繁多且每个产品涉及的技术并不为其所属领域的相关人员普遍知悉和容易获得,具备商业秘密不为公众所知悉的特性"。❶因此,法院在考量"不为公众所知悉"要件时,需要注意仔细考察"一般(整体)"与"细部(具体)"之间的关系。

2. 能为权利人带来经济利益并具有实用性

商业秘密所具有的商业价值,主要表现为这些信息给权利人带来的经济利益或竞争优势。根据《最高人民法院关于审理不正当竞争民事案件应用法律若干问题的解释》第10条的规定,有关信息具有现实的或者潜在的商业价值,能为权利人带来竞争优势的,应当认定为"能为权利人带来经济利益、具有实用性"。在最高人民法院公布2012年中国法院知识产权司法保护10大创新性案件——"衢州万联网络技术有限公司与周慧民等侵害商业秘密纠纷上诉案"中,法院也明确认为,商业秘密的实用性要求商业秘密必须转化为具体的可以实施的方案或形式。❷也就是说,一种信息要想得到法律的保护,必须转化为具体的可以据以实施的方案或者模式,法律并不保护单纯的构想、大概的原理和抽象的概念。如果某一信息尚在摸索、未被具体化或在实际应用的阶段,即不能被确定为商业秘密。商业秘密的价值性要求使用该商业秘密可以为权利人带来经济利益,提升竞争优势。这种利益包括现实的经济利益,也包括潜在的经济价值。所谓潜在的经济价值主要表现在能够改进技术、提高劳动生产率或产品质量,能够有助于改善企业经营管理绩效、降低成本和费用等方面。

---

❶ "东莞市鸿宝精密机械制造厂等与杨某侵犯商业秘密纠纷上诉案",(2011)粤高法民三终字第228号民事判决书。

❷ "衢州万联网络技术有限公司与周某某等侵害商业秘密纠纷上诉案",(2011)沪高民三(知)终字第100号民事判决书。

在本案中，AI 系列智能仪表产品系宇电公司的核心产品，为公司带来显著的经济效益。2009~2010 年，宇电公司在营业收入和营业毛利上收益颇丰，对国家税收贡献巨大，在厦门高新技术企业中名列前茅。上述证据表明，作为该产品最核心技术的芯片程序（含程序芯片和校正芯片）显然属于公司重要的生产技术资料。可见其经济效益可观，具备较强的实用性。

3. 经权利人采取保密措施

根据《最高人民法院关于审理不正当竞争民事案件应用法律若干问题的解释》第 11 条第 3 款第（5）项的规定，"签订保密协议"属于商业秘密权利人采取的一项保密措施。对商业秘密所采取的保密措施，要求权利人采取的保密措施万无一失是不现实的，将导致巨大的社会成本，也是过于苛刻的。因此，保密性实际上是指权利人为防止信息泄露所采取的与其商业价值等具体情况相适应的合理保护措施。

在本案中，原告王某某与第三人宇电公司签订的《保守商业秘密协议书》《劳动合同》《劳动合同解除书面协议》都明确约定原告王某某不得泄露宇电公司内部的"科研资料、生产技术资料"等商业秘密的义务及相应责任。工资签收表也体现原告王某某在宇电公司工作期间每月领取保密补贴。可见，第三人对能为其带来一定经济效益的重要技术信息，已经采取相应的保密措施。

综上所述，被告在行政处罚决定中认定涉案的 AI 系列智能仪表产品的芯片程序为宇电公司的商业秘密并无不当。

（二）王某某的行为是否构成侵犯商业秘密

根据我国《反不正当竞争法》第 10 条的规定，侵犯商业秘密的行为主要包括以各种不正当手段获取权利人的商业秘密；披露、使用或者允许他人使用以前项手段获取的权利人的商业秘密；违反约定或者违反权利人有关保守商业秘密的要求，披露、使用或者允许他人使用其所掌握的商业秘密。第三人明知或者应知前述违法行为，获取、使用或者披露他人的商业秘密的，视为侵犯商业秘密。本案中，王某某的行为是否构成侵犯商业秘密，思明区人民法院采用"接触+实质性相似"规则。即从商业秘密这一构成要件出发，围绕具有"实质性相似"特征的两件信息资料，认定原告王某某有"非法接触"的事实,包括以各种不正当手段获取权利人的商业秘密;而并无证据证明"合法来源"的事实,包括善意使用或披露、自行研发、反向工程以及以其他合理方式获取相同的商业秘密,最终判定王某某的行为构成侵犯商业秘密。

所谓"接触+实质性相似"规则,是指法院在审理侵犯商业秘密案件中,如果被告所使用的商业信息(包括技术信息和经营信息)与权利人的商业秘密相同或实质性相似,同时权利人又有证据表明被告在此前具备掌握该商业秘密的条件,那么就必须由被告来证明其所使用之商业信息的合法来源,否则即应承担侵权赔偿责任。"接触+实质性相似"规则在我国的知识产权法律渊源中虽然只有国家工商行政管理总局于1998年颁布的《关于禁止侵犯商业秘密行为的若干规定》中作过一些简单的规定,但它在我国侵犯商业秘密案件的审判实践中得到了非常广泛的运用。

1. 接触

对"接触"的理解,是该规则深刻内涵之核心所在。在本案中,原告王某某2007年11月进入宇电公司工作,工作岗位为总经理助理,职务仅次于总经理,作为权利人的前雇员是侵犯商业秘密法律关系中能够直接从权利人处获得商业秘密的人。基于其特殊的身份,其接触行商业秘密的事实不证自明,法律已免去权利人对此的证明责任。与宇电公司签订《保守商业秘密协议书》,每月领取保密补贴,由于原告王某某都是与权利人直接发生往来关系,所以他对所接触的商业秘密是从权利人处获得应当是明知的,因而对该商业秘密归属权利人所有也应该是非常清楚的。故原告王某某"接触"宇电公司技术信息已经具有法律层面上的高度盖然性。

2. 实质相似

商业秘密是一种未公开而为持有人通过保密措施予以维系权益的技术信息或经营信息。在商业秘密侵权案件中,权利人应该且能够对于自己控制的权利事实进行举证,如秘密性、保密性、对方获取商业秘密的可能性等,但对于相对人获取同一商业秘密的途径和方法往往存在举证困难。这是因为商业秘密不具有绝对意义上的独占性,同一秘密信息可能为多个主体所拥有，其合法获取的途径也不尽相同，如自行构思、善意取得、反向工程等。因此，不少学者和法官主张对被告取得技术秘密的手段采取举证责任倒置的方式，进行过错责任推定。❶

在商业秘密侵权诉讼中，权利人须对"实质性相似"负举证责任，即要证明"被申请人所使用的信息与自己的商业秘密具有一致性或者相同性"，受保护的秘密信息与被控侵权使用的信息是"相同信息"。被告即被控侵权人则就"合法来源"要素即取得或者使用商业秘密的合理性事实提供证明，此即在程序上倒置的举证责任。

在本案中，艾克特公司产品的外观、线路板、原材料的使用、元器件的布置等与宇电公司产品基本相同，功能、用途基本一致。而根据福建中证司法鉴定中心〔2012〕数检字第10号电子数据鉴定意见可知，送检的宇电公司和艾克特公司的人工智能温控器/调节器的主控芯片中的机器代码一致，且经反汇编后的汇编代码也一致，两者为同一来源。即两者构成"实质相同"。

3. 合法来源

在"接触+实质相似"成立的情况下，原告王某某需证明其获得涉案技术信息具有合法来源才能免于承担侵权责任。原告主张自己是通过反向工程获得涉案产品，根据原告的陈述，其是委托他人破解涉案芯片程序，支付费用后购买获得，自己并未破解该芯片程序。思明区人民法院认为，我国《反不正当竞争法》所称的"反向工程"，是指通过技术手段对从公开渠道取得的产品进行拆卸、测绘、分析等而获得该产品的有关技术信息。王某某所称的"购买"芯片程序的行为并不属于法律规定的"反向工程"。王某某主张其通过反向工程获得涉案芯片程序的说法没有法律依据。

本案事实上属于"事后反向工程抗辩"的情形。在反向工程的案件中，无论任何时候接触过他人秘密信息，都将否定合法反向工程的存在。实践中，实施反向工程而同时接触他人秘密信息的情况大有存在。在反向工程开始前，反向工程实施人接触到秘密信息，从而在公有领域寻找相当的信

---

❶ 郃中林："关于知识产权诉讼证据的若干热点问题"，见最高人民法院知识产权审判庭编：《知识产权审判指导与参考》（第1卷），法律出版社2000年版，第87页。

息，再结合产品制定反向工程进程。无论是哪一种接触信息的方式，只要接触，合法的反向工程就被推翻了。各国法律都明确规定，一方以不正当手段获得他人的商业秘密之后，又以反向工程为由主张获取行为合法性的，不予支持。本案中反向工程实施人在原告王某某处接触秘密信息后，所为的也只能是非法的反向工程行为。

根据《最高人民法院关于审理不正当竞争民事案件应用法律若干问题的解释》第12条第2款的规定，当事人以不正当手段知悉了他人的商业秘密之后，又以反向工程为由主张获取行为合法的，不予支持。此外，作为参考，江苏省高级人民法院《关于审理商业秘密案件有关问题的意见》第16条也规定，通过反向工程获取商业秘密的，不构成侵犯商业秘密。但产品系通过不正当手段获得除外。通过不正当手段获得他人商业秘密的，事后以可通过反向工程获得为由抗辩的，不应支持。

上述做法也能在比较法上找到相应的支持。例如，美国伊利诺伊州法院认为，当被告使用原告的秘密信息时，具有对公开获得的产品进行反向工程的能力并不能阻却商业秘密盗用责任的承担。❶ 特拉华州法院判决指出，如果他人采取不正当手段生产诉争产品，则合法反向工程的可能性不能阻止法院对原告请求诉前禁令的授予。❷ 美国俄亥俄州法院也认为即使原告的商业秘密本可以通过独立发现或反向工程获得，但法院禁止被告使用通过违背保密关系所获得商业秘密。❸

在本案中，王某某所称的"向他人购买破解的芯片"是否属于法律规定的"合法来源"？原告提供QQ聊天记录、光大银行账户明细查询单及汇款凭证欲证明其获得涉案芯片程序具有合法来源。但是，原告提供的QQ聊天记录是单方打印件，证据形式不符合法定要求。且在内容上，QQ聊天记录、光大银行账户明细查询单及汇款凭证均无法证明所谓芯片破解人的真实身份、收款人的真实身份、两者之间的关系、破解芯片的具体信息等。

---

❶ ILG Industries, Inc. v. Scott, 273 N. E. 2d 393 (Il. 1971).

❷ Technicon Data Systems Corp v. Curtis 1000, Inc., 224 U. S. P. Q. 286, p.291 (Del. Chan. Ct. 1984).

❸ Valco Cincinnati, Inc. v. N & D Machining Service, Inc., 492 N. E. 2d 814 (Oh. 1986).

因此这些证据无法形成充分有效的证据链证明王某某获得涉案芯片的来源是真实、有效、合法的购买行为。另外，原告王某某称其没有获取宇电公司涉案芯片程序中的"校正芯片程序"，其修正仪表的精度是通过自己读取宇电公司产品存储芯片中的"偏差数据"并保存应用到原告产品上的方式，系原告自己的独特方式。但经审核相关检验报告并讨论后，专家组亦否认了原告所称的校正过程。

综上所述，被告关于原告王某某侵犯第三人商业秘密的认定，事实清楚，证据充分，思明区人民法院予以支持。另外，由于王某某获取涉案技术信息没有合法来源，现场组装的仪表是否检定合格已不影响侵权行为的成立。

五、典型意义

本案是一起颇具代表性的知识产权行政案件，涉及原告与第三人民事主体之间的侵犯商业秘密纠纷，原告与被告之间的行政主体与行政相对人之间的行政诉讼纠纷。从程序上看，本案庭审时，鉴定人、专家均出庭参加诉讼，在庭审程序上具有一定的代表性。在实体上，本案的焦点系原告是否侵犯第三人的商业秘密。在"接触+实质相同"要件成立的前提下，思明区人民法院对原告获取涉案技术的来源进行合法性分析，认定原告所称的向他人购买涉案"芯片技术"不是我国法律规定的"反向工程"，最终确认厦门市工商局行政处罚所认定的原告侵犯第三人商业秘密的事实清楚。本案在法律适用方面进行的探索对于司法实践具有一定的参考价值。

（曾争志　刘　禹）

萧某某假冒注册商标罪案研析

一、案情简介

2010~2012年,被告人萧某某指使他人在广东省汕头市生产并在厦门销售假冒"素手浣花"黑糖棒棒糖。"素手浣花"黑糖棒棒糖的商标注册人为黄某某,与萧某某并无授权关系。萧某某所生产、销售的"素手浣花"黑糖棒棒糖后被鉴定机构证明为假冒注册商标的商品。厦门市产品质量监督检验院亦对这些假冒的"素手浣花"黑糖棒棒糖进行检测,检测结果符合糖果卫生标准。2011~2012年,被告人陈某甲向被告人萧某某购买了假冒的"素手浣花"黑糖棒棒糖155件,而后于2011年12月至2012年5月在厦门进行销售。2012年8月,被告人萧某某因涉嫌销售假冒注册商标的商品罪被公安机关刑事拘留,同年9月14日因涉嫌假冒注册商标罪被逮捕;2012年陈某甲也因涉嫌销售假冒注册商标的商品罪被公安机关刑事拘留,同年9月14日被逮捕。厦门市思明区人民检察院以假冒注册商标罪和销售假冒注册商标的商品罪对被告人萧某某和陈某甲提起刑事诉讼。

二、裁判结果

厦门市思明区人民法院经审理认为,被告人萧某某已销售的数额高达人民币117万元,情节特别严重,构成假冒注册商标罪,判处有期徒刑4年6个月,并处罚金人民币60万元。被告人陈某甲明知是假冒注册商标的商品而予以销售,销售金额达6万余元,数额较大,已构成销售假冒注册商标的商品罪,判处有期徒刑6个月,并处罚金人民币4万元。

三、争议焦点

本案的争议焦点有：

（1）假冒注册商标罪中的非法经营数额如何确定？

（2）假冒注册商标罪与其他罪名之间的关系如何？

四、案例评析

（一）假冒注册商标罪中的非法经营数额如何确定

根据我国《刑法》第 213 条规定，未经注册商标所有人许可，在同一种商品上使用与其注册商标相同的商标，情节严重的，处 3 年以下有期徒刑或者拘役，并处或者单处罚金；情节特别严重的，处 3 年以上 7 年以下有期徒刑，并处罚金。由此可见，"情节严重"是假冒注册商标罪的构成条件，而情节的"严重"与"特别严重"又是刑事司法量刑中的分水岭。对于如何确定情节的"严重"和"特别严重"，《刑法》本身却没有更多详细的规定。

2004 年最高人民法院和最高人民检察院公布的《关于办理侵犯知识产权刑事案件具体应用法律若干问题的解释》可以为如何确定假冒注册商标罪中的情节"严重"和"特别严重"提供依据。根据此解释的第 1 条，假冒注册商标罪中的"情节严重"是指非法经营数额在 5 万元以上或违法所得数额在 3 万元以上的，或者是假冒两种以上注册商标，非法经营数额在 3 万元以上或者违法所得数额在 2 万元以上的；而"情节特别严重"是指非法经营数额在 25 万元以上或者违法所得数额在 15 万元以上的，或者是假冒两种以上注册商标，非法经营数额在 15 万元以上或者违法所得数额在 10 万元以上的。❶ 由此可见，"非法经营数额"和"违法所得数额"是划分情节严重和情节特别严重的重要依据。确定非法经营数额和违法所得数额，对于假冒注册商标罪的情节轻重，对于刑事司法的量刑，都是至关重要的。

---

❶ 最高人民法院、最高人民检察院《关于办理侵犯知识产权刑事案件具体应用法律若干问题的解释》，2004 年 12 月 8 日，法释〔2004〕19 号。

1. 非法经营数额的内涵

我国在司法实践中对于非法经营数额内涵的认识，经历了一个发展的过程。1990年4月，国家工商行政管理局商标局在给福建省工商行政管理局的批复中认为对于非法经营数额的计算要分三种情况：其一，商品全部销售的，销售金额为非法经营数额；其二，商品未销售的，则购入的总货款为非法经营数额；其三，商品部分销售的，已售部分的销售款总数加上尚未售出的部分的购入货款之和为非法经营数额。❶1994年国家工商行政管理局发布《关于执行〈商标法〉及其〈实施细则〉若干问题的通知》。在此通知中，工商总局首先明确了侵犯商标权的侵权人所经营的全部侵权产品，包括已销售的和尚未销售的，都应当纳入非法经营额的计算中。其次，这种非法经营额的计算方法应为销售侵权商品的收入与库存侵权商品的实际成本之和。❷2004年最高人民法院和最高人民检察院公布的《关于办理侵犯知识产权刑事案件具体应用法律若干问题的解释》第12条将非法经营数额的外延从销售数额的范围扩大至行为人在实施侵犯知识产权行为过程中，制造、储存、运输、销售侵权产品的价值。

不仅是司法实践中，在学者中，对于"非法经营数额"的内涵也存在一定的争议。有学者认为，一般而言，"对于侵权人所经营的全部侵权商品（已经销售的及库存的）均应计算为非法经营额。对于生产、加工侵权商品的，其非法经营额为其侵权商品的销售收入与库存侵权商品的实际成本之和；对于因侵权人的原因导致实际成本难以确认的，视其库存数量与该商品销售单价之乘积为实际成本；没有销售单价的，视其库存商品的数量与被侵权的同种商品的销售单价之乘积，为库存商品的实际成本"。❸还有学者认为，经营行为在整体上看是一种营利性活动的全过程，因而非法经营数额是指基于营利目的而非法从事的特定经营活动所投入和所获得的全部数额。因此，非法经营数额和销售金额外延差不多，严格地讲，非法经营

---

❶ 国家工商行政管理局商标局《关于商标侵权案件中非法经营额问题的批复》（工商标字〔1990〕第77号）。

❷ 国家工商行政管理局《关于执行〈商标法〉及其〈实施细则〉若干问题的通知》（工商标字〔1994〕第329号）。

❸ 姜伟主编：《知识产权刑事保护研究》，法律出版社2004年版，第92页。

数额在外延上比销售金额的范围更广。

基于假冒注册商标的经营性,《关于办理侵犯知识产权刑事案件具体应用法律若干问题的解释》中对非法经营数额内涵与外延的界定是合理的,即应当从行为人实施侵犯知识产权的行为开始,整个过程中的制造、储存、运输和销售侵权产品的价值,都应当纳入非法经营数额之中,以确定行为的严重程度。一方面,单单依靠销售金额来认定假冒注册商标行为的严重性是不够的,因为对于已经构成犯罪的假冒注册商标的行为来说,其行为的严重程度已经不在于其行为人通过这一犯罪行为的获利是多少,而是给法律所保护的法益造成多大的侵害。即使行为人什么都没有得到,他对法益的侵害也是确实存在的,没有从非法行为中得到利益并不能抹杀违法行为的社会危害性,因而不能单纯以此作为定罪与量刑的依据。就假冒注册商标罪所实施的行为来看,行为人实施假冒注册商标的行为,在自己生产和销售的商品上使用与他人注册商标相同的商标,其目的是商品进入流通领域,可以在市场上获得非法利润,而当其罪行暴露时,其商品的销售状态不能确定,可能已经售出也可能没有售出。但实际上,不论其售出与否,对于假冒注册商标罪所保护的法益已经造成侵害,因为其行为一开始就已经对法益造成侵害,并且这种侵害体现在假冒他人注册商标的各个环节。另一方面,《关于办理侵犯知识产权刑事案件具体应用法律若干问题的解释》第12条第1款对"非法经营数额"的解释包括假冒注册商标罪的行为人从实施行为开始的整个过程,包括制造、储存、运输和销售。由此可见,非法经营数额的范围大于销售金额。用"非法经营数额"来作为认定情节是否严重的标准,能更好地体现犯罪的本质,比销售金额和违法所得额更加科学。

2. 非法经营数额的计算

虽然"非法经营数额"作为确定假冒注册商标罪的罪与非罪,罪轻与罪重的分水岭的内涵可以确定为包含整个侵犯知识产权的行为过程中所产生的价值,包括制造、储存、运输和销售侵权产品的价值,但是要确定其计算的方法,在实践中又存在许多问题。

最高人民法院、最高人民检察院、公安部、司法部联合颁布的《关于办理侵犯知识产权刑事案件具体应用法律若干问题的解释》第12条规定:

已销售的侵权产品的价值,按照实际销售的价格计算;未销售的侵权产品的价值,按照标价或者已经查清的侵权产品的实际销售平均价格计算;侵权产品没有标价或者无法查清其实际销售价格的,按照被侵权产品的市场中间价格计算。由此可见,有四个价格可以作为计算非法经营数额的依据,即实际销售价格、标价、实际销售的平均价格及市场中间价。

然而这个标准在运行中产生了问题,如2011年的李某假冒注册商标罪案。在李某假冒注册商标罪案中,被告人李某在未获得商标所有权人许可的情况下,在2.2万件白坯衫上使用与"鄂尔多斯"注册商标相同的商标,包装成假冒的"鄂尔多斯"羊绒衫;在4 633件白坯衫上使用与"恒源祥"注册商标相同的商标,包装成假冒的"恒源祥"羊毛衫并将这些假冒的羊毛衫用于销售。案发后,公安机关在李某店内扣押吊牌价每件人民币2 180元的假冒"鄂尔多斯"羊绒衫4 351件,吊牌价每件人民币1 680元的假冒"鄂尔多斯"羊绒衫17 403件;吊牌价每件人民币968元的假冒"恒源祥"羊绒衫4 433件。未销售的羊绒衫以吊牌价计算共计达人民币4 000余万元。此案经鄂尔多斯中级人民法院审理认为,李某的行为构成假冒注册商标罪,虽然其已经销售的数额无法查清,但是未销售的部分,根据吊牌价即标价计算,为人民币4 000余万元,其情节特别严重。根据最高人民法院、最高人民检察院《关于办理侵犯知识产权刑事案件具体应用法律若干问题的解释(二)》第4条规定,对于侵犯知识产权犯罪的人民法院应当判处一定的罚金。罚金数额可以按照非法经营数额的50%以上1倍以下确定。在李某假冒注册商标案中,鄂尔多斯市中级人民法院以未售出的商品的标价计算得出的非法经营数额为人民币4 000余万元,因此判处人民币2 000余万元的罚金。这一案件被称为天价罚金案,并引起轩然大波。后经内蒙古高级人民法院发回重审后,一审的鄂尔多斯中级人民法院查明被告人实际销售的平均价格为人民币100余元,且其主观意图也并不是将这些假冒的羊绒衫按吊牌价出售,因此重新计算其非法经营数额为人民币398万余元,修改其罚金为人民币199万余元。

天价罚金案也带来许多思考。有学者就《关于办理侵犯知识产权刑事案件具体应用法律若干问题的解释》第12条所提出的计算标准提出质疑,认为这种计算标准存在瑕疵，行为人可能利用这一标准逃避法律的制裁。例如，两人都生产相同的假冒某品牌的裤子（该品牌裤子的市场中间价格为300元），其中一个人标价30元，另一个人没有标价也未能查清其实际销售价格，按上述的计算标准，前者非法经营数额为30×件数，后者为300×件数，由此造成的结果是相同的行为不同的罪责。❶ 这是不合理的。理解这一标准，要克服认识的片面性。

在本案中，厦门市思明区人民法院在认定被告人萧某某的非法经营数额时，对于其已经销售的数额，根据现有证据《棒棒糖成品生产表》和《棒棒糖成品出货表》中对于2010～2011年生产销售的棒棒糖的单价和数量的详细记载，经过计算可以得出其销售的金额达117万余元。而被查扣的涉案产品的价值，根据规定，未销售的按照标价或者已经查清的侵权产品的实际销售平均价格计算。侵权产品没有标价或者无法查清其实际销售价格的，按照被侵权产品的市场中间价格计算。本案中，因为涉案的假冒"素手浣花"黑糖棒棒糖无标价，依据法律应当按照已经查清的侵权产品的实际销售平均价格计算。但是，思明区人民法院考虑到本案中销售时间较长，销售价格相差较大，以产品被扣的当年度的平均销售价格认定更符合客观实际，故被告人萧某某被查扣的100件"素手浣花"黑糖棒棒糖的价值以2012年的销售平均价格计算，价值为3.6万余元。鉴于被告人已销售的数额已经达到"情节特别严重"的量刑标准，而未销售的相对而言金额较小。因此，思明区人民法院在认定上以已经销售的数额作为被告人萧某某的犯罪数额，以未销售的数额作为酌定从重的情节，这种考虑不仅对侵害注册商标的犯罪行为进行了追诉，同时也对被告人的利益给予了适当的考虑，达到了法律效果与社会效果的有机统一。

另外在庭审中，被告人萧某某的辩护律师辩称，被告人的犯罪对其所在社区没有不利影响，请求法院判处3年以下有期徒刑并适用缓刑。被告人陈某甲的辩护律师辩称陈某甲销售的多数棒棒糖并未流入社会，未对社会造成不良影响，请求法院判处1年以下有期徒刑并适用缓刑。这种"未

---

❶ 陈芳："假冒商标产品非法经营数额认定的探讨"，载《福建质量管理》2005年第5期。

流入社会"和"对社区"没有不利影响是否能成为法院考虑从轻的情节呢？

从假冒注册商标罪侵犯的法益来看，这种请求是不成立的。对于假冒注册商标罪的客体，刑法理论界有几种不同的观点。有的学者认为，假冒注册商标罪的客体是"国家对商标的管理制度"，也可以称为国家商标管理活动或者国家商标管理秩序；❶ 有的学者认为，假冒注册商标罪的客体应为"商标专用权"；❷ 有的学者认为，假冒注册商标罪的客体为"国家的商标管理制度和他人注册商标的专用权"。❸ 在这些学说中，将本罪的客体界定为复杂客体最为恰当，因为国家商标管理制度和他人注册商标专用权都是假冒注册商标行为所直接侵害的社会关系，主要有以下两个理由。

其一，假冒注册商标犯罪行为破坏了国家对商标的管理制度。商标管理制度是指国家为了维护社会主义市场经济秩序，促进商品交易和对外贸易的正常进行，提高商品质量，保护商品生产者和消费者的合法权益，通过颁布有关商标的法律法规，对商标实行统一管理，对注册商标给予法律保护，禁止假冒、伪造、仿造、销售他人注册商标的侵权行为。与此同时，国家工商行政管理机关根据商标法的规定，通过管理商标注册的申请，商标注册的审查核准，注册商标的续展、转让和使用的许可，注册商标争议的裁定，商标使用的管理以及对注册商标专用权的保护活动，行使对商标的统一管理职能。商标一经注册，就受到法律保护，未经注册商标所有人许可，任何人不能在同一种商品上使用与其注册商标相同的商标。假冒注册商标的行为，在破坏国家对商标的统一管理的同时也破坏了国家的商标管理秩序。因此，即使只是假冒了注册商标而未进行销售，只要情节严重，也达到了本罪的追诉标准。

其二，假冒注册商标犯罪侵犯了他人的注册商标专用权。在当今市场经济时代，商标不仅起着提示商品来源的作用，而且体现着商品的质量、价格、服务乃至企业的经营形象和市场声誉，代表着社会对某一特定商品

---

❶ 杨春洗、杨敦先主编：《中国刑法论丛》，北京大学出版社1994年版，第341页。
❷ 周振想主编：《刑法学教程》，中国人民公安大学出版社1997年版，第454页。
❸ 赵秉志、王淑敏：《刑法各论问题研究》，中国法制出版社1996年版，第214页。

的评价。注册商标专用权在市场经济体系中具有重要作用，因而受到法律的特殊保护。我国《民法通则》第 96 条明确规定："法人、个体工商户、个人合伙依法取得的商标专用权受法律保护。"根据《商标法》第 3 条第 1 款规定，经商标局核准注册的商标为注册商标，注册商标所有人享有商标专用权，受法律保护。行为人假冒注册商标的行为，正是侵犯了注册商标所有人的注册商标专用权，非法占有了本属于注册商标所有人的市场占有份额，进而使注册商标所有人遭受严重的经济损失，从这个层面看，注册商标专用权构成假冒注册商标罪所侵犯的法益之一。注册商标专用权包括使用权和禁止权两方面，使用权是注册商标所有人自己合法使用、转让或许可他人使用的权利；禁止权是注册商标所有人禁止他人使用、转让的权利。从上述的法律规定可以看出，假冒注册商标的犯罪行为必定侵犯了他人的商标专用权。

综上所述，假冒注册商标罪侵犯的法益不仅是注册商标专用权人的利益，更是国家对商标的管理制度，所以，这一法益的侵害并不能以假冒注册商标的商品尚未进入流通领域作为一个请求法院从轻考虑量刑的理由。

（二）假冒注册商标罪与其他罪名之间的关系如何

1. 假冒注册商标罪与销售假冒注册商标的商品罪

在本案中，萧某某先于 2012 年 8 月因涉嫌销售假冒注册商标的商品罪被公安机关刑事拘留，后于同年 9 月因假冒注册商标罪被逮捕。从被告人的行为来看，此两罪都可以评价被告人在不同阶段的行为，那么如何确定这种情况下被告人的罪数与罪名呢？

刑法确定罪名是以行为侵犯的法益为基础，以"全面评价"和"禁止重复评价"为原则进行确定。"全面评价原则是指罪数的评价应当包含行为侵犯的全部法益"，"禁止重复评价原则是指禁止对同一法益的同一次侵犯进行重复的评价"。判断行为侵犯的法益是否为同一法益既要判断法益在种属上是否同一，在此除了要考虑刑法分则的章节分类还要考虑法益的主体和内容，也要判断作为法益的载体是否同一。对于是否是同一侵犯过程的判断，应当从社会的相关观念予以综合判断，有三种情形可以认定为同一侵犯过程，一是为实现侵犯某一法益的目的而先后实施的多个行为；二是渐进侵犯同一法益的多个行为；三是前一行为使法益处于持续被侵犯的状态，后一行为对该法益的侵害未能超出前一行为的侵犯的情形。❶

行为人未经注册商标所有人许可在同一种商品上使用与其注册商标相同的商标，又销售了该假冒注册商标的商品，在商品的生产和销售过程中涉及两个罪名，分别是假冒注册商标罪和销售假冒注册商标的商品罪，两个罪名侵犯的客体都是国家的商标管理制度和注册商标专用权。由于立法方面的原因，假冒注册商标罪对行为的评价能够包容销售假冒注册商标的商品罪对行为的评价，因而仅成立一个犯罪构成的评价足以，所以以假冒注册商标罪评价之即可。

在本案中，被告人萧某某虽然既在生产过程中涉及假冒注册商标罪，又在销售过程中触及销售假冒注册商标的商品罪，但是后一行为对法益的侵犯仍然是国家的商标管理制度和他人的注册商标专用权，没有超过前一行为所侵犯的法益，因而对被告人定罪为假冒注册商标罪是较为妥当的。

2. 假冒注册商标罪与生产、销售伪劣产品罪

生产、销售伪劣产品罪是指商品生产者、销售者违反产品质量管理法规和工商管理法规，生产、销售伪劣产品，销售金额较大的行为。实践中，假冒注册商标罪和生产、销售伪劣产品罪存在一定的交叉之处。对于这两者的区分，应当从其差异和联系入手。

其存在的差异在于，假冒注册商标罪侵犯的是复杂客体，既有国家的商标管理制度，又有他人的商标专用权。而生产、销售伪劣产品是简单客体，即国家对于商品的质量监督管理制度，且生产、销售的是不合格的产品。生产、销售伪劣产品罪的认定重点在于商品的质量问题，譬如对商品掺杂、掺假，以次充好，以不合格产品冒充合格产品。如果行为人生产的产品质量并无问题，而是未经商标专用权人许可，在相同产品上使用相同的商标，则只能以假冒注册商标罪定罪处罚。

更复杂的情况是，如果行为人将假冒的他人注册商标用于生产、销售伪劣产品，是处以一罪还是数罪呢？从实施的行为上看，该行为实际上是

---

❶ 庄劲：《犯罪竞合：罪数分析的结构与体系》，法律出版社2006年版，第49~66页。

两个相对独立的行为，一个是使用假冒的注册商标，另一个是生产伪劣商品。但是这两个行为又存在牵连关系，假冒注册商标是为了生产、销售其伪劣商品，应当作为牵连犯从一重罪论处。最高人民法院、最高人民检察院、公安部联合颁布的《关于办理侵犯知识产权刑事案件适用法律若干问题的意见》也明确了，实施生产、销售伪劣商品犯罪，同时构成知识产权等其他犯罪的，依照处罚较重的规定定罪处理。❶

在本案中，厦门市产品质量监督检验院对这些假冒的"素手浣花"黑糖棒棒糖进行检测，得到这些棒棒糖符合糖果卫生标准的检测结果。因此本案只以假冒注册商标罪论处。如果这些棒棒糖经检测不符合糖果卫生标准，则应当以生产、销售伪劣商品罪和假冒注册商标罪择一重罪论处。

五、典型意义

被告人萧某某生产、销售假冒的"素手浣花"台湾黑糖棒棒糖，金额100余万元，并销往包括厦门在内的全国多个地区，其在厦门的其中一个销售批发商就是被告人陈某甲。而关于"素手浣花"棒棒糖，厦门市思明区人民法院同时受理了商标权利人黄某某诉恬蜜公司等销售假冒"素手浣花"棒棒糖的系列民事侵权纠纷，而这些经销商的假货来源与被告人萧某某生产的假货有联系。该案体现了厦门市思明区人民法院在打击知识产权犯罪方面的决心。

更重要的是，涉及"素手浣花"商标的案件体现了厦门市思明区人民法院知识产权审判"三合一"的特点，显示了刑事、民事相结合打击侵害知识产权行为的优势。知识产权纠纷案具有关联案件持续增多、涉案当事人身份多样化和当事人取证举证难度大三大特点。知识产权侵权行为一般隐蔽性大，专业性强，尤其是涉及网络、计算机侵权案件，因电子证据的无形性和脆弱性往往导致证据取证难，存储难，当事人也存在取证难、举证难等问题。长期以来，知识产权的刑事案件由刑事审判庭适用刑事诉讼法审理，民事案件由民事审判庭适用民事诉讼法审理，行政案件由行政审

---

❶ 最高人民法院、最高人民检察院、公安部《关于办理侵犯知识产权刑事案件适用法律若干问题的意见》（法发〔2011〕3号）。

判庭适用行政诉讼法审理，这样一种"差序格局"，无端耗费审判的人力物力财力，不但裁判尺度不易统一，而且给当事人造成讼累。面对这些难题，建立知识产权三审合一制度有利于统一司法尺度、节约审判资源、提高审判效率、强化知识产权保护和培养知识产权法官专业素质，可以避免出现"三审分立"机制下知识产权刑事、民事法官知识产权知识相对缺乏的现象。

该案入选2014年福建法院知识产权司法保护十大案例。

（李缘缘　王灵烨）

张某某假冒注册商标罪案研析

一、案情简介

自2012年2月以来,被告人张某某使用厦门市翔安区的一所房子作为生产场所,并向他人购买印有"金门高粱酒"的标签、瓶盖、酒瓶、纸箱、散装白酒和灌装机器,在上述场所生产假冒金门高粱酒并进行销售。2012年3月17日,被告人张某某雇佣的工人张某甲在上述场所外搬运酒箱到小货车上时,厦门市公安局大嶝边防派出所的民警对其进行盘查并在该场所内查获多种"金门"高粱酒。

经金门酒厂实业股份有限公司鉴定,上述查扣的酒非该公司生产,系假冒"金门"高粱酒;厦门市同安区价格认证中心出具《价格鉴定结论书》,确定查扣的黑色823"金门"高粱酒1200瓶价值共计人民币405 600元、红色823"金门"高粱酒1680瓶价值共计人民币567 840元,总计人民币973 440元。

二、裁判结果

厦门市思明区法院经审理认为:被告人张某某犯假冒注册商标罪,判处有期徒刑2年,并处罚金人民币10万元;扣押在案的赃物3262瓶假冒注册商标的"金门"高粱酒、扣押在案的作案工具——假酒生产线一条予以没收。

三、争议焦点

本案的争议焦点有:

（1）涉台酒商标是否受商标法保护？
（2）被告的行为是否构成假冒注册商标罪？

四、案件评析

（一）涉台酒商标是否受商标法保护

商标保护具有地域性，一般采属地原则。知识产权在历史发展上原是封建君主以特许权的形式所授予的钦赐特权，只能及于君主权力所辖之地域范围，而各国于建立商标法律制度时，按国家主权原则，亦仅对于依本国法律取得的商标权加以保护，在他国所发生之与商标有关的事实，对本国并无拘束力，此即商标保护之"地域性原则"。《保护工业产权巴黎公约》（以下简称"巴黎公约"），亦采取此一原则。

我国商标权的取得采取注册主义，即商标之使用者或者预定使用者，须将其商标向主管机关申请注册获准后，方能取得商标专用权而受法律保护。当然，商标注册后，商标所有人仍有实际使用与继续使用之义务，否则将构成商标权被撤销之事由。注册主义除了可以鼓励商标之创设使用人及早申请商标注册以纳入管理之外，还可以避免孰先使用之证明上之困难，此亦为注册主义之优点。

因此，一个标识受到商标法保护的先决条件，受制于属地主义与注册主义原则。中国台湾地区与中国大陆的商标注册分属不同系统，是以涉台的"金门高粱酒"商标是否应受我国商标法的保护需要进行讨论。

金门高粱酒为台湾知名高粱酒，由金门酒厂实业股份有限公司（以下简称"金门酒厂"）生产，于2000年筹备，2004年正式进驻大陆市场，陆续依商标法注册许多商标，2010年金门高粱酒被国家工商总局认定为"中国驰名商标"。2013年进一步扩大商标注册，目前金门酒厂所有的有效商标以及待审商标共计149件。

本案所涉及的"金门高粱酒"商标依照商标法与国务院工商行政管理部门商标局之规定注册，依照我国《商标法》第3条的规定，经商标局核准注册的商标为注册商标，包括商品商标、服务商标和集体商标、证明商标；商标注册人享有商标专用权，受法律保护。

(二) 被告的行为是否构成假冒注册商标罪

TRIPs 协议第 61 条规定："成员至少应对具有商业规模而故意仿冒商标或侵害著作权之案件，订定刑事程序及罚则。救济措施应包括足可产生吓阻作用之徒刑及（或）罚金，并应和同等程度之其他刑事案件之量刑一致。必要时，救济措施亦应包括对侵权物品以及主要用于侵害行为之材料及器具予以扣押、没收或销毁。会员亦得对其他侵害知识产权之案件，特别是故意违法并具商业规模者，订定刑事程序及罚则。"

TRIPs 协议之规定为强制性质，成员之内国法保障须符合条约所定之最低标准，由于我国为世贸组织之成员方，故有义务遵守 TRIPs 协议之规定。观诸 TRIPs 协议第 61 条，并非规定一切商标侵权之行为均必须以刑罚加以制裁，其规范者为蓄意仿冒商标之行为（willful trademark counterfeiting），且客观上须达到商业规模（commercial scale），而刑事制裁手段则可选择自由刑、罚金或两者并行，但重点在于足以产生吓阻作用（sufficient to provide a deterrent），由此可知 TRIPs 协议刑事制裁之思维应是采取一般预防理论。

而内化外国法为本国法，我国商标的刑法保护，商标法规定刑事罚则的是《商标法》第 67 条；在刑法罚则上，则有《刑法》第 213~215 条。本案涉及假冒注册商标罪之法条为《刑法》第 213 条，即未经注册商标所有人许可，在同一种商品上使用与其注册商标相同的商标，情节严重的，处 3 年以下有期徒刑或者拘役，并处或者单处罚金；情节特别严重的，处 3 年以上 7 年以下有期徒刑，并处罚金。《刑法》第 213 条的主观要件，法条并未明文，但参考 TRIPs 协议的立法要求，同时考虑《刑法》第 15 条过失犯罪，以及法律有规定的才负刑事责任的体系观察，加上观诸刑事责任的最后手段性原则与比例原则，本条主观要件应以故意为要件而不包含过失。而其客观要件，为在同一种商品，使用与其注册商标相同的商标，情节严重的（呼应 TRIPs 协议的商业规模要求），是以将本案情形在构成要件该当性上进行分析。

就本案而言，首先，被告人在主观上具备故意。金门高粱酒为知名酒类，更是经国家认证的驰名商标，其商标的商标性使用时间长、范围广，本案被告使用此知名酒类的商标，殊难想象其使用出于过失而不知，于一般社会常识经验有违。又本案被告人经自认，承认其主观的故意。犯罪人自认虽不得为唯一认定的证据，但是辅以其他间接、辅助证据，加上社会常识判断，本案被告人之主观上故意，应属无疑问。

其次，被告人在同一种商品上使用与其注册商标相同之商标。本案被告人所贩卖之商品为高粱酒，与金门酒厂所制造贩卖的商品相同，在分类上同属于3301类含酒精的饮料。本案中报告人张某某于2012年2月开始着手生产假冒金门高粱酒并进行销售，并于2012年3月17日被破获。

由于被告人张某某使用商标皆与金门酒厂现有产品上之商标相同，因此在本案中还应考虑金门酒厂的商标是否注册，并具体受到假冒的商标为哪一个。国家工商行政管理总局商标局商标检索系统筛选得出：商标申请人为金门酒厂实业股份有限公司，该商标为已注册的国际分类号为33号的酒类商标，2012年被告人张某某着手前已注册并受商标法保护（见图1）。

金門高粱酒

图1

此商标已于2002年7月申请，2005年10月已注册，之后又经续展，使用期限直到2024年。与犯罪实施期间重合，唯其用字为金门高"粱"酒，依照最高人民法院、最高人民检察院《关于办理侵犯知识产权权刑事案件具体应用法律若干问题的解释》第8条之规定，《刑法》第213条规定的"相同的商标"，是指与被假冒的注册商标完全相同，或者与被假冒的注册商标在视觉上基本无差别、足以对公众产生误导的商标。该商标中的"粱"与高粱之"粱"之间仅仅在视觉上基本无差别、足以对公众产生误导。依照比较主要部分原则、通体观察原则、隔离观差原则，"粱""粱"商标近似，又在同一种商品上，难谓没有造成混淆的可能。

再次，被告人行为属情节严重的。为合乎比例原则与最后手段性，TRIPs协议第61条要求，侵害商标权的行为，客观上须达到商业规模，才达到刑法的需罚性。《刑法》第213条要求的情节严重应参照最高人民法院、最高人民检察院《关于办理侵犯知识产权权刑事案件具体应用法律若干问题的解释》,非法经营数额在25万元以上或者违法所得数额在15万元以上的,即属于情节特别严重。本案涉案金额达人民币973 440元,依照前述解释标准,属于情节特别严重,显然已达商业规模。

因此,被告人的行为满足主观故意、同一种商品、使用与其注册商标相同的商标、情节严重的情形,符合《刑法》第213条规定的构成要件,构成假冒注册商标罪。

五、典型意义

假冒酒类的犯罪态样有其特殊性:酒类商品单价贵,附加价值高,具有犯罪者预期报酬值高的特点;制造假酒,危害消费者健康甚巨,社会成本巨大,犯罪严重性大;一般消费者识别不易,难以识破举报。对于犯罪者而言,提供了预期制裁低而预期报酬高的诱因。

本案显示了侦查机关加大执法力度的成果,也向社会宣示了制裁概率的增加。当制裁的严厉程度值法定的情况下,加大执法力度,在执法上投注心力,提高侦查以及法院制裁的机率,将可以提高制裁的边际概率与边际严厉程度,进而提高制裁的预期值,并降低犯罪人的边际利益。当犯罪边际利益小于边际预期制裁成本时,往往理性的人不会去做,从而有效地保障了权利人的法益。

打击商标犯罪能促进企业良性发展,确保商标所区别的商品或服务的竞争成果不受人榨取。商标上承载着公司的商誉,往往也反映着商誉的价值。打击商标犯罪以降低侵权人的边际利益,降低侵权动机,同时提高商誉价值的边际贡献,提供企业良性发展的诱因,促进经济发展。本案为涉台商标维权的正面案例,可以鼓励涉台商标注册。

金门高粱酒是我国台湾地区非常著名的酒类,进入大陆市场后广受欢迎,由于酒类行业系知识产权附加价值较高的行业,知名品牌与一般品牌的酒,价格往往差异较大。一些不法分子利用酒类产品高附加价值、易被仿制的特点,非法生产、销售他人具有知名品牌的产品,以此获取巨额暴利。近年来,福建多个地区市场上就出现了相当数量的假冒金门高粱酒。

假酒生产条件差、质量无保障,易给人民群众生命健康造成严重损害。只有不断加大知识产权保护力度,严厉惩处假冒商标的犯罪分子,透过严格缓刑适用,加大打击力度,有力地维护权利人的合法权益,才能规范市场秩序。

本案被福建省高级人民法院评为2014年消费者权益保护典型案例。

(李缘缘　曹宇君)

林某某、王某某等8人销售假冒注册商标的商品罪案研析

一、案情简介

美国匡威公司所有的"CONVERSE"商标是世界知名的运动鞋品牌。2009~2010年,被告人林某某、王某某等8人先后伙同徐某(化名王平)、"小丽"、宋某共同或者单独在福州、厦门两地,通过在淘宝网上开设网店的方式销售假冒"CONVERSE"商标的胶鞋,并在厦门租用仓库用以储存。2010年8月30日,厦门公安机关抓获刘某某、林某某、林某某、严某、严某、王某某,并于当日上午查获假冒"CONVERSE"牌的胶鞋81 000双,货值金额为人民币18 788 574元。其中,鞋盒上有标价的货值金额共计人民币17 830 180元,无标价的最低销售额共计人民币958 394元。经鉴定,上述胶鞋系假冒"CONVERSE"注册商标的产品。2010年12月7日,公安人员抓获被告人林某某。2011年1月5日,被告人王某某主动到公安机关投案。

二、裁判结果

厦门市思明区人民法院经审理认为,被告人林某某、王某某等8人明知是假冒注册商标的商品,先后共同或者单独在福州、厦门两地通过网络予以销售,货值金额共计人民币18 788 574元,其行为均已构成销售假冒注册商标的商品罪。故依法认定各被告人构成销售假冒注册商标的商品罪,分别判处两年到六年不等的有期徒刑,并分别处以10万~300万元不等的

罚金。

三、争议焦点

本案的争议焦点有：
（1）假冒注册商标的侵权商品的销售数额如何计算？
（2）涉案商品真伪的"鉴定意见"的证明效力如何？

四、案例评析

（一）假冒注册商标的侵权产品的销售数额如何计算

销售假冒注册商标的商品罪，是指明知是假冒注册商标的商品而予以销售，销售金额数额较大的行为。销售假冒注册商标的商品罪属于数额犯，在解决该类知识产权侵权与犯罪的实务中，必须处理的一个问题是犯罪数额的认定。对已经销售的侵权产品，由于存在实际销售价格，在计算数额时直接按照其实际销售价格计算即可，但对未销售的侵权产品价格，由于并未实际销售，不可能直接像已经销售的侵权产品按照实际销售价格计算其价格，具体如何计算则需要考虑其他因素。在本案审理过程中，对查获的未销售的假冒注册商标的胶鞋如何计算其总金额产生了分歧。公诉人主张按照产品鞋盒上的标价计算；8名被告人则主张按照产品的最低销售价格计算，或者是依照产品的实际销售平均价格计算。

1. 犯罪数额的确定

为正确处理《刑法》中涉及犯罪数额的案件，必须明确理解和准确运用此类案件中涉及的犯罪数额法律概念。一般来说，《刑法》中数额犯中犯罪数额计算的主要标准有销售金额、货值金额、非法经营数额、违法犯罪所得等。知识产权犯罪大多为数额犯。犯罪数额的确定，对于认定和处罚侵犯知识产权类犯罪具有重要意义，关系罪与非罪、此罪与彼罪、量刑轻重等方面的界定，也是司法机关办理侵犯知识产权犯罪案件的一大难点。尤其是在立法和司法实践中，销售金额、货值金额、非法经营数额三者之间界限模糊，容易引起混淆，因此有必要先对这三个犯罪数额的认定标准做一厘定。

林某某、王某某等8人销售假冒注册商标的商品罪案研析

根据2004年最高人民法院、最高人民检察院《关于办理侵犯知识产权刑事案件具体应用法律若干问题的解释》第9条之规定,"销售金额"是指销售假冒注册商标的商品后所得和应得的全部违法收入。就本案涉及的销售假冒注册商标的商品罪而言,其中的销售"所得"是指行为人销售假冒注册商标的商品后实际所获得的违法收入的情况;而其中的"应得"则是指行为人销售假冒注册商标的商品后尚未实际收到货款的情况。❶

关于"货值金额",目前我国《刑法》中并没有明确规定。2001年最高人民法院、最高人民检察院《关于办理生产、销售伪劣商品刑事案件具体应用法律若干问题的解释》第2条第2款规定,"伪劣产品尚未销售,货值金额达到刑法第一百四十条规定的销售金额三倍以上的,以生产、销售伪劣产品罪(未遂)定罪处罚"。就货值金额的计算,上述解释规定,"货值金额以违法生产、销售的伪劣产品的标价计算;没有标价的,按照同类合格产品的市场中间价格计算;货值金额难以确定的,按照国家计划委员会、最高人民法院、最高人民检察院、公安部1997年4月22日联合发布的《扣押、追缴、没收物品估价管理办法》的规定,委托指定的估价机构确定"。在司法实践中,绝大多数案件缴获的往往是尚未销售的伪劣商品,对于伪劣产商品的实际销售情况往往无账可查、无价可询、无据可证,因此司法机关最终只能依据缴获的尚未销售的伪劣商品的货值金额对生产者、销售者进行定罪量刑,货值金额认定的重要性可见一斑。上述司法解释的基本精神对于销售假冒注册商标的商品罪的认定同样具有参考价值。

根据2004年最高人民法院、最高人民检察院《关于办理侵犯知识产权刑事案件具体应用法律若干问题的解释》第12条之规定,"非法经营数额"是指行为人在实施侵犯知识产权行为过程中,制造、储存、运输、销售侵权产品的价值。从文义解释的角度来讲,非法经营数额是指行为人在从事非法经营活动中所涉及的侵权产品的总价值,即包括非法制造的侵权产品的获利数额,亦包括非法运输的侵权产品的获利数额、非法储存的侵权产品的获利数额以及销售侵权产品的获利数额等。❷ 由此可见,"非法经营数

---

❶ 刘宪权:"侵犯知识产权犯罪数额认定分析",载《法学》2005年第6期。

❷ 胡云腾、刘科:"知识产权刑事司法解释若干问题研究",载《中国法学》2004年第6期。

额"所涵盖的范围比销售数额要广泛得多。

综上所述,所谓销售金额,是指产品销售后已经得到或者可以得到的金额,货值金额一般用以计算尚未销售部分产品的总金额,而非法经营数额则不但包含前述两者而且包括其他的获利。

在本案中,主要涉及的是未销售商品"货值金额"的认定问题。在司法实践中,各地法院往往参考司法解释对非法经营数额的规定来计算货值金额。2004年最高人民法院、最高人民检察院《关于办理侵犯知识产权刑事案件具体应用法律若干问题的解释》第12条对"非法经营数额"作了规定,即"制造、储存、运输和未销售的侵权产品的价值,按照标价或者已经查清的侵权产品的实际销售平均价格计算。侵权产品没有标价或者无法查清其实际销售价格的,按照被侵权产品的市场中间价格计算"。据此,就销售假冒注册商标的商品罪而言,应按照以下先后顺序来认定尚未销售的侵权产品货值金额:(1)有明码标价或者已查清的侵权产品销售价格的,以实际销售平均价格计算;(2)没有明码标价或者无法查清侵权产品销售价格的,以被侵权产品的市场中间价格计算。

2. "标价"与"实际销售平均价格"的适用顺序

综上所述,认定侵权产品的货值金额,首先应当按照明码标价或者已经查清的实际销售平均价格计算。但是,侵权商品的标价和实际销售平均价格两种标准之间的适用关系如何,即二者之间是否存在适用顺序的问题,相关司法解释并未予以明确。仅从语言表述的逻辑关系上来看,产品标价与侵权产品的实际销售平均价格应属于并列关系,司法机关可以从两个标准中任选一种作为货值金额的计算标准。

事实上,在司法实践中如何选择货值金额的计算标准,应当依据案件的具体情形加以确定。在司法实践中涉及的案件情况十分复杂,每个案件都有其特殊之处。因此,最可取的方法应当是允许法院根据案件的不同情况采用相应的计算标准。例如,在另外一个涉及销售假冒注册商标的商品罪案件——"萧某某、陈某某销售假冒注册商标的商品罪案"中,因为该案涉案产品无标价,思明区法院判决认为尚未销售的"素手浣花"黑糖棒棒糖的货值金额就按实际销售平均价格计算。❶ 由于涉案产品销售时间较长，销售价格相差较大，以产品被扣押的当年度的平均销售价格认定更符合客观实际，反映了法院办案的灵活性和客观性。

在本案中，辩护人也提出应按照假鞋实际销售价格，即每双 40~80 元的合理价格来计算货值金额，不应该以产品的标价计算，因为鞋盒上的标价（STAR 经典版低帮轻便胶鞋每双标价 265 元、高帮 295 元）从出厂时即印刷完毕，只是为了达到以假乱真的效果，并非鞋子实际销售的参考价。从遏制侵权发生、加大知识产权保护力度的角度来看，若行为人为逃避处罚，故意将假冒商品标价很低，而其实际销售价格往往较高，按照标价计算犯罪金额可能会轻纵制假售价的行为。以较高的实际销售价格计算货值金额恰恰体现了刑事制裁的严厉性，有利于打击假冒行为。同时，在本案中被告人一方亦并没有提供证据证明其销售的侵权产品的实际销售平均价格为多少，导致法院无法采纳其意见。为了体现司法上对制假售假的打击力度，思明区法院最终以鞋盒上的标价来计算货值金额。考虑到本案的特殊背景和社会危害性，该判决认定是从严把握的。

3. 侵权产品尚未销售或者部分销售情形的定罪量刑

在本案中，被告人明知是假冒注册商标的商品而予以销售，其中已销售金额为人民币 1 009 079 元，尚未销售的假冒注册商标商品货值金额共计人民币 18 788 574 元，均系数额巨大，存在假冒注册商标的商品部分销售与部分尚未销售并存的情况，处于犯罪既遂和未遂并存的状态，对此应以"重刑吸收轻刑"的方法从一重刑论处。根据 2011 年最高人民法院、最高人民检察院、公安部《关于办理侵犯知识产权刑事案件适用法律若干问题的意见》第 8 条的规定，"假冒注册商标的商品的销售金额和未销售货值金额分别达到不同的法定刑幅度或者均达到同一法定刑幅度的，在处罚较重的法定刑幅度内酌情从重处罚"。思明区法院在判决书中明确指出尚未销售的假冒注册商标的商品，系犯罪未遂，依法可以从轻或者减轻处罚。这里的"从轻或者减轻处罚"指的是比照未遂部分的既遂犯，从轻或减轻对被

---

❶ "萧某某、陈某某销售假冒注册商标的商品罪案"，（2013）思刑初字第 766 号刑事判决书。

告人进行处罚。

（二）涉案商品真伪的"鉴定意见"的证明效力如何

经"CONVERSE"商标权利人匡威公司的代理人耐克体育（中国）有限公司鉴定，涉案胶鞋系假冒匡威公司"CONVERSE"注册商标的产品。这里引出本案涉及的另一个问题，即商标权利人一方出具的涉案商品真伪"鉴定意见"可否作为证据予以采信。在刑事诉讼中，"鉴定意见"具有什么样的证据属性，其证明力大小如何。在侵犯商标权刑事犯罪案件中，商标权利人出具涉案商品真伪鉴定书的现象十分普遍。在公安机关、检察机关和审判机关的法律文书中，一般将商标权利人一方出具的这类鉴定文本称为鉴定意见。但是，此项鉴定文书是证据法意义上的"鉴定意见"还是属于被害人陈述仍有争议，解决这个问题对判定其证明力大小有重要影响。

1. 涉案商品真伪鉴定书在刑事诉讼中的证据属性

所谓鉴定意见，是指在诉讼活动中鉴定人运用科学技术或者专门知识对诉讼涉及的专门性问题进行鉴别和判断所形成的意见。

根据2011年《最高人民法院关于办理侵犯知识产权刑事案件适用法律若干问题的意见》第3条的规定，公安机关、人民检察院、人民法院在办理侵犯知识产权刑事案件时，对于需要鉴定的事项，应当委托国家认可的有鉴定资质的鉴定机构进行鉴定。一般来说，鉴定机构受司法机关委托进行鉴定，处于中立地位，与被害人、被告人无利害关系，其出具的鉴定意见不具有主观偏向性。根据商标局的相关批复，商标注册人也可以受委托进行鉴定，并且其出具的"鉴定意见"可以作为证据予以采用。❶

诉讼程序中的鉴定人必须是与案件没有利害关系的人。尽管受工商局委托，商标权人一方作为利害关系人，其出具鉴定文本并不是诉讼法中严格意义上的"鉴定意见"，而属于被害人陈述。所谓被害人陈述，是指刑事被害人就其遭受犯罪行为侵害的情况和其他与案件相关情况向公安机关、

---

❶ 根据商标局2005年作出的《关于假冒注册商标商品及标识鉴定有关问题的批复》，在查处商标违法行为过程中，工商行政管理机关可以委托商标注册人对涉嫌假冒注册商标商品及商标标识进行鉴定，出具书面鉴定意见，并承担相应的法律责任。被鉴定者无相反证据推翻该鉴定结论的，工商行政管理机关将该鉴定结论作为证据予以采纳。

人民检察院、人民法院所作的陈述。被害人陈述和鉴定意见同属于言词证据,是以人的陈述为存在和表现形式的证据材料。两者的区别主要有:其一,被害人陈述具有不可替代性,而鉴定意见具有可替代性。其二,被害人陈述具有偏向性,而鉴定意见具有中立性。❶ 其三,在侵犯商标权刑事犯罪案件中,商标权利人处于被害人地位,其就假冒商品或者商标所作的真伪辨别属于被害人陈述而非鉴定意见,无须满足鉴定资质的要求。

在实务中,被告人也多会以商标权利人与案件存在利害关系、不具有鉴定资质为由提出抗辩。毫无疑问,上述抗辩所依据的事实是客观存在的,然而,辩方不能以此为依据来排除商标权利人出具的鉴定文本的证明效力。尽管其不可作为鉴定意见加以采用,但是可以作为被害人的陈述加以采用。上述做法为司法实务所采纳。例如,在"顾某、张某某销售假冒注册商标的商品罪上诉案"中,上海市第一中级人民法院认为被害人的委托代理人博邦公司出具的书面《鉴定情况说明》并非刑事诉讼证据中的鉴定意见,其内容为被害单位的辨认,其证据属性应当归类于刑事诉讼证据中的被害人陈述。❷

2. 涉案商品真伪鉴定书的证明效力

商标权利人出具的鉴定书具有当然的证明效力,除非被告人有相反证据予以推翻。商标权利人为了维护其商标和商品不受侵害,往往会投入较大的维护成本,其中就包含一定的技术要素,这类技术要素通常只有商标权利人掌握并且秘而不宣,并且商标权人对自己的商品更加了解,对仿冒商品也更为敏感,其出具鉴定书不仅方便易行,还可以减少一定的司法鉴定时间和成本。

但是商标权人出具的鉴定书并不能保证相对中立,客观存在的利害关系会对证据效力产生消极影响,因此对该类鉴定文本的内容不能照单全收,而应当根据具体情况,从证据与待证事实的关联程度、证据之间

---

❶ 唐震:"商品权利人出具的商品真伪鉴定意见的证据属性及其审查",载《人民司法》2013年第6期。

❷ "顾某、张某某销售假冒注册商标的商品罪上诉案",(2012)沪一中刑知终字第3号刑事判决书。

的联系等方面综合全案证据进行审查。由于被害人与犯罪嫌疑人、被告人之间固有的利害关系，尽管商标权利人出具的关于商品真伪的鉴定意见具有当然的证明效力，仍然需要结合其他证据予以综合审查，与其他证据共同指向同一待证事实，不存在无法排除的矛盾和无法解释的疑问，才能作为定案的根据。

在本案中，除了"CONVERSE"商标权利人匡威公司一方出具的《鉴定书》外，还有福建中证司法鉴定中心《司法鉴定检验报告书》、厦门市诚兴德会计师事务所《专项审计报告》、厦门市产品质量监督检验所《检验报告》等鉴定意见、其他书证、物证、证人证言等。经过分析，上述证据内容共同指向同一待证事实，即被告人销售假冒注册商标的商品的事实，上述证据内容与商标权利人一方出具的鉴定意见相互印证，能够佐证鉴定意见的证明内容增强其证明效力。

五、典型意义

福建省是世界鞋类品牌的重要代工生产基地，拥有几千家制鞋企业，产品销往世界各地。但是近年来，福建省一些地区仿制国外高端胶鞋产品的案件频发，损害了商标权人的合法权益，扰乱了市场秩序，同时也侵害了消费者的合法权益。对该类制假售价行为进行有效打击，是净化市场环境、彰显福建省对知识产权保护工作的力度和决心的现实要求。

本案案情错综复杂、取证难度高、打击难度极大。一方面，本案涉及的仿冒"CONVERSE"商标的假鞋产品也是高仿鞋，在审判程序中经厦门市产品质量监督检验所鉴定，符合标准合格品要求。因此，本案涉及的违法行为极具隐蔽性。另一方面，本案涉及区域广、涉案人员众多，是福建省迄今为止最大的网络销售假鞋案，假鞋生产涉及莆田、武平等地，销售范围则遍及全国各地。

在法律适用方面，本案体现了思明法院对于大力打击制假售假行为的决心。尤其是本案对尚未销售的假冒注册商标的商品货值金额计算方法的处理，及对知识产权犯罪案件中不可避免的鉴定真伪问题的解决，对同类案件具有普遍的借鉴意义。

　　鉴于本案的重大现实意义，本案判决书已经入选"最高人民检察院2012年度打击侵犯知识产权犯罪十大典型案例"，具有全国性影响力和示范意义。

（刘德芬　田双莉）

叶某、张某某销售假冒注册商标的商品罪案研析

一、案情简介

2013年6月,被告人张某某受林某某的委托购买一批贵州茅台酒。被告人张某某、叶某为牟取非法利益,由叶某提议,两人共同商定后,由被告人叶某以每瓶人民币500元的价格向他人购买了20件共计240瓶500ml标有"MOUTAI"商标标识的酒,被告人张某某与林某某谈妥销售价格每瓶930元。同年6月12日,被告人叶某将酒运至厦门高崎国际机场时被公安人员全部缴获。经贵州茅台酒股份有限公司鉴定,上述酒均系假冒贵州茅台酒厂有限责任公司注册的"MOUTAI"商标,对应真品市场零售价格为人民币999元/瓶。6月25日,公安人员到贵州省贵阳市找到被告人张某某及叶某,二人承认出售上述"茅台酒"。6月27日,二被告人随同公安人员回到厦门并于6月28日被刑事拘留。经鉴定,上述假酒达到国家食品卫生标准,不属于有毒有害食品。

二、裁判结果

厦门市思明区人民法院经审理认为,被告人叶某、张某某明知是假冒注册商标的商品而予以销售,销售金额达人民币223 200元,数额较大,其行为已构成销售假冒注册商标的商品罪。被告人叶某、张某某系共同故意犯罪,被告人叶某是犯意的提出者和货源的组织者,被告人张某某在明知涉案商品是假酒的情况下,仍然积极与买家联系,商谈销售价格。二人在共同犯罪中作用相当。两被告人因意志以外的原因犯罪未能得逞,是犯罪

未遂，依法可以从轻或减轻处罚。两被告人到案后如实供述罪行，在法庭上自愿认罪，赃物被全数查获未流入社会，依法可以从轻处罚。综上所述，法院决定对两被告人从轻处罚，但对辩护人宣告缓刑的辩护意见不予采纳。判决被告人叶某犯销售假冒注册商标的商品罪，判处有期徒刑一年四个月，并处罚金人民币10万元。被告人张某某犯销售假冒注册商标的商品罪，判处有期徒刑一年二个月，并处罚金人民币8万元。扣缴在案的240瓶500ml标有"MOUTAI"商标标识的假酒，予以没收销毁。

三、争议焦点

本案的争议焦点有：
(1) 被告人的行为构成何罪？
(2) 被告人的行为构成既遂还是未遂？

四、案例评析

（一）被告人的行为构成何罪

厦门高崎国际机场查获的这批高仿茅台酒的包装、防伪标识、酒瓶外观甚至酒的味道几乎和正宗的茅台酒相差无几，本案的关键问题在于：被告人低价买进这批高仿茅台酒并高价卖出的行为构成生产、销售伪劣产品罪还是销售假冒注册商标的商品罪？

生产、销售伪劣产品罪是指生产者、销售者违反国家有关产品质量、安全监督管理的法律法规，在产品中掺杂、掺假，以假充真，以次充好或者以不合格产品冒充合格产品，销售金额达5万元以上的行为。销售假冒注册商标的商品罪是指违反商标管理法规，销售明知是假冒注册商标的商品，销售金额达5万元以上的行为。单纯从概念上考察，上述两罪的内涵和外延似乎相去甚远。但是在司法实践中，两罪往往存在交叉竞合的情况，从而导致认定和处理上存在分歧。有鉴于此，厘清生产、销售伪劣商品罪与销售假冒注册商标的商品罪的界限，在理论和实践层面都有重要意义。

1. 销售假冒注册商标的商品罪与生产、销售伪劣产品罪的区别

两罪在犯罪构成方面的区别主要表现在以下两个方面：

第一,侵害的法益不同。销售假冒注册商标的商品罪侵害的是国家商标管理制度和商标权人的注册商标专用权,也涉及消费者的合法利益,但侧重保护的是商标权人的权益;生产、销售伪劣产品罪侵害的是国家产品质量监督管理制度和消费者的合法权益。

第二,危害行为的表现不同。销售假冒注册商标的商品罪表现为他人未经注册商标所有人许可,在同一种商品上违法使用与其注册商标相同的商标,行为人知晓并进行产品销售的行为。生产、销售伪劣产品罪的危害行为主要表现为生产、销售的产品质量不符合原产品标准或行业标准,并不一定涉及假冒他人商标行为。

2. 销售假冒注册商标的商品罪和生产、销售伪劣产品罪的竞合

在生产、销售伪劣产品罪中,"伪劣"一词中"伪"也取"假冒、仿冒"的意思,这也说明该罪与销售假冒注册商标的商品罪的竞合关系。具体说来,行为人销售的假冒商标的商品可以分两种:伪而不劣、又伪又劣;伪劣产品也分两种:劣而不伪、又伪又劣。"伪而不劣"即行为人对外销售假冒注册商标的商品,但该商品具有产品说明所示的使用性能,产品质量合格,不属于劣质产品。因此,若行为人构成犯罪,只能单独以销售假冒注册商标商品罪追究其刑事责任。"劣而不伪"即行为人销售质量不合格的商品,但是未假冒他人的注册商标,若销售金额达到刑法规定的犯罪数额较大的入罪要求,则应认定为销售伪劣产品罪。如果行为人销售的是"又伪又劣"商品,即销售的是假冒他人注册商标的商品,同时该商品又是伪劣商品,这种情况下则会出现认定罪名分歧的情况。

理论界有对此问题有两种观点。按照"法条竞合论",销售假冒注册商标的商品罪与生产、销售伪劣商品的犯罪之间存在法条竞合关系。法条竞合是犯罪所侵犯的社会关系错综交织的现实状态造成的,无论犯罪是否发生,人们都可以通过对法律条文内容的分析而确定各个法条之间原本依刑事立法就实际存在的重合或者交叉关系。❶ 即使没有犯罪行为的发生,但是根据现有的刑法规定,行为人在生产、销售伪劣商品的同时可能也假冒了

---

❶ 高铭暄主编:《刑法专论》,高等教育出版社2006年版,第384页。

他人的注册商标，而销售假冒他人注册商标的商品也可能同时是伪劣商品，在这种情况下同一行为可以被两个法条评价，符合两个犯罪的构成要件。所以，生产、销售伪劣商品罪与销售假冒注册商标罪之间存在法条竞合的交叉关系，即两个法条之间各有一部分构成要件相互重合，体现了"你中有我、我中有你"的情形，形成一种选择适用的问题，应依照重法优于轻法原则加以处理。

按照"想象竞合论"，销售"又伪又劣"的商品是一行为同时触犯两个罪名，属于想象竞合关系，应当从一重罪处罚。因为销售假冒注册商标的商品，可能是质量合格的商品，也可能是劣质商品；生产、销售的伪劣商品，可能没有假冒他人的注册商标，也可能假冒了他人的注册商标，涉及两罪名的法条之间并不存在必然的重合或交叉关系，不符合法条竞合的情形。销售"又伪又劣"的行为符合想象竞合犯，即两个罪名发生关联，是以行为人实施特定的犯罪行为为前提，而不是因法条之间的内在联系，没有销售"又伪又劣"商品的犯罪行为也就没有想象竞合情形的出现。

对于法条竞合和想象竞合的关系，有的学者主张大竞合理论，不必严格区分两者。❶ 若考虑到刑法定罪量刑的目的，就在于对违法性及有责性事实进行全面评价，从而宣告一个罪刑相适应的刑罚，则销售假冒注册商标的商品罪和生产、销售伪劣产品罪无论是法条竞合关系还是想象竞合关系，并不妨碍案件的处理，即依据两理论都主张的"从一重罪论处"，这也符合我国法律解释的规定。最高人民法院、最高人民检察院《关于办理生产、销售伪劣商品刑事案件具体应用法律若干问题的解释》第10条规定，实施生产、销售伪劣商品犯罪，同时构成侵犯知识产权、非法经营等其他犯罪的，依照处罚较重的规定定罪处罚。该解释虽然没有明确指出是法条竞合还是想象竞合，但依据其中规定在不违背刑法基本原则的前提下能解决实务问题即可。

在本案中，被告人销售假酒的行为侵犯了他人注册商标专用权，且销售的假酒达到了国家食品卫生标准，思明区检察院和思明区法院将被告的

---

❶ 陈洪兵："不必严格区分法条竞合与想象竞合"，载《清华法学》2012年第6期。

行为定性为销售假冒注册商标的商品罪，是符合我国现行法律规定的。

（二）被告人的行为构成既遂还是未遂

本案涉及的另一个问题是，被告人张某某与买方谈妥价格，在准备交货过程中，将酒运至厦门高崎国际机场时被公安人员全部缴获，被告人的行为构成犯罪既遂还是未遂。

所谓数额犯，是指以法定数额作为犯罪构成要件定量标准的犯罪。销售假冒注册商标的商品罪系典型的数额犯，社会危害性的大小主要取决于犯罪数额的大小。目前，我国学界针对数额犯是否有未遂问题一直有争论。

1. 作为数额犯的销售假冒注册商标的商品罪是否存在未遂形态

目前，学界针对数额犯是否有未遂形态的理论，大致有以下三种：

第一种观点为"否定说"，即否定数额犯存在未遂形态。此种观点的理论基础是"刑法分则规定是以犯罪成立模式"构建，即刑法分则所规定的构成要件是犯罪的成立条件，而不是犯罪的既遂条件。因此，如果刑法分则将危害结果规定为犯罪构成要件，则没有发生该结果的，一律不构成犯罪，当然也不能以未遂犯论处。❶ 以本案涉及的销售假冒注册商标的商品罪为例，持此观点的学者认为，销售金额只存在于已经销售假冒注册商标的商品中，如果相关商品还没有销售或者销售金额没有达到法定数额，则不存在数额较大而构成犯罪的情况，当然也不存在未遂问题。但是，该观点未能区分行为数额犯与结果数额犯，将数额犯构成要件中的法定数额都视为结果数额犯的数额要求，把行为数额犯的未遂排除出去，有悖于立法精神。在很多实务案例中，假冒注册商标的商品尚未成功销售，没有实际销售金额，但是也不能否定该行为的法益侵害性。

第二种观点为"肯定说"，即肯定数额犯存在未遂形态。这种观点根据我国传统刑法理论所认同的"刑法分则规定是以犯罪既遂模式"构建的论点，认为刑法规定的各种犯罪构成及其刑事责任，是以既遂罪为标准的，即以一定数额的危害结果的实际发生为构成要件，齐备了犯罪构成要件的是犯罪既遂；如果由于行为人意志以外的原因，犯罪数额未达到法定标准，

---

❶ 张伟："数额犯若干问题研究"，载《中国刑事法杂志》2010年第3期。

就是犯罪的未遂。但是,"肯定说"将社会危害性尚未达到应当追究刑事责任的行为作为犯罪来对待,以致扩大了数额犯未遂的成立范围,混淆了"行为未遂"与"犯罪未遂"两个不同的概念。销售假冒注册商标的商品罪以销售金额人民币5万元作为犯罪既遂的标准,一旦销售金额不足5万元,同时与尚未销售的商品的货值金额累加不足15万元的,若判定为犯罪未遂则未免打击面过大,有悖刑法谦抑性原则和罪责刑相适应原则。

第三种观点为"折中说"。该观点也建立在"刑法分则规定是以犯罪既遂模式"的基础之上,并将数额犯分为结果数额犯和行为数额犯两类。其一,结果数额犯是以发生符合法定数额标准的结果作为犯罪构成要件,只有发生符合法定数额标准的结果,犯罪才能成立,因而不存在犯罪的未完成形态。立法上对结果数额犯的数额规定主要有两类:造成实际损失的数额和违法所得数额。例如,销售侵权复制品罪是指以营利为目的,销售明知是刑法规定的侵权复制品,违法所得数额巨大的行为。其二,行为数额犯存在犯罪既遂、未遂之分。如果犯罪行为造成标志犯罪完成的基本结果,属于犯罪既遂;如果由于意志以外的原因未发生犯罪的基本结果,但行为数额达到法定的定罪标准的,属于犯罪未遂。❶ 对比销售侵权复制品罪中的"违法所得数额"与销售假冒注册商标的商品罪中的"销售数额",从立法用语角度看,前者规定的是结果数额,而后者的"销售金额"指行为人已经销售或正在销售假冒注册商标的商品所得和应得的全部金额,并未将数额限定为结果数额,包含结果数额和应得数额在内。依据此观点,作为销售假冒注册商标的商品罪存在未遂形态。

2. 销售假冒注册商标的商品罪成立未遂形态的数额标准

一般而言,刑法中对于行为数额犯的定罪数额标准,是既遂行为与未遂行为的共同标准。无论犯罪行为是既遂还是未遂,只要行为数额达到法定的定罪标准,就应当依法追究行为人的刑事责任。所不同的应当是刑罚上的区别对待,即对于未遂犯,可以比照既遂犯从轻或者减轻处罚。

但是,并非所有着手之后的未遂行为都应处罚,其成立犯罪必须以具

---

❶ 刘之雄:"数额犯若干问题新探",载《法商研究》2005年第6期。

有严重的社会危害性为条件。我国刑法秉持"以处罚既遂犯为原则,以处罚未遂犯为例外"的原则,数额犯的未遂行为在例外的情况下才应当作为未遂犯予以处罚。另外,从我国《刑法》关于数额犯的刑罚配置来看,刑罚都比较轻,大多在3年以下有期徒刑,而法定最高刑在3年以下有期徒刑的犯罪通常被视为轻罪。既然在达到既遂状态的情况下,轻罪的社会危害性就比较小,那么在轻罪的未遂状态下更应该控制将其纳入刑罚范围。从司法实践看,未遂状态下的犯罪数额若没有达到较大标准,并没有对合法权益产生直接、现实的刑法意义上的威胁,应适用《刑法》第13条的但书规定,即属于情节显著轻微、危害不大,不以犯罪论处,这种情况可以适用行政手段加以规制。

我国司法解释中对销售假冒注册商标的商品罪未遂标准的规定就体现了上述精神。根据最高人民法院、最高人民检察院、公安部、司法部联合颁布的《关于办理侵犯知识产权刑事案件适用法律若干问题的意见》(以下简称《意见》)第8条第1款规定,销售明知是假冒注册商标的商品,具有下列情形之一的,以销售假冒注册商标的商品罪(未遂)定罪处罚:(1)假冒注册商标的商品尚未销售,货值金额在15万元以上的;(2)假冒注册商标的商品部分销售,已销售金额不满5万元,但与尚未销售的假冒注册商标的商品的货值金额合计在15万元以上的。一方面,《意见》肯定该罪存在犯罪未遂,并不违背《刑法》总则对犯罪未遂的规定以及数额犯存在未遂的基本法理,体现了"从严"的一面;另一方面,为限制该罪的入罪范围,《意见》将成立未遂罪的数额标准从既遂标准的5万元以上提高到了15万元以上,又体现了"从宽"的一面。这种解释理念体现了刑法谦抑精神的要求,也符合《刑法》第13条"但书"之规定。❶

3. 销售假冒注册商标的商品罪中"销售"的认定

在具体判断销售假冒注册商标的商品罪的犯罪停止形态时,首先明确行为人是否已经着手实施犯罪行为,再讨论犯罪数额问题。若行为人着手实施且完成销售行为,则销售金额达到5万元即构成犯罪且既遂;若行为

---

❶ 李晓君:"销售假冒注册商标的商品罪之未遂形态争议问题探析",载《知识产权》2014年第11期。

人着手实施犯罪行为但由于意志以外的原因销售行为未完成,则货值金额达到15万元就构成犯罪未遂。本罪最主要的客观表现为销售行为,必须将"销售"的含义予以厘清才能准确判断具体案件中行为人是否着手实施了犯罪。

本罪中的"销售"是指将假冒注册商标的商品的所有权通过有偿的形式出让给他人。销售行为包括批发、零售、代销等各种形式,一般来说要求同时具有买进和卖出两个行为。有人认为,销售行为具体实施的前提条件是要有明确的买卖双方,销售者在购买者出现之前为了实现销售商品的目的而实行的任何活动都只能是销售的准备活动,因而只有销售者找到购买者之时,才能认定销售行为已经着手。因为销售假冒注册商标的商品罪中偏重于处罚卖出假冒注册商标商品的这一行为,单纯买进假冒注册商标的商品且尚未卖出的行为并不按照本罪来处理,一般运用行政手段加以处罚。也有人认为,销售涵盖从买入到卖出侵权商品的全过程,为了卖出而买入侵权商品,即告"着手",一旦完成货物交付,即告"完成"。

买入侵权商品后一定要找到买方才是犯罪着手的说法值得商榷。行为人明知是侵权商品而买入应是本罪的"着手",尽管侵权商品尚未销售,没有进入流通环节,也不能否认该行为的社会危害性,放纵以销售为目的而买入假冒他人商标的商品的行为。同时,为避免扩大刑法的入罪范围,若尚未销售侵权商品的货值金额没有达到刑法规定的数额标准,对行为人可用行政手段加以规制,若达到刑法规定的数额标准,则具有刑法意义上的社会危害性,应受到刑法规制。这也符合我国刑事司法相关解释对销售假冒注册商标商品罪的规定,即买入假冒注册商标的商品尚未销售,但货值金额达到15万元即构成犯罪未遂,这里的"尚未销售"应主要指的是行为人以营利为目的买入侵权商品但尚未卖出的情形。

对于本罪中销售行为的完成问题,一般认为,销售行为的完成是行为人已经将假冒注册商标的商品销售出去,货物所有权发生转移,而且实际所获的销售金额达到法律规定的数额较大的程度。反之,对货物尚未交付、所有权还未转移的,应认定为尚未销售,属于犯罪未遂。

在本案中,被告人从贵阳买进侵权商品,虽然有明确的买家,与购买者也已达成商品购销的合意,并约定了茅台酒的销售价格和运输方式,但是双方既未实际交付定金或货款,也未完成假冒注册商标的商品交付,全部侵权商品被公安机关查扣。该种情况中销售活动并未完成,其对法益尚未造成实质的、现实的侵害,故思明区人民法院认定为犯罪未遂。

五、典型意义

在司法实践中,销售假冒注册商标的商品罪大致占知识产权犯罪案件总数的一半,而制售假酒正是其中一个重要的多发类别。

制售假酒犯罪主要以假冒茅台、五粮液等著名国产白酒,以及马爹利、蓝带等进口知名品牌洋酒为主,甚至已成为一个行业的潜规则,社会影响恶劣,危及大量终端消费者的身体健康,本案的审理对打击此类犯罪活动以及保护商标权人和消费者的合法权益具有示范作用。

厦门市思明区人民法院在本案的审理过程中,妥善解决了销售假冒注册商标的商品罪构成既、未遂的标准问题,有助于统一裁判标准,对类似案件具有指导意义。该案获评福建省法院2016年消费者权益保护典型案例。

(林 鸿 田双莉)

Study on Zhao Moumou vs. Fu'an bang Co. & South Hotel Copyright Infringement Dispute

I. Case Brief

Zhao Moumou, the plaintiff of this case, argued that he is a painter and the editor of *Facial Makeup in the Peking Opera*, published by Zhaohua Publishing House in 1992. This book was republished in the name of *Album of Facial Makeup in the Peking Opera of China* in 2003. All the 568 types of facial makeup designs used in the Peking Opera along with more than 20 portraits of Peking Opera characters are the original works of the plaintiff. He found that some pictures on the billboard of Fu'an bang Co., Ltd. (hereafter "Fu'an bang Co.") , the defendant of this case, were using 12 of the facial makeup drawings from his book without his permission and paying any licenses fees. The South Hotel is the owner of the building that hangs the billboard. The plaintiff filed a lawsuit against the two defendants, seeking injunction relief and apologies for their infringing acts in *Amoy Daily*, as well as damages of RMB 182 000 for the economic losses and RMB 2 000 for reasonable expenses.

The defendant claimed that, first of all, the facial makeup of Peking Opera is a form of folk art in China, passed from one generation to another for a long period of time. The plaintiff, as the editor of his book, has the copyright on the compiling of the whole book, but no copyright on each of the facial makeup in the book. Secondly, the plaintiff provides no evidence to show the facial makeup drawings used in the advertisement are copied from his book. On the contrary, these facial makeup drawings are selected from the public domain by the advertisement company, but not from the plaintiff's book. The defendant also contended that it has no subjective intent to commit an infringement for there are so many facial makeup available that the defendant has not to copy those in the plaintiff's book, and it was just a very short time when the defendant released the advertisement before the proceeding, thus its use didn't make any profits and cause any actual economic losses to the plaintiff.

II. Decisions

After hearing, the Siming District People's Court ruled that the plaintiff Zhao Moumou has the copyright of the facial makeup drawings of Peking Opera in the book *Album of Facial Makeup in the Peking Opera of China*, and therefore should be protected. The defendant Fu'an bang Co. used the facial makeup drawings of the plaintiff on the advertisement without permission should stop using these works and pay a total of RMB 22 000 of compensation to the plaintiff. As to the apology claim of the plaintiff, the courts ruled that the infringing acts of the defendant did not cause any damage to the plaintiff's mental health and reputation, therefore did not withhold this claim.

III. Key Issues

The key issues of this case are as follows:
Firstly, whether the plaintiff has copyright in the facial makeup drawings?
Secondly, whether the defendant infringed the plaintiff's copyright?

IV. Analysis

Zhao Moumou is a famous artist in China for his paintings of Peking Opera characters. Since 2003, after the republishing of *Album of Facial Makeup in the Peking Opera of China*, the plaintiff found some of the facial makeup drawings in this book were used without his permission. So he filed several lawsuits against the infringers in the courts all over China, included the city of Beijing, Shanghai, Chongqing, Shanxi, and Inner Mongolia, Zhejiang, Hebei, Hunan and Fujian provinces. The decadents involve Internet operator, producer of souvenirs, retailers, plazas, advertising companies, hotels, food suppliers as well as decoration companies. In these cases, the plaintiff argued that the facial makeup drawings he drew are original; the defendants' breach his copyright and should be liable for injunctions and damages.

A. Whether the plaintiff has copyright in the facialmakeup drawings?

The plaintiff asserted that the defendant infringed his copyright, which mainly includes the following layers of meaning: Firstly, the plaintiff is the original copyright holder or a legal right holder of the facial makeup designs; secondly, these facial makeup deigns constitute "works" in copyright law; thirdly, the rights of the plaintiff based on the facial makeup designs are not abandoned, therefore do not enter into public domain. The second point is the most critical. According to Article 2 of the *Implementation Regulation of Copyright Law* of the People's Republic of China, the term "works" as stated in the Copyright Law shall include original works of literature, arts and sciences with intellectual results which can be reproduced in a tangible form. It is obvious that the facial makeup designs are in the area of arts. Therefore, it is a decisive step to judge whether the facial makeup designs are original or not and whether it is a "work" in the copyright law.

Originality refers to the work protected by copyright should be the creation of the author, meaning that it is not copied from other people and should be creative to some extent. Common law system and civil law system have different requirements on originality. In general, originality standard in the common law system is relatively low. For example, in *University of London Press Ltd. v. University Tutorial Press Ltd.*, a UK case, the court held that in order for a work to gain copyright protection, it must originate from the author and contains a minimum creativeness. It is the classic interpretation of the meaning of originality and has been cited even in modern cases. In *Feist Publications, Inc., v. Rural Telephone Service Co.*, the Supreme Court of the US ruled that the work should contain a minimum creativeness in order to fulfill the originality requirement. ❶ However, the civil law system is different from the common law system in deeming the work as a reflection of the personality of the author, not as a simple form of property. Accordingly, the originality civil law system civil law system adopts a strong link between the rights and the personality of the author. Therefore, anything could be produced by the common people should not be protected, even though those do not exist before it was produced. ❷

There is no provision made to determine whatoriginality is in Chinese copyright laws and regulations, nor the judicial interpretations. In practice, no dispute exist on the understanding that the originality requires the work are not copied, but lies in the threshold of creativity, that's to say, whether it should be novel or original and to what extent it should be. The lack of unification of the original requirement in the judicial practices leads to uncertainties of obeying and applying the copyright rules.

The most important points in determine the meaning of "creativity", are whose perspective should be chosen and to what extent the creation should be. That is, whose perspective should be chosen, the judge, the expertise or someone else? Besides, to what extent the creation should be? Is a one-for-all criterion or different criteria for different types of works working?

There are four kinds of answers to the first question. The first one, also the most common one, is that the judge can decide the extent of creation at his discretion. The second one is that the question of creativity should be left to the expertise. Because originality is a question of fact in the most cases, for which the judge could not do it on his own. The judge should rely on the expertise form certain

---

❶ *Feist Publications, Inc., v. Rural Telephone Service Co.*, 499 U. S. 340 (1991).
❷ M. Rehbinder, *Copyright Law*, translated by Zhang Enmin, Law Press 2004, p. 117.

area like judicial appraisal bodies to evaluate the originality of the work disputed in certain case. Therefore, the judge could be freed from those fact-finding affairs, which they are not good at and can put more attention on the legal issues such as finding infringement.❶ The third one is that the court should bear the duty to decide by referring to the expertise. Copyright Law protects various kinds of works, but the judges are not competent because the originality of a work should be examined by referring to multidisciplinary knowledge. Besides, there is no detail requirements and standard concerning to originality in Copyright Law, it might be even the expertise would face the same difficulties when dealing with such kind of issues.❷ The forth one is that both the judge and expertise are not competent in deciding the originality of a work, because it is dangerous by leaving the duty to evaluate the work to those who have been trained by legal training, it is also wrong to deny the copyright protection by referring to the public's low bad tastes.❸ However, leaving the duty of judging the value of a work to a panel also means resurrection of censorship of literature and Article❹ The originality is not only a matter of law but also a matter of art appreciation. Therefore, the duty of deciding originality should be chiefly assigned to the judge; the parties can employ expertise or judicial appraisal to support their claims, of course, the judge can decide if these testimonies could be accepted.

As to the second issue, that is the extent of creativity. There is no specification on this issue in the laws and regulations in China, so it is left to the judge decide at discretion. However, the judge should remember that the extent of creativity would not keep balancing of public interests and author protection. The judge should focus on the incentive of creator and leaving enough to the public, as

---

❶ Zhao Rui, "Rethinking and Cognizing of Originality of Copyrighted Work", in Intellectual Property, 2011 (9).

❷ Liu Hui, "Commentaries of the trichotomy of Originality of Copyrighted Work", in Intellectual Property 2011 (4).

❸ *Bleistein v. Donaldson Lithographing*, 188 U. S. 239 (1903).

❹ Liu Wenjie, "Copyright in the WeChat Platform", in Legal Research, 2012 (6).

well as limit the monopoly power without harming the public.

There are two kinds of opinions in dealing with the facialmakeup drawings cases. For example, in *Zhao Moumou vs. Chongqing Meiduo Food Co.*, Chonging People's High Court ruled that the plaintiff's 586 facial makeup drawings in the book *Album of Facial Makeup in the Peking Opera of China* are original work of art based upon the folk art of traditional Peking Opera and the understanding of the traditional mask art, by using his mastery of painting skills, therefore should be protected by Copyright Law.[1] However, some courts deny. For example, Changsha Intermediate People's Court ruled that the facial makeup drawings painted by the plaintiff are lack of originality. Because even if the plaintiff's outline lines, strokes and traditional facial features are different, but the Peking Opera facial makeup drawings is mainly through the spectrum and color to the audience to pass information, leaving the already formed face spectrum and color, subtle strokes change also lost a separate meaning of existence. People enjoy the opera in the audience, can clearly see the actor's performance, hear the actor's singing, but it is difficult to distinguish the subtle differences in the face. Unless the plaintiff to draw lines on the lines, strokes of the changes lead to the use of traditional facial spectrum and color to show the characteristics of different characters, otherwise this change is not enough to make it creative Because the Peking Opera is a category of traditional culture, The originality of its similar works should be put forward higher requirements, the plaintiff did not prove that the relevant face relative to the traditional mask of creativity and significantly different, not because the plaintiff draw, published Peking Opera a book and found the plaintiff *The spectrum of graphics* itself is copyrighted.[2]

The fundamental reason for these different opinions is that the standard the originality held by the local courts is not uniform. This difference becomes clearer when dealing with works based on folk arts. To decide whether facialmakeup draw-

---

[1] (2011) Yu Gaofa Minzhong No. 188.
[2] (2006) Changzhong Minsan Chu No. 0399.

ings are original, the first thing to do is to be cautions about the raw materials of folk art and the works based upon folk Article Put another way, it is important to filter those belong to the public domain before dealing with the issues concerning the originality of the facial makeup drawings.

The facial makeup of Peking Opera is a traditional folk art in China, with an over 300 - year history. The facial makeup of Peking Opera is not totally imaginary, but is the result of long-term practice, observation of the phenomenon of life, experience, and comprehensive, analyzing characters by the artists and gradually formed a set of complete artistic techniques. The Peking Opera facial uses various colors to make an exaggerated sketch of the actor's face; these different colors and patterns are using to reflect the character, status and status of the characters. Every character in the operas has fixed facial makeup, with unique colors and design. For example, red represents loyalty, white represents cunning, Bao Zheng has a moon on his forehead. Any person who paints a specific picture of a Peking Opera character is bound to follow these particular patterns and colors. However, the way of expression Peking Opera is not unique, a variety of genre print the face method has been formed in the long-term development of Peking Opera, for example school of Hao, school of Qiu, each these schools has its own characteristics on the techniques of painting the facial makeup drawings.

Furthermore, to put on a facial makeup does not mean that one can just copy the former patterns, the actors should adjust the pattern according to their face and feature of acting, in order vividly reflect the appearance of the characters, emotional and personality characteristics, so that the facial makeup drawings and performance could be fully integrated. Therefore, as long as the facial makeup could reflect the main feature of the characters, there is no need to require complete agreement in the drawing method and pattern. When the artist in the form of an artwork displays the facial makeup of Peking Opera, in which embodies the author's style and characteristics of the creation, the lines, the composition of the composition of the pattern, etc., therefore, reflect the different delineation of originality.

Siming District People's Court affirmed that the facial makeup drawings could be original works and should be protected by Copyright Law. First of all, according to Copyright Law, the citizen, legal entity or other organization whose name is mentioned in connection with a work shall, in the absence of proof to the contrary, be deemed to be the author of the work. In this case, the author of *Album of Facial Makeup in the Peking Opera of China* should be Zhao Moumou because his name was announced on the cover, therefore, Zhao Moumou could be the author of the facial makeup drawings in this book and his copyright should be protected. Secondly, although the patterns, colors and designs of facial makeup drawings are relatively the same, the actor could adjust the pattern and adopt a different method. These different lines, arrangements and proportion reflect the originality of these facial makeup drawings. The plaintiff used his skill in combination with the understanding of the Peking Opera art, in the form of art for each specific facial makeup for re-creation of the characters. All these works are reflecting the creative labor of the author, which is not just compiling some existing facial makeup in one book. Therefore, the facial makeup drawings in this book are original and should be protect by Copyright Law.

B. Whether the defendant infringed the plaintiff's copyright?

In the case that the album has been original, it is necessary to further judge whether the defendant's use of thePeking Opera face constitutes infringement. In judicial practices, "contact + substantial similarity" is the basic standard used to determine whether a defendant has infringed the reproduction right of a copyright. That is to say, if the accused work is substantially similar with the copyright holder's work, at the same time, the copyright holder could show that there is evidence that the defendant had the contact with his/her work, and then the defendant should prove that the work has legal sources, otherwise he/she shall bear damage liabilities.

Specifically, "contact" refers to the defendant previously studied or copied the plaintiff's works, or has the opportunity to read, research, copy them. Put another way, the creation is not originated from the creator, which is a further evidence of the plagiarism of the defendant. According to the basic legal theory, "contact" is a matter of fact, such factors as the subject, behavior and mind state should be taken into account when dealing with contact issue. The subject of contact could be any one, the behavior of contact could be legal (transfer or employment) and illegal (theft, force and deceit), and the mind state of contact could be on the purpose of infringing and accidental contact subsequently arising the intention of infringement.

To prove "contact", the plaintiff mainly through the following two ways, one is to collect and put forward the direct evidence, such as evidence can show the defendant has read, seen, bought the plaintiff's work or the defendant once worked in the plaintiff's office, etc. Secondly, through indirect evidence, for example, the plaintiff's works have been earlier made public through issuance, exhibition, performance, screening, broadcasting, etc., or the plaintiff has his works registered before, and such works are available to public. In the judicial practices, the judges usually adopt a high probability standard to decide whether the defendant has the opportunity to contact with the plaintiff's work. According to Rule 108 of *Interpretation of Civil Procedure Law of People's Republic of China* launched by the Supreme Court, as to the evidence provide by the party who bears the burden of proof, upon examination and combining with the relevant facts, the courts should make sure the existence of such fact is of highly likeliness, therefore shall be deemed as the fact existing.

Under the doctrine of "substantial similarity", the main portion of an accused infringing work should be found substantially similar with the original part of the plaintiff's work. Put another way, the defendant takes the original part of the plaintiff's work as his/her own. The Abstraction−Filtration−Comparison test (AFC) is a method of identifying substantial similarity for the purposes of applying copyright law. Differ from the abstract observation method in applying the "three – step" test, in the judicial practice, there is another method called "overall observation", which emphasis the "overall concept and feeling", by treating a variety of creative elements (including unprotected elements) as a whole, in order to identify whether the legal work constitutes substantial similarity.❶ Usually, in the analysis of the "substantial similarity", the priority should be given to the "abstract observation method", and the "overall observation method" should be treated as an auxiliary pole, namely applicable results only in the former cannot be applicable or unreasonable to apply the latter obviously. It should also be pointed out that hoe much similarity of the works can be considered substantial to constitute an infringement is anther question worthy of consideration. However, in judicial practices, a large number of references to other people's works or references to the essence of the work will constitute "substantive use".❷

Back to this case, in the identification of "contact", Siming People's Court adopted the high degree of probability standard. The court ruled that because the plaintiff's work and the defendant's work is basically the same, and the plaintiff's work is published before the defendant's work, so the defendant is very likely to have accessed these facial makeup designs. At the same time, the defendant did not provide any evidence when he rebutted the facts advocated by the plaintiff; therefore, his assertion of "no contact" shall not be supported. In terms of the determination of the "substantial similarity", the court didn't adopt the AFC approach, instead, the court made its decision directly from the "overall concept and feeling", seen all the creative elements as a whole for the 11 pieces of facial makeup drawings are substantially similar with the plaintiff's works, therefore the infringing acts should lie.

---

❶ *Roth Greeting Cards v. United Card Co.*, 429 F. 2d 1106 (9th Cir. 1970).

❷ Wu Handong, "On the Judicial Standard of Contact + Substantial Similarity", in Legal Science 2015 (8).

V. Significance of this Case

This case is one of the typical cases in the infringement cases of Peking Opera. Since modern times, Peking Opera has become an important medium to introduce and disseminate traditional Chinese art and culture around the world, and is known as China's "national essence". On 16 November 2010, Peking Opera was listed as a representative list of intangible cultural heritage of human beings. Peking Opera bears cultural connotation and spirit value, and can be of great help of national spirits building, national values of reengineering, national culture revival, as well as for the construction of socialism with Chinese characteristics and harmonious human society has important practical significance. Therefore, how to protect traditional culture has become a major task in our country.

The typical significance of this case is that it makes clear that the art of the Peking Opera is a kind of creative material, which should be protected by law. Creators by using his own painting skills combined with the understanding of the Peking Opera art in the form of art, and different from other existing works, it is the use of Peking Opera art re-creation of folk art, reflecting some kind of intellectual creative labor, which is required by the originality in copyright law. To confirm and protect copyright facial makeup works not only won't limit the inheritance and development of Peking Opera art, but is important to encourage the Peking Opera artist's artistic creation, is beneficial to the prosperity and development of the Peking Opera art, as well as conducive to the protection of the similar traditional cultural heritage.

(Zeng Zhengzhi & Zhao Tao)

Study on Huasheng Co. vs. Kansai Co. Copyright Infringement Dispute

I. Case Brief

The Fuzhou Times Huasheng Copyright Agency Co., Ltd. (hereafter "Huasheng Co."), which is specializing in copyright operation, has obtained the exclusive right to exercise the right of projection of 100 Music Videos (MVs), 58 of which were involved in this case, such as *When Love has not yet been Told*, in Amoy and it has the right to negotiate with the users, give permissions, collect the payments, and initiate legal proceedings in the name of right owner. Kansai Amoy Entertainment Co., Ltd (hereafter "Kansai Co."), a KTV operator, stored 58 MVs including *When Love has not yet been Told* in its song-selecting system for its consumer demand, and played these MVs in commercial sense without the permission of the right owner. Thus, Huasheng Co. brought an action against Kansai Co., alleging that Kansai Co. violated its projection right based on 58 pieces of work.

The plaintiff requested the court to order the defendant to immediately stop the infringement, pay RMB 58 000 as compensation for the economic losses and the reasonable expenses of RMB 9 000 for stopping the infringement, and bear all legal costs of the case.

The defendant argued mainly from the following aspects: firstly, the plaintiff has no right to represent the copyright owner to claim compensation; secondly, the plaintiff's copyright licensing agreement is defective; thirdly, the use of the song system is provided by the operator, its increase or delete by the operator, the defendant has no intention of infringement; fourthly, the plaintiff claims the amount is unreasonable.

II. Decisions

After hearing, Siming District People's Court ruled that the plaintiff has received the right of showing in Amoy area according to Transferring Agreement, therefore is eligible to be a plaintiff to file a lawsuit. The defendant, Kansai Co., should be reliable for its negligence of scrutinizing the right of the MTVs which have been stored in its song-selecting system, and its commercial play of these MTVs constitutes infringement of the projection right of the plaintiff. As to the amount of compensation, the court held that, because the plaintiff did not specifically prove its losses, and there is no evidence of the specific profits the defendant got from the infringement, the court made its decision by applying the Statutory Compensation Standard which takes the degree of the defendant's subjective fault, duration of infringement as well as the reputation of the works in question and other factors into account. The court further noted that the plaintiffs could have resolved the disputes in economic reasonable ways, such as proposing tort warning to the defendant, but it straightly brought a lawsuit, a relatively-high-cost way, which contributed to a large amount of expenses including notary fees, lawyer fees, etc. Those expenses were held unreasonable, which means the plaintiff itself shall bear part of them. Therefore, the court ruled that Kansai Co. should stop the infringement immediately, and should compensate the plaintiff economic losses and reasonable expenses totaling RMB 32 000.

III. Key Issues

The key issues of this case are as follows:

Firstly, does the defendant violate the plaintiff's right of showing?

Secondly, whether the defendant could claim the lawful source defense? Thirdly, are the plaintiff's anti-infringing actions reasonable?

IV. Analysis

A. Does the defendant violate the plaintiff's right of showing?

KTV companies mainly engaged in products is MTV, each KTV on demand system has tens of thousands of MTV. KTV operators mainly through the following three channels to obtain MTVs: one is buy from some illegal operators; the second is download from the Internet in person and install them in the on-demand system with the help of the technical staff; the third is to join the China Audio-Video Copyright Association (hereinafter "CAVCA"), pay the annual royalties and get license from the CAVCA's unified music library. In general, the first two channels are suspected of violating the MTV copyright, but what specific kind of copyright is violated, needs to analyze the different situation.

First of all, different types of objects represent different nature of behavior. In the present market, most of the MTVs fully embody creative labor, that is, the choice of the screen, the arrangement and the mood of the lyrics with each other, with the light and shadow to create the mood of the song, the atmosphere, the use of color performance music emotions, the use of sports modeling to form a strong impact on the visual, etc. All of these creative labors are from the writer, director, actor, editor and synthesizer. These kind of MTVs have meet the standard of the originality required by the copyright law and they are created in a way similar to cinematography, so they can be treated as "similar to cinematographic works" in copyright law. According to the Copyright Law of China and its Implementing Regulation, the copyright of cinematographic works and "similar to cinematographic works" shall be enjoyed by the producer, therefore, the producer have the right of reproduce, translate, network disseminating and so on articulated in Article 10 of Copyright Law. If the scripts, music in those works can be used independently, the author of those independent works shall have the right to exercise the copyright separately. However, in the judicial practice, there are still a small part of MTVs do not meet the requirements of copyrighted work. Such MTVs only mechanically store scenes of nature, people or others, and their function is to record and copy. Even in order to ensure the quality of the sound and picture, there are some adaptation of the camera position and simple editing; it is not up to the originality of the work. Such MTVs can only be identified as video products. According to the provisions of the Copyright Law of China, the first producer of video products enjoy the neighboring right of those video products, and has the right to copy, issue, lease, network disseminate and so on, but has no projection right. Therefore, when deciding what kind of rights the defendant has infringed on, we should first judge whether the object being played is a "cinematographic work" or an "audio-visual product", and then judge whether the plaintiff is entitled to the litigation qualification, the focus is to judge whether he is the author of the MTV works, or has already acquired the license of the author or the producer, and finally based on the specific behavior of the defendant, we can determine whether the defendant's actions fall into the scope of the control of the exclusive right.

Secondly, different operating systems represent different nature of behaviors. At present, the operating system on the market mainly includes stand-alone operating system and VOD system. The former refers to the system without the support of the network, but through an independent computer or other terminal to complete the selection of songs and songs of the two systems. In the stand-alone operating system, the spread of MTV is a traditional one-way behavior, does not involve the issue of interactive communication. Each box has its own set of on-demand equipment and corresponding server equipment. KTV operators store MTVs in these technical devices, thus, it is only reproductions of MTV works (or products) which have already existed in the device, there is no problem of network transmission. VOD system, also called network system, is a user-driven interactive system. It uses network and stores songs on the server. Through a variety of computer rooms without disk, disk set-top boxes, diskless set-top boxes and other terminal equipment, it can complete the selection and play process of songs, users can get access to those MTVs in their chosen time and place. The use of VOD system often leads to the work being played, screened, etc., but with the traditional one-way communication or there is a fundamental difference, it is with the development of network technology to produce an interactive or on-demand communication behavior. At present, at least 80% of the KTV provide VOD system for consumers to provide song accompaniment service. There is an essential difference between VOD system and stand-alone operating system. In a stand-alone operating system, KTV operators are likely to infringe the right of reproduction, projection, receiving remuneration, but it won't infringe the right of network transmission. In the VOD system environment, the KTV operator may infringe the right of network transmission.

It is worthy of further discussion that the defendant's playing behavior usually involves copying and spreading two links at the same time. The purpose of replication is often to follow-up. Correspondingly, it may also violate the right of reproduction and the right of information network transmission. Then whether the plaintiff can not only advocate the right to copy, but also advocate the right to information network communication? What is the difference between the right of broadcasting and the right of information network communication?

As to the first question, there are different attitudes in judicial practice. When the plaintiff both advocates the right of reproduction, but also advocates the right to broadcast or information network communication rights, the court usually agrees that the right of reproduce has been infringed, and find that the defendant also violated the right to broadcast or information network communication rights. But some courts do not believe that the right to reproduce has been violated. For example, in *Huayi Co. vs. Beijing Baiyun Suosi Haojing Internet Service Co.*, Beijing Xicheng District Court ruled that, the plaintiff advocates that the defendant's actions have infringed upon the right of reproduction and the right of showing, due to the misunderstanding of the copyright-related legal concept, the defendant provide the cinematographic works through the local area network spread to the public without permission, so that the public may access these works from a place and at a time individually chosen by them, so the rights of information network transmission has been violated.❶

No mater whether it is a single-machine version of the song system or the VOD system, the music works are usually uploaded to the terminal equipment of the independent compartment and the non-temporary copy of the work is formed. Therefore, whether the operator violates the right of reproduce might not be disputed. The real question is, when an act that has already constituted the infringement of the rights of information network, whether it is necessary to carry out a separate and critical issue on the right of reproduction. This is the right of request in civil law; the plaintiff can advocate the right of information network transmission and the right of reproduction infringement at the same time. But the scope right of reproduction is narrower than the right of information network transmission, so the legal protection is limited when the plaintiff claims the rights of reproduction. Based on the principles of disposition and no trial without complaint in procedural law, the court should not be decided on violations of the right of information network transmission.

Specifically, the purpose of reproduction by the KTV operators to is to distribute. If it only reproduces some works, without distributing them, the degree of its harm for copyright infringement is obviously quite low. Accordingly, the scope of liability for the mere violation of reproduction rights should also be limited to injunction, that is, the "cessation of infringement" and "the elimination of influence" under Article 47 of the Copyright Law, and the right holder claims that damages are generally difficult to obtain. However, infringement of information network transmission rights is more serious than the infringement of reproduction

---

❶ (2008) Xi Minchu No. 2431.

right, not only because the formation of non-temporary copies, but also the wide spread of copied, which interfere with the genuine KTV works (products) market and normal use, unreasonably damage the legitimate interests of the right holder, so the right holder is entitled to injunction relief to eliminate the impact, and can also require the infringer to bear the responsibility for compensation for the losses. In addition, according to *Regulations on the Protection of Information Network Transmission Rights*, the form of liability for infringement of the right of information network communication includes stopping the infringement, eliminating the influence, apologizing and compensating for the losses. The infringement to the right of reproduction only refers to the liability of restoration, but does not involve the issue of damages, so if the right holder wants to claim damages, the basis of the right to claim could only be the protection of information network transmission rights, not the right to reproduce. However, if the right holder only wants to gain injunction relief, to eliminate the impact, he/she could either choose the right to reproduce or the right of information network transmission as the foundation of copyright infringement litigation.

The second question is the difference between the right of showing and the right of information network transmission. According to Article 10 of Copyright Law of China, the right of showing refers the right to show to the public a work, of fine art, photography, cinematography and any work created by analogous methods of film production through film projectors, over-head projectors or any other technical devices. Whereas, the right of information on network transmission refers to the right to communicate to the public a work, by wire or wireless means in such a way that members of the public may access these works from a place and at a time individually chosen by them. Through the definition we can find, the biggest difference between the right of showing and the right of information network transmission is that the forms of work distribution are not the same: the right of showing mainly regulates distribution through the "projector, slide projector and other technical equipment", but the right of information network transmission regulates the interactive presentation of works by "wired or wireless" network. Behind the distinction between the above two rights reflects the upgrading communication technology of copyrighted works. As to the KTV infringement litigation, if the operator to take a stand-alone version of the song system (each room has a set of independent on demand equipment), even if consumers can "select time" "selected location" on demand works, because it is not taken "wired or wireless" way of transmission, the behavior does not constitute the dissemination of information networks, but belong to the technical equipment through the public reproduction of the work, which falls in the scope of the right of showing. However, when the KTV operators use the MTV works uploaded to the local area network, and through the server and the terminal between the terminal equipment connected, not a specific third person in its selected time, place on-demand music TV works, at the same time to meet the interactive communication and "wired or wireless" to provide the public with three requirements, therefore, KTV operators constitute a violation of the right of information network transmission. However, it may be argued that, whether through wired or wireless network, and whether there is no interactive communication, that through the information network to disseminate the work is through "other technical equipment to reproduce the works" is logical, in other words, even if the right to information network communication does not regulate this form of information network transmission, it can also be included in the exclusive scope of the right to be adjusted, because "other technical equipment" can be interpreted as including information network equipment. The definition of the right to information network transmission in our country stems from the expression of Article 8 of the World Intellectual Property Organization Copyright Treaty (WCT). ❶ The reason for the introduction of the right to information network transmission to involve the interactive communication network is the traditional communication rights are built on the one-way, passive means of

---

❶ Hu Kangsheng ed., *Interpretation of Copyright Law of People's Republic of China*, Law Press, 2002, p. 56.

transmission. The aim of Article 8 of WCT is to make national copyright legislations to involve "interactive" communication in the copyright owner's exclusive rights. ❶ Therefore, when the Copyright Law has made specific provisions on this particular mode of transmission, other special provisions cannot be applied to other general provisions.

In this case, Siming District People's Court affirmed that the MTVs are copyrighted works and ruled that the defendant violated the right of showing based upon the specific facts of this case.

B. Whether the defendant could claim the lawful source defense?

The most common defensive strategy used by KTV operators is that the vendor provides the on-demand system provider also installs the music video-on-demand system and songs, so the songs have legitimate source. But is it really the case? In order to answer this question, it is necessary for us to have a deeper understanding of the legitimate source defense of sellers.

The legitimate source defense also called goodwill tort rules; its theoretical basis is derived from the protection of bona fide third parties. From the perspective of fairness and justice, the law needs to distinguish between good and malicious people, so that people with different subjective attitudes bear different civil liability. If the actor is in good faith and pays the appropriate consideration, the rights of the bona fide actor shall be protected in accordance with the principle of fairness. From efficiency point of view, if the seller is required to conduct a nuanced investigation of the products provided by the supplier to ensure all the goods they sell will not infringe anyone's right, it will unreasonably increase transaction costs, reduce transaction enthusiasm, and become the barrier of social and economic development. But when the seller is only of subjective goodwill, but can not point out the legitimate sources of infringing goods for the right owner to pursue the perpetrators, seller should still bear the relevant legal responsibility, because from

---

❶ Wang Qian, *Copyright Protection in Internet*, Law Press, 2011, p. 114.

the point of view of the importance of the value of the law, in this case, justice takes precedence over the efficiency of the transaction.

In Chinese legal system, legitimate source defense is mainly embodied in the Patent Law (Article 70) and Trademark Law (Article 60), but Copyright Law does not specify whether the seller can use such rule to defend. According to the Article 53 of Copyright Law, "where the publisher or producer of replicas is unable to prove that the publication or production is legitimately authorized or where the distributor of replicates or the licensor of replicates of film works or works created using methods similar to film making, computer software or audio-visual recordings is unable to prove that the distribution or lease of replicas has a legitimate source, legal liability shall be borne." This provision only provides the publisher and producer's legal liability, but does not explicitly mention whether the seller, the service provider can claim legitimate source defense. To solve this problem, the Supreme People's Court has promulgated the "Interpretation of Several Issues Concerning the Application of Law in the Trial of Copyright Civil Dispute Cases" and "Notice on the Trial Work of Internet Copyright Cases Involved", but whether the seller of the infringing goods directly advocating the issue of legitimate sources of defense remains unspecified. Although Copyright Law of China does not clearly treat the "legitimate sources" as a defense, copyright products sellers have the right to claim legitimate sources defense. The main reasons are as follows: First of all, in the field of Copyright Law, the "issuer" contains "the seller", "issuer" usually refers to the natural person or legal person who provides the original works or copies to the public by way of sale or gift. That is to say, selling is included in issuing. Secondly, in order to maintain the legislative system of IPR balanced and consistent, it is necessary to make such an explanation. Patent Law and Trademark Law clearly defined, if the seller is in good faith, and can provide the legitimate source of the product, he does not need to take responsibility for the damage. In order to maintain the consistency of the legislation, the same provision should be also stipulated in the Copyright Law. Finally, after all, the seller is not the source of infringement, if the law prohibits the seller from quoting "legitimate source defense", but treats the manufacturers who are the source of infringement and sellers of goodwill as the same, it is unfair. What's more, too heavy duty of care will make the issuer, the licensor too cautious to make deals, and even reduce their will to distribute or sell goods. This will not be conducive to the dissemination of cultural products and the construction and development of China's cultural industry.

In addition to the legitimate source, another element of legitimate sources of defense is the mind sate of the defendant. The subjective attitude of the seller can be divided into the following three types: firstly, the seller knows that the goods they sell are infringing the copyright; the second is that the seller should know that the goods they sell are infringing the copyright, but the seller does not actually know; thirdly, the seller does not know, should not know that the sale of goods is copyright infringement. If the seller knows that he is selling the infringing products, in this first case, the seller cannot be exempted from liability. The second case is negligent, that is, to presume to know the situation; the third case is "do not know" the situation is self-evident. What is controversial is whether the second case should be included in the "do not know". In the case of intellectual property infringement, the principle of non-fault is applied to injunction, and the principle of presumption of fault is applied to damages. In judicial practice, the seller of the infringing commodity usually uses the "do not know" as a defense, so we need to know whether it should have known. Because the second case is fault, the sellers as market operators, should bear the duty of reasonable care. When it does not fulfill the duty of reasonable care in the process of purchasing, it should be deemed as should has known but do not know, which can not directly exempt from the seller's liability.

To sum up, the legitimate sources of defense matters must be established at the same time have two elements: one is a legitimate source; the other is subjective on the no fault. In this case, the court correctly pointed out that the defendant did not provide the appropriate evidence to prove that these music video works have legitimate sources; the court shall not adopt this defense. The defendant did not obtain the permission and authorization of the copyright owner and use these music works for profit, thus constitute infringement. From the decision, it can be seen that the judgment of the court on the fault is to take the objective criterion, that is, through the defendant's behavior to speculate on the subjective content of the actor, the defendant without permission for the use of music-related works, subjective with a certain fault.

C. Are the plaintiff's anti-infringing actions reasonable?

According to the Article 49 of the Copyright Law of China, the compensation amount shall also include reasonable expenses incurred by the rights holder to stop the infringement acts. In accordance with the above provision, the perpetrator requested the court to adjudicate the defendant to pay the reasonable fee paid in order to stop the infringement on the premise that the rights act itself should be within the reasonable boundaries permitted by law. The legal basis of the provision is *obliegenheiten* (German) in civil law. *Obliegenheiten*, also known as indirect obligations, it refers to the relative relationship between the legal person can not ask the obligor to fulfill the obligations of the defendant will not be liable to damage, but only to bear the obligations of those who suffer the right to derogation or loss of obligations, in short, is the rights of their own interests to protect their duty of care. Because the violation of *obliegenheiten*, in essence, is negligence or giving up, the opposite party is not wrong, and therefore cannot be attributed to the opposite party. The main feature of *obliegenheiten* is that the right holder is usually not required to perform, and that it will not be liable for damages in violation of it, and only the party who is responsible for the obligation is subject to derogation or loss. For example, if another party for breach of contract harms one party, it should be timely to take measures to prevent the losses expansion, which is not a real obligation. The theory of obliegenheiten is not based on the principle of good faith. In the contractual relationship, if a party defaults to the other party to the loss, non-breach of contract to expand the loss and sit idly by, to the next party to the request for damages, which will obviously result in a huge waste of resources, but also an abuse of their rights integrity behavior. In the damages litigation, the infringer's rights to take obvious behavior or the high cost of rights and does not meet the usual affair, but look forward to get compensation from the infringer, which is contrary to the principle of good faith, for this part beyond the reasonable scope of the cost, the opposite party is not wrong, the right should be responsible for their own.

In this case, the plaintiff registered on 12 January 2011, get the author's authorization on 14 January, and apply for a notary public to collect evidence on 17 January. It is not difficult to see that the plaintiff's company was set up in order to carry out the litigation of the involved works, and the purpose of the litigation was to be analyzed from the plaintiff's preparation of the lawsuit and the proceedings and the plaintiff's obtaining the authorization period, the type of rights and the area in which the rights were exercised. Not just to stop the infringement, but to seek to seek non-normal economic interests through litigation. The plaintiff, after three days of authorization, obtained notary evidence, indicating that the plaintiff knew that the defendant had the management of the work, but the plaintiff did not file a warning of infringement, but notarized evidence and prosecution. In the case of infringement warning may stop the case of infringement, the plaintiff directly using a higher cost of litigation rights, is clearly not reasonable, which is the abuse of the rights of the plaintiff, the resulting expansion of the cost of maintaining the rights of the plaintiff of the fault, and the defendant is no fault, so for the expansion of this part of the rights of rights, should be borne by the plaintiff.

V. Significance of this Case

This case is a typical case among KTV series of infringement cases, and was selected as one of "Top 10 Cases of Amoy Courts 2012".

KTV companies mainly engage in music products, each KTV on demand system has tens of thousands of music and television works. From the current situation, copyright infringement in Chinese KTV industry is more serious. This is mainly due to the copyright owner and KTV companies cannot reach one-on-one authorization. Therefore, in the cases involving KTV copyright infringement, the role of sound collection collaboration for industry organizations should be fully considered. Especially in the identification of infringement, for those who joined the sound collection association, accept the unified management of industry organizations, and in accordance with the provisions of the payment of royalties, music from the library to obtain a music KTV company, should be protected by copyright.

The typical significance of this judgment in this case, is to promote the major KTV companies in Amoy to actively join the sound collection association, accept the unified management of industry organizations, and actively fulfill the obligation to respect and protect intellectual propertyrights; purification of KTV industry market environment has played a significant role in promoting. Copyright owners, KTV companies can benefit from, but also to a substantial reduction in similar infringement, and achieved good legal results. In addition to the judicial judgments in this case, Siming District People's Court issued to the Amoy Entertainment Industry Association issued a judicial proposal for KTV and other entertainment industry companies, proposing self-discipline industry, also achieved good social results.

In addition, the Siming District People's Court ruled against the plaintiff's rights improperly lead to unreasonable increase in the cost of the phenomenon of a special analysis, and the plaintiff company to bear some of the unreasonable rights fees, also provide a verdict to learn from to the future similar cases.

(Zeng Zhengzhi & Zhao Tao)

Study on Xingmao Co. vs. Yuhai Co. & Dongben Co. Trademark Infringement & Unfair Competition Dispute

I. Case Brief

Amoy "Gulangyu" is a famous scenic spot in Amoy City, Fujian Province, where a large number of domestic and foreign tourists come here for the beautiful scenery. "Gulangyu" was originally one of administrative districts of Amoy City, but it is no longer one of county level administrative divisions after Gulangyu becomes one part of Siming District.

As well as the name "Gulangyu", the pie product here is also marketing at home and abroad. Many businesses sale pies and mark "Gulangyu" "Gulangyu specialty" "Gulangyu flavor" "Gulangyu pie" and other slogans. In this way, they can use Gulangyu names to increase the competitiveness of other similar products. In fact, "Gulangyu" is also a commercial trademark owned by Amoy Xingmao Trading Co., Ltd. (hereafter "Xingmao Co."), and was used in the production of pies as early as the 1980s. Xingmao Co. claims that these businesses on the use of "Gulangyu" are all infringements of their trademark rights and thus filed a lawsuit, sued Amoy Yuhai Food Co., Ltd. (hereafter "Yuhai Co.").

In 1983, "Gulangyu" registered trademark owner, Gulangyu food factory, began in the production of Amoy pies and other food on the use of "Gulangyu" trademark. After years of extensive publicity and sales, "Gulangyu" pies and pastries in the industry enjoyed a high reputation. From 1983 onwards, "Gulangyu" pie won many provincial and national level honorary titles. On 18 June 2010, Zeng Moumou was granted the above-mentioned Gulangyu trademark and authorized Xingmao Co. to use it exclusively, as well as the rights and interests of trademark rights and related anti-unfair competition. In April 2013, the plaintiff Xingmao Co. found that Yuhai Co. 's production of pies on the box highlights the use of "Gulangyu pie" and other words, and use the same size of the product box and packaging with the plaintiff in the stores of Amoy Dongben Trading Co., Ltd. (hereafter "Dongben Co."); the decorations of the box inside and outside, including the style and pattern of color, shape are all with a high degree of similarity, so that when the plaintiff and Yuhai Co. 's packaging is placed separately, the consumer is difficult to distinguish. And Yuhai Co. described the product as "Gulangyu pie made in accordance with the traditional craft and exclusive formula", in an attempt to let consumers mistakenly believe that their products is authentic "Gulangyu pie", with obvious malicious infringement. Due to Yuhai Co. 'sperennial sales of infringing products, the plaintiff caused huge economic losses.

The plaintiff hold that the defendant's behavior against its registered trademark exclusive right and constitute unfair competition, it requested the defendant to immediately stop the production and sale of products containing the use of "Gulangyu" words and with the plaintiff's "Gulangyu pie" packaging decorated with an approximate box, immediately destroy all the infringement of the plaintiff registered trademark exclusive right and the unfair competition of product packaging, and compensation for infringement to the plaintiff caused economic losses of RMB 200 000, asked the defendant to publish an apology statement on "Amoy Daily", openly apologize to the plaintiff.

II. Desisions❶

Siming District People's Court ruled that the plaintiff legally owned "Gulangyu" trademark of the registered trademark of the exclusive right, and can sue inthe names of their own. The pie with the plaintiff trademark "Gulangyu" words (see Figure 1), violated the plaintiff registered trademark exclusive right, should stop infringement and compensation according to law. The words "Gulangyu Pie" in the title page of the "Gulangyu Specialties" (see Figure 2), is the legal use of geographical names and therefore does not constitute infringement. Dongben Co. has proven the source of the pie legal, so there is no liability. It is legally ordered by Yuhai Co., should immediately stop in its production and sales of products using the "Gulangyu" words box (see Figure 1), and compensation for the plaintiff Xingmao Co. economic losses and reasonable costs RMB 80 000. In addition, because the case does not involve personal rights, so the plaintiff's apology advocates do not support.

Figure 1   Figure 2

---

❶ Similar case concerning "Gulangyu" Pie trademark infringement and unfair competition dispute, please refer to (2015) Xia Min Chu Zi No. 1473 decision issued by Amoy Intermediate People's Court on 31 July 2017, and (2017 Min Min Zhong No. 899 decision issued by Fujian High People's Court on 18 December 2017.

III. Key Issues

The key issues of this case are as follows:

Firstly, whether Xingmao Co. is eligible to bring this lawsuit?

Secondly, whether the use of "Gulangyu" words by the defendant on the box is legal?

Thirdly, whether the box used by the defendant constitutes an unfair competition?

IV. Analysis

A. Whether Xingmao Co. is eligible to bring this lawsuit?

According to Article 4 of the *Interpretation on Several Issues Concerning the Application of Law in the Trial of Civil Disputes in Trademarks* by the Supreme People's Court, the licensee of the exclusive use license contract may bring a lawsuit to the court when the exclusive right of the registered trademark is infringed.

"Gulangyu" trademark in Amoy pies and other food has a long history of registration and use. Early in 1983, the owner of "Gulangyu" registered trademark, Gulangyu food factory, began to use the trademark in the production of Amoy pies and other food. After the enterprise restructuring, the owner of "Gulangyu" changed to a third party Zeng Moumou. In 2005, Zeng Moumou obtained registration of "Gulangyu (art body)" trademark (No. 3847042) in the Trademark Office, the approved use of goods include the pie (snacks), pies, meat pie, cake, cookies (cookies), bread, fruit pies, sugar (pastry), dumplings, moon cake. In 2011, Zeng Moumou obtained registration of "Gulangyu" trademark (No. 1571341) in the Trademark Office, the approved use of goods include sugar, candy, biscuits, cakes, dumplings, rice, ice cream, fish skin peanuts, crisp sugar, south sugar. On 18 June 2010, the third party Zeng Moumou was granted "Gulangyu" trademark, and authorized Xingmao Co. to exclusive use it, as well as the independent rights and interests of the trademark rights and related anti-unfair competition rights.

The owner of the trademark agreed the plaintiff's actions; therefore, the plaintiff legally obtained "Gulangyu" trademark rights, and can sue in their own name, Xingmao Co. is suitable for the plaintiff.

B. Whether the use of "Gulangyu" words by the defendant on the box is legal?

"Gulangyu" is a place name trademark. The name of the trademark, as the name suggests, is the "place name" as a limiting condition, with a place name for the content of the product logo. Firstly, one of the basic attributes of the trademark is significant. The significance of trademark includes inherent distinctiveness and business significant, and the place name trademark does not have a strong inherent distinctiveness because it has another meaning denoting a place. Secondly, the name of the trademark is usually used in public. Article 10 (2) of the Trademark Law of China stipulates that the place names of administrative divisions above the county level or foreign names known to the public shall not be trademarks, but the names have other meanings or as collective marks, Unless the registered trademark of the place of use continues to be valid. ❶

The principles of trademark registration of geographical names as in China are: firstly, as the names as a collective trademark, registered Trademark Law

---

❶ The so-called administrative divisions above the county level, including county-level counties, autonomous counties, county-level cities, municipal districts; prefecture-level cities, autonomous prefectures, regions, allies; provincial provinces, municipalities and autonomous regions; two special administrative regions, namely China Hong Kong, China Macao and China Taiwan region. The names of the administrative divisions above the county level shall be governed by the "Administrative Division of the People's Republic of China" published by the Ministry of Civil Affairs of China. Above the county level administrative division names, including the full name, referred to as the county and above the provinces, autonomous regions, municipalities, provincial capital cities, plans to separate cities, the famous tourist city phonetic form. The following three cases, place names can be used as a trademark: Firstly, the names have other meanings. The so-called place names have other meanings, meaning that the place name as a vocabulary has a definite meaning and the meaning is stronger than the meaning of the place name, and will not mislead the public. Secondly, place names as a collective trademark, to prove the components of the trademark. Thirdly, the registered trademark of the use of geographical names, according to the law continues to be effective.

can protect place name trademarks. The place names protected as collective marks and registered trademarks at this time are geographical indications. Secondly, the administrative divisions above the county level and public awareness of foreign names in two cases can be protected by Trademark Law, that is, the place name has been registered trademark or the place name has other meanings. Thirdly, administrative divisions above the county level and public names other than foreign names can be registered as a trademark, but can not cause public misunderstanding or have a negative impact.[1]

Geographical names are different from geographical indications. Geographical indications refer to the identification of the quality, reputation or other special characteristics of a commodity in association with its geographical origin to facilitate the identification of the origin of the goods. The geographical names shall have the exclusive right of the trademark owner, and the geographical indication shall not be exclusive; the place name and trademark shall be legally transferred or permitted to be used by others after the legally registered property of the property right, and the geographical indication Not exclusive for the individual, can not be free to transfer.

Gulangyu was a district of Amoy before, belonging to the county level above the names, due to the change of administrative division, Gulangyu District has become a part of Siming District since 2003, Gulangyu is no longer a county-level administrative divisions. "Gulangyu" as a place name trademark has been reasonable after that. A variety of goods registered "Gulangyu" trademark, even in the bathroom also appeared.

Trademarks can effectively strengthen the exchange of information between buyers and sellers, if there is no reasonable trademark protection system, consumers in the purchase process are difficult to get information. Therefore, the trademark not only condensed goodwill, but also allows consumers to link goods or

---

[1] Du Ying, "The Registration of Geographical Names and Their Rational Use", in Legal Science 2007 (1).

services with its providers correctly together. Similarly, the Trademark Law not only protects the goodwill of owners of the trademark, but also protects the consumer to correctly identify the source of the goods. To this end, Article 57 of the Trademark Law provides that any of the following acts shall be an infringement of the exclusive right to use a registered trademark: (1) uses a trademark that is identical with a registered trademark in relation to identical goods without the consent of the owner of the registered trademark; (2) uses a trademark that is similar to a registered trademark in relation to identical goods, or uses a trademark that is identical with or similar to a registered trademark in relation to similar goods, without the consent of the owner of the registered trademark, and liable to create confusion.

So the consumers may be confused with the source of the goods or services, which is a necessary condition for the infringement of the trademark. It may impose a legislative ban on the behavior that may cause the trademark confusion and can effectively protect the interests of the consumers.

According to the *Interpretation on Several Issues Concerning the Application of Law in the Trial of Civil Disputes in Trademarks* by the Supreme People's Court, similar marks refer to those are "easy to make the relevant public goods on the source of misunderstanding or that its source and the plaintiff registered trademark goods have a specific link" (Rule 10); and similar goods refer to those for the general public generally believe that there is a specific link, or easily be confused (Rule 11). When determine whether there is a confusion, the judge need to stand in the relevant public point of view, to determine whether the trademark involved is sufficient to affect the consumer to determine the source of goods or services.

Back to the case, "Gulangyu" is no longer an administrative division name, according to the Trademark Law it can be registered as a legitimate trademark. However, "Gulangyu" is also a place name, which means that, enterprises can use Gulangyu for ordinary use. In this way, we need to find out under which circumstances we can use "Gulangyu". In general, since Gulangyu has become a reasonable trademark, in order to protect the normal Gulangyu trademark, the other Enterprises cannot violate the "Gulangyu" trademark. Therefore, in order to use Gulangyu as geographical name, we have to use these three words as a place name, for example, "Gulangyu specialty" "Gulangyu flavor", which is not highlighted use.

Firstly, the highlighted use of the trademark is an infringing act.

The use of generic names and geographical names shall be "justified" in accordance with Article 49 of the *Regulations on the Implementation of the Trademark Law* (hereinafter "Regulations"). Although "Gulangyu" is a very famous place name, "pie" is also a common name in the food industry, but in Figure 1, "Gulangyu" and "pies" in the front of the box presented in two lines, the defendant did not use the Gulangyu Pie as an indivisible part, but instead highlighted the words "Gulangyu". In addition, the "Gulangyu" words used in the middle of the box, the front is also the largest of all the text on the box, and the defendant's "Zhenshixuan" trademark is located on the left and the front is small. Because of the word "Gulangyu" in the middle of the box, consumers might note the word "Gulangyu" instead of "Zhenshixuan" trademark. The highlighted "Gulangyu" might make the relevant public confused, therefore, this is not the proper use of geographical names under the Regulations.

Secondly, the ordinary use of "Gulangyu" does not constitute a trademark infringement.

In Figure 2, the word "pie" is marked in the middle of the box, and with a smaller font of "Gulangyu specialty" is on the left side of the "pie", "Gulangyu" and "specialty" are interrelated unity. Gulangyu is not only the plaintiff's trademark but also is a well-known place name. In accordance to Article 49 of Regulations, the plaintiff cannot prohibit other people to use "Gulangyu" as a geographical name. Although the plaintiff has registered "Gulangyu" as its trademark, the defendant also has its registered trademark "Zhenshixuan", at the same time, uses "Gulangyu specialty" along with this mark without highlighting the word "Gulangyu". Here consumers will not be confused when they buy the product, so the defendant marked "Gulangyu specialty" on the packaging is not wrong, this behavior should be deemed as fair use.

Thirdly, the use of "Gulangyu pie" on the title page is not an infringing act.

There is neither any evidence to prove that the pie and Gulangyu have a specific contact, nor any evidence that "Gulangyu pie" has become a commodity generic name or well-known commodity-specific name. The company was located in Gulangyu before it moved to other place, so it was expressed as "Gulangyu pie" in the title, which means "Gulangyu" is used as a place name. In addition, the "Gulangyu pie" located on the cover of the title page will not lead confusion or misunderstanding.

C. Whether the box used by the defendant constitutes an unfair competition?

Unfair competition refers to the operator and other relevant market participants to take fair and honest credit and other recognized business ethics means to fight for trading opportunities or undermine the competitive advantage of others, damage to the legitimate rights and interests of consumers and other operators, and disrupt the society and economic order.

The law encourages legitimate competition and prohibits unfair competition. Article 5 of the Anti-Unfair Competition Law of the People's Republic of China prohibits such unfair competition as anyone who uses the unique name, packaging, decoration and the name of the well-known commodity, which could be confused with that well-known commodity or mistakenly believe that the well-known goods are from the plaintiff. Because it is an improper means to engage in market transactions, might cause damage to the competitors. According to Rule 4 of the *Interpretation on the Application of Law on the Trial of Unfair Competition Civil Disputes* by the Supreme People's Court, the protection of the unique name, packaging, decoration of well-known commodity's can refer to the same or similar to determine the principles as trademark protection.

The reason why the unique names, packaging and decorations of well-known commodities are protected by the Anti-Unfair Competition Law is these symbols have the function of identifying the source of the commodity and become the distinguishing mark of the source of the commodity. If they are not protected, the market gains of the user could not be maintained, the market confusion of consumers could not be prevented.

In this case, the packaging and decorating of the commodity is the packaging and decoration that is not common to the relevant commodity and has the distinguishing feature of the commodity source. According to Article 5 of Anti-Unfair Competition Law, "specific packaging, decoration of well-known commodity" refers to the packaging, decoration of the distinction, that is, to identify the meaning of the source of goods.

First of all, the box used by the plaintiff is not unique. Other pie brands are also used the same paper material. The evidence is not enough to prove that the plaintiff only uses the material and decoration. Secondly, there are many differences on the two boxes: (1) In the front of the plaintiff's box is a more prominent architectural pattern, but the defendant's box cover is text and red seal; (2) the plaintiff's box is a flower which is larger than the defendant's; (3) There is no pattern in the middle of the defendant's box cover (4) the color of the four sides of the plaintiff's is red, but the defendant's color is brown; (5) the cover of the plaintiff's covers the extension of the body of the "Gulangyu" trademark, but not the defendant's not. In summary, there are many differences between them; the defendant's box does not constitute an unfair competition.

V. Significance of this Case

The typical significance of this case is that the court correctly delineates the scope of the protection of geographical names and the boundaries of trademark infringement. The coincidence of place names and trademarks is often encountered in judicial practice. Gulangyu was originally a district of Amoy, belonging to the above county level names. Due to administrative division reform, Gulangyu District merged into Siming District in 2003. From then on, Gulangyu is no longer a county-level administrative division. When this prohibited rule did not apply, Gulangyu as a national well-known scenicspot was quickly registered as trademarks.

Intuitively, Gulangyu is both a trademark and a place name. If the trademark is protected, it will affect the normal use of the place name. However, if the name is protected, the trademark cannot be properly and properly protected. As to the word "Gulangyu" in use, the conflict between the use of geographical names and trademark arises. This trademark, which has the dual meaning of registered trademark and place name, is of the greatest difficulty in balancing the use of names by trademark owners and the public at the trial.

For the pie packages involved in this case, one of which is the single word of "Gulangyu"; the other is putting "Gulangyu" and "pie" together. Finally the court ruled that the highlight use of "Gulangyu" was trademark infringement, and the use of "Gulangyu" along with "pie" is using a place name, which is a fair use, does not constitute trademark infringement. This decision did a clever distinction between the infringement and fair use in the commercial use of the word "Gulangyu" in the packaging, provides a very good guide to the public as well as similar cases involving place name in the trademark.

(Li Yuanyuan & Zhang Weichang)

Study on Amoy Baodao vs. Fuzhou Baodao Unfair Competition Dispute

I. Case Brief

Plaintiff Amoy Baodao Glasses Co. Ltd. (hereafter "Amoy Baodao") alleged that it was founded in 1997, after a long-term business development, has established a good business reputation, the plaintiff's trade name after a long-term practice in the consumer has a high reputation, "Baodao Glasses" enjoys popular support. Recently, the plaintiff in Amoy Siming Hexiang Road West, No. 266, found a glasses sales shops name as "Baodao Glasses Co. Ltd. —619th Store of China", the defendant the 13th department of Fuzhou Baodao Glasses Co. Ltd. (hereafter "Fuzhou Baodao"), but its not the plaintiff's chain store. The defendant, the 13th department of Fuzhou Baodao using the words "Baodao Glasses Company" as its shop signs, also on other accessories, issued invoice as "Baodao Glasses (National Chain Stores)", and stamped "Baodao Glasses Co. Ltd. —619th Store of China".

Plaintiff Amoy Baodao claims that the defendant's unauthorized use of the plaintiff's trade name, misleading consumers, is an unfair competitive behavior. The defendant is a branch of Fuzhou Baodao, Fuzhou Baodao should be delt with Amoy 13th department of Fuzhou Baodao joint and several liable for the infringement.

The defendant Fuzhou Baodao argued that the plaintiff's request is the scope of administrative proceedings, but this case is belonged to the scope of civil cases, the court should dismiss the plaintiff's request; the defendant Amoy 13th department of Fuzhou Baodao is legally registered enterprises, the trade name rights should be protected according to law; the defendant enjoys a high reputation in the community, the defendant Amoy 13th Department of Fuzhou Baodao is legitimate to use the trade name.

II. Decisions

Siming District People's Court held that the defendant Amoy 13th department of Fuzhou Baodao uses "Baodao GlassesCo. Ltd. —619th Store of China" in its store plaque, and in its merchandise, packaging as "Baodao Glasses (National Chain Stores)", the use of the simplified name in Amoy city is enough to make the relevant public confuse, should be considered as infringement to the plaintiff's trade name, is unfair competition, should compensate the civil loss. The court made the following verdict: the defendant shall stopped using the simplified term of "Baodao Glasses" in its shop; the defendant Fuzhou Baodao shall pay compensation to the plaintiff RMB 10 000.

III. Key Issues

The key issues of this case are as follows:

Firstly, whether the plaintiff's original claim is within the scope of civil action?

Secondly, whether the defendant's conduct violated the Anti-Unfair Competition Law?

Thirdly, whether the compensation requested by the plaintiff was reasonable?

IV. Analysis

A. Whether the plaintiff's original claim is within the scope of civil action?

The plaintiff argued that the defendant used it trade name withoutits permission which might cause consumer confusion therefore should constitute an unfair competition, so the defendant should stop using its trade name and pay all the damages arising from its advertising. The object of this case is whether the defendant's behavior infringed the plaintiff's trade name right, whether the defendant constituted unfair competition and whether civil liability should be borne. The plaintiff requested is belonged to the scope of civil proceedings. Siming People's District People's Court shall not support the defendant's claim that it's the scope of administrative proceedings respondent.

B. Whether the defendant's conduct violated the Anti - Unfair Competition Law?

Trade name is an important symbol of recognition of the enterprise. Similar to the function of the name refer to a natural person. The use of trade names can also bring certain economic benefits to its owners. Enterprises engage in business activities, provide excellent goods and services, cultivate and establish a good corporate image, and call it a good business reputation. Through the trade name the consumers can identify the enterprise, and make the final choice of the actual consumption between many enterprises to provide goods or services.

a. Methods to protect trade name

Under the current legal system, the methods of trademark protection are as follows.

The first one is administration of trade name registration. The concept of trade name right can be subdivided into the right to use and the right to exclude. The right to use a trade name is the right of the enterprise to legally use the name. The right to exclusive use of the trade name is to exclude others improper use of the same or similar trade name rights. The "Trade Name Registration Regulations" in the specification, is also divided into two areas: one is the use of the name of the enterprise to make a specification, to establish the conditions for the use of specific trade names, to ensure that the registered names will not overlap with each other, legally registered and then protected. The other is the protection of the exclusive use right of the name of the enterprise, the infringement of the name will be punished with a penalty.

The second one is protection of Trademark Law. The core scope of the protection of the Trademark Law is the trademark. But there is effect of indirect protection to trade name rights within. Because the trade name and trademark have their similarity. Formally, the trademark consists of "any visible sign that distinguishes the goods of natural persons, legal persons or other organizations from others' goods, including text, graphics, letters, numbers, three-dimensional symbols and color combinations, and the above elements combination, can be registered as a trademark application", but in the case of the word mark, trademark and trade name are similar. The function of the mark is for the product or service tag, to distinguish between different products or services, to avoid confusion, can be used as consumer products or service experience of the induction object, function to carry goodwill. And the function of trade name is a corporate mark, to distinguish between different companies, consumers can also be used as a product or service experience, the object of induction, also be able to carry goodwill they have similar functionality, for example, where the product manufacturer places the firm prominently in products, brochures, advertisements and brochures, packaging and business premises, or where the service provider has a service mark, when there is no material carrier in this case, the trademark and the trade name could been difficult to distinguish. Therefore, although the scope of the protection on Trademark Law is focused on trademark itself, but in some case the function and form of the trademark coincide with trade name, it can be said that the Trademark Law also has an indirect protection of trade name on functions and forms.

The third one is protection of Anti-Unfair Competition Law. The use of the name of another enterprise, causing goodwill to cling to others, confusion caused by consumer misconduct, etc. caused by unfair competition, is in scope of Anti-Unfair Competition Law. According to Article 5 of Anti-Unfair Competition Law, unauthorized use of other people's trade name or name, made mistaken for other people's goods, should be punished.

The last one is protection of "Civil Law". There are two kinds of persons on civil law, natural persons and legal persons, of which the legal person also has the right to name, we can say civil law protects the trade name also, but just isn't its core purpose.

b. Type of confusion

The key is sue of trade name infringement is whether the consumers are confused. Trade names, trademarks are able to carry goodwill, distinguish between each other's functions, if it's not function properly it may cause confusion to the consumer. In practice, there are three possible scenarios as follows.

The first one is confusion between trade names. According to Article 7 of the *Provisions on the Administration of the Registration of Trade names*, the enterprise shall consist of the name (or trade name), trade or business characteristics, and the form of organization, and shall be labeled with the name of the administrative division of the place where the enterprise is located. The name of the enterprise shall be used after registration, and shall enjoy the exclusive right within the prescribed scope. In different administrative regions, two legally registered trade name are exactly the same may happen.

The second one is confusion between trade name and trademarks. The conflict between a trademark right and a trade name means that the trademark or enterprise name that uses the same or similar characters is different from the right holder, and the consumer has confused the source of the goods or services and mistakenly recognizes the two as the same person, or there is a specific link between the two. The possibility of the conflict between the trade name and the trademark comes from the similarity and different systems of the two.

Trademarks and trade names have similarities, in the form of trademarks any natural persons, legal persons or other organizations of goods and others distinguish the goods visibility signs, including text, graphics, letters, characters, three-dimensional signsand color combinations, and combinations of these elements, may be registered as trademarks, but in the case of a ward only trademark, the trademark and the trade name are formally similar. The function of the mark is for the product or service tag, to distinguish between different products or services, to avoid confusion, can be used as consumer products or service experience of the induction object, function to carry goodwill. The function of trade name is a corporate mark, to distinguish between different companies, consumers can also be used as a product or service experience, the object of induction, also is able to carry goodwill.

Trademark and trade name have similar functionality, for example, where the product manufacturer places the firm prominently in products, brochures, advertisements and brochures, packaging and business premises, or where the service provider has a service mark, when there is no material carrier in this case, the trademark and the trade name could been difficult to distinguish. On the other hand, trademark and trade name belong to different systems; the competent authorities are not the same. Trademark Law regulates the same kind of goods or services cannot be registered as the same or similar trademarks. This exclusivity is nationwide, in order to prevent the emergence of similar trademarks.

And the trade name is regulated with the *Provisions on the Administration of the Registration of Trade names*. The uniqueness of a trade name need not necessarily to be nationwide, but should be within the area under the jurisdiction of the registered industrial and commercial administrative department. It's clearly regional only. Because of the two different system and scope, with similar functions and forms, may also be legally registered, may result in trademark rights and trade names to conflict, that is, the use of the same or similar text trademarks and trade names belong to different rights holders, and the source of goods or services to consumers confused, to mistakenly believe that the two are the same source, or there is a special connection between those two.

Third one is that trademarks may be confused with each other. This is one of the traditional core issues of the Trademark Law, so we will not go into details.

c. This case

The defendant Fuzhou Baodao was founded in 1992, in accordance with the *Trade Name Registration Administration Regulations*, the name of the enterprise was Fuzhou Baodao Glasses Inc. The plaintiff Amoy Baodao was established in 1997, the name of the enterprise was Amoy Baodao Glasses Inc. Both sides are legally registered in accordance with the *Trade Name Registration Administration Regulations*. The two companies' trade names and organizational forms are the same; the only distinction is the trade names in the administrative divisions are different.

This case belongs to the conflict between trade names, in two administrative-divisions, two legally registered trade names are not the same in seeking protection, and each of them has its uniqueness. The name of the industry, organization, and administrative region are the same, not the main difference between the signs. Name itself is the core of the trade name and the most important distinction mark, the public often through the name to remember and distinguish between different enterprises. However, the key names of the two enterprises are the same, and they are only distinctive by administrative divisions. Resulting in a difference in form, registration is fully legal, but in essence, likely to cause confusion.

Siming People's Court held that there is specific rules lied in the laws and regulations. The defendant who was founded in 2010 did not use its registered name, instead of using "Baodao Glasses Co. Ltd. —619th Store of China", and "Baodao Glasses (National Chain Stores)" on its product packaging. Its simplification of the use of corporate name is not reported to the registration authority for the record, although the plaintiff is not unauthorized use of other trade name, but does not belong to the proper use of trade names. Its simplified use of the name of the business did not report the registration of the competent authorities for the record, does not belong to the use of the name of the enterprise. The civil disputes between the enterprise name and the prior rights shall be dealt with in accordance with the principle of good faith, safeguarding fair competition and protecting the interests of the earlier legal rights holders. Under normal circumstances, the name of the enterprise industry, organizational forms, administrative regions and other common, not the main symbol of the distinction between enterprises. Font size is the core of the enterprise name and the most important distinction between the logo, the public often through the size to remember and distinguish between different enterprises. But the special case of this case is that these two businesses are exactly the same in the name, industry, organization form, the only difference between the two trade names is the administrative division The In the course of use, the administrative division in the name of the enterprise becomes the only sign of distinguishing the two companies. Through a long-term business development since 1997, the year when it registered, the plaintiff's trade name has a high reputation among consumers. Although the defendant Fuzhou Baodao was established in 1992, but the defendant Fuzhou Baodao Amoy 13th Business Department was established in Amoy in 2010. Amoy has already been well-known under the premise of the later set up the defendant Fuzhou Baodao, Amoy thirteenth business department, omit the head office and the plaintiff's name in the only distinction between the name, that is, the name of the enterprise Of the administrative division "Fuzhou", simplified use of "Baodao Glasses Co. Ltd. - 619th Store in China", "Baodao Glasses (National Chain Stores)" approach is not unauthorized use of the plaintiff's name, but enough to make it difficult for consumers to distinguish between two Enterprises, mistakenly believe that the defendant and the plaintiff there is a specific relationship between the relationship, causing confusion. Therefore, it should be confirmed that the defendants committed unfair competition, and violated the plaintiff's business name.

d. Other possible solutions

As mentioned above, this case is unique to apply Anti-Unfair Competition Law.

However, it may be possible to seek protection on the Trademark Law with indirect protection. According to Article 1 (1) of the *Interpretation on the Application of Law concerning Trademark Disputes* by Supreme People's Court, to highlight the use of the same or similar characters in the same or similar commodities as the trade name, and to easily mislead the relevant public, violates the exclusive right of a registered trademark.

In this case, Amoy Baodao has numerous "Baodao Glasses" trademarks, although some of them are graphic trademark, but in fact they are graphics presenting as text, does not detract the meaning of the text.

Amoy Baodao may claim that they have the right to use the logo shown in the graphic meaning similar to the text, and the conduct of defendant, has caused confusion to the public, causing other damage to its registered trademark exclusive right. In this way, the trade names are not necessarily the same in the infringement case, similarity is enough. It is more flexible then applying the Anti-Unfair Competition Law.

According to Article 53 of Trademark Law, the effect can be civil and administrative reliefoptions; the way may be more favorable to the plaintiff then applying Anti-Unfair Competition Law.

Due to the uniqueness of this case, the names of the two legally registered enterprises are identical; they are not registered trademarks of others; trademarks and trade names themselves are not well-known commodities; the court held that it is not the unauthorized use of the plaintiff's trade name; nor forged on the goods falsely marked. Resulting in difficulty to classified within the Anti-Unfair Competition Law system.

However, the litigant in the litigation advocates the emphasis on the Anti-Unfair Competition Law, thus the court is bounded to made judge in this area. Under those limitations, the court cannot apply the more convenient settle way with Trademark Law. Put the Court in the dilemma of substantive justice and procedural justice, but it still found a way of taking both sides into consideration. Maintain the procedural justice, and promote the development of intellectual property rights, banning the infringement of trademarks or trade name can promote the healthy development of enterprises. To ensure that the competition for the goods or services distinguished by the mark is not squeezed. Trademarks carrying the company's goodwill, often also reflects the value of goodwill. It is a good intention to suppress the trademark infringement and reduce the marginal interests of the infringer, reduce the infringement motive, improve the marginal contribution of the goodwill value, provide incentives for the benign development of enterprises and promote economic development.

C. Whether the compensation requested by the plaintiff is reasonable?

Siming District People's Court held that the plaintiff requested the defendant to compensate the economic loss and stop the infringement to pay a reasonable cost of 10 million, but the plaintiff failed to provide the appropriate evidence to prove its actual loss and the defendant's profit, Siming District People's Court will take into account the infringement, the consequences and the subjective fault of the defendant and other factors, to determine the amount of compensation requested by the plaintiff, as appropriate.

V. Significance of this Case

Conflicts between trade names of enterprises in different enterprises are very typical of a kind of intellectual property disputes. The businesses usually promote their own name to allow consumers to identify, remember, and agree with their business purposes through market practice.

The defendants in this case practice their own legally registered trade name, but still constitute an infringement. The most critical issue in this case is how to determine the legitimacy of the use of the names of two legally registered trade names with identical name beside the region name. The time of establishment the business, place, visibility, brand impact area will be the factors have to be taken into consider. The most important consideration in this case is the actual consequences of the use of prior rights and name in specific regions. Although the defendant Fuzhou Baodao is legally registered, even earlier than the establishment of the plaintiff Amoy Baodao, but it is established in Fuzhou. In this specific area of Amoy, the plaintiff firstly established and after decades of development and publicity has enjoyed a higher reputation. There is a clear business point and identity, so the plaintiff has enjoyed the previous right of the name of Baodao Glasses in Amoy. The defendant Fuzhou Baodao in Amoy established the Fuzhou Baodao Amoy 13th Department, who simplify the use of "Baodao Glasses", although it does not belong to the alleged use of other people's trade name, but enough to allow consumers to mistakenly believe that the Department and the plaintiff has special connections between the plaintiff's previous rights. The behavior of the defendant was identified as unfair competition, infringed the plaintiff's trade name rights. Because the defendant's trade name has been legally registered, the court only supports the symbolic compensation according to this fact.

Banning the infringement of trademark or trade name can promote the healthy development of enterprises. To ensure that the competition for the goods or services distinguished by the mark is not squeezed. Trademarks carrying the company's goodwill, often also reflects the value of goodwill. To reduce infringement motive, at the same time to improve the marginal contribution of the value of goodwill, will provide incentives for the sound development of enterprises and promote economic development.

(Zeng Zhengzhi & Cao Yujun)

Study on Yinju Co. vs. Joint Co., et al Unfair Competition Dispute

I. Case Brief

Plaintiff Amoy Yinju Spatial Geographic Information Co., Ltd. (hereafter "Yinju Co.") claims that the defendant Li Mou, Chen Moumou and Amoy Joint Survey Information Co., Ltd. (hereafter "Joint Co.") infringe its trade secret, constitute acts of unfair competition, files a civil lawsuit to the court, and request for injunctions, formal apologies and compensation for the loss of RMB 1.

The defendant Joint Co., Li Mou, Chen Moumou commonly argue that Japan's customer information can be collected and checked from Japanese related websites, no secret, so the customer is not monopolized by the plaintiffs, after the departure, whether engaging in the same or similar industry with the plaintiff, Amoy Labor Arbitration Committee rules that the defendant Li Mou and Chen Moumou have no breach, and the plaintiff did not fulfill relevant payment obligation, finally rules to dismiss the plaintiff demands. That is the defendants did not misapproprate the plaintiff's trade secrect, so did not violate the Anti-Unfiar Competition Law.

II. Desisions

After hearing, Siming People's Court ruled that, the defendant Li Mou, Chen Moumou, has set up new firms with similar business to the plaintiff when they haven't resigned from the plaintiff Yinju Co., after the defendant Li Mou joins the defendant Joint Co., still maintains business relationships with customers when he worked in the plaintiff, infringes the plaintiff's commercial secrets, and seek profits for the defendant Joint Co., therefore, the acts of defendant Li Mou, Chen Moumou and Joint Co. belongs to acts of unfair competition, and the infringement should be immediately stopped in accordance with the law. The defendant Li Mou, Chen Moumou are employees of Joint Co., and the behavior interest engaged in office belongs to the defendant Joint Co., and the duty behavior, and ruling that defendant Joint Co. compensates the plaintiff's loss of RMB 1. Because the case does not involve in the personal rights, rejects request for plaintiff's apology.

III. Key Issues

The key issues of this case are as follows:

Firstly, does the defendant infringe the plaintiff's trade secrets?

Secondly, does defendant Li Mou, Chen Moumou violate any competitive restriction?

IV. Analysis

A. Does the defendant infringe the plaintiff's trade secrets?

Business secret, refers to technical information and business information, security measures taken by the holder, unknown to the public, which can bring economic benefits to obligee with practicality. It's known from the definition, the business secrets should have secrets, economic value and take security measures. Since business secret itself has great economic value, at the same time the commercial secret also has the character of "once leaks, always leak", so once the commercial secret is lost, it likely brings obligee irreparable damage. Legislation protection for business secret is mainly embodied in the Anti-Unfair Competition Law, in addition, there are also protection on Civil Procedure Law, Contract Law, Labor Contract Law, Criminal Law and a series of administrative rules and regulations. This case mainly involves the protection of business secrets in Anti-Unfair Competition Law.

To identify the precondition of trade secret infringement behavior is to identify whether the infringement object is trade secret, namely the cognizance of commercial secrets. There are three elements to recognize business secret, first of all, judge whether the information is "unknown to the public". The *Interpretation to Several Applicable Law Problem on the Trial of Unfair Competition Civil Cases* issued by the Supreme People's Court rules that, the information, not commonly known and easily obtained by the relevant personnel in the field information belongs to, is "not known to the public", at the same time, if the information is common sense or industry practices of people in the economic or technical field, or the information just involves in product size, structure, materials, simple combination of, components, and other contents, or after entering the market, the relevant public can directly obtain through products observation, or the information has been publicly disclosed in public publications or other media, or the information has been the publicized by public report, exhibitions and other ways, or the information can be obtained from other open channels, or the information without paying a certain cost to easily obtain, doesn't belong to the category of "unknown to public". Secondly, economic value judgment, and the relevant information has actual or potential commercial value, and can bring competitive advantage to obligee, namely, "can bring economic benefits to obligee, with practicality". Finally, security measures judgment, according to the characteristics of information carrier, confidential will of obligee, identifiable degree of security measures, difficulty degree to obtain by the way, and other factors, judge whether obligee adopts reasonable protection measures appropriate to the specific situation of its commercial value to prevent information leakage. For it, relevant judicial explanation also outlines some reasonable security measures legislation example, if the obligee, within the known range of restricted classified information, only must inform relevant personnel the content, or take prevention measures such as locking for classified information carrier, or mark confidential marks on the carrier of the classified information, or use password or code for classified information, etc., or sign a confidentiality agreement, or restrict visitors entering to confidential machine, factory, workshop and other places or propose confidential request, or ensure other reasonable measures of the information secret, and under normal circumstances, it is enough to prevent leak classified information, so the obligee shall be deemed as taking confidential measures.

The client list involved in commercial secrets in this case, generally refers to special customer information composed of the client's name, address, contact information and trading habits, intention, content, differing from related public information, including the customer list gathering many customers, and the specific customer maintaining long-term and stable trade relations. In this case, Yinju Co., had signed cooperation agreement on geographic data measurement, with Asahi Sailing Commercial Co. in September 2005, and still keep cooperation relationship. Whether the information about Asahi Sailing Commercial Firm is the commercial secret, we should judge from three aspects of the commercial secret, first of all, general information of Asahi Sailing Commercial Firm, such as the company's address, contact information, etc., which can be achieved through the network retrieval, the part of information belongs to the public knowledge. But beyond that, the specific contact information company, trading habits, trading content between Asahi Sailing Commercial Firm and Yinju Co. is "not known to public", which meets the requirements of secrecy. Secondly, for Yinju Co., Asahi Sailing Commercial Firm is the important customer, and has many economic transactions, of course, this information has important economic value, meeting "obligee can bring economic benefits, with practicality". Finally, Yinju Co., by making confidential system, signing confidentiality clause with employees, asking resigned employees to sign confidentiality commitment and other measures to actively prevent disclosure information, meet the requirements of "taking security measures". So, customer information, transaction content related to Asahi Sailing

Commercial Firm shall be regarded as trade secrets.

After recognizing business secrets, it is necessary to judge whether related behavior constitutes an act of infringing business secret. Yinju Co. had entered into cooperation agreement about geographical data measurement with Asahi Sailing Commercial Co. in September 2005, which is reached between Asahi Sailing Commercial Co. and Li Mou, representing the company, hereafter, Li Mou is also involved in a series of exchanges, quite familiar with and understand cooperation relations, the current situation, trading content and the request between Yinju Co. and Asahi Sailing Commercial Firm. Later, Li Mou set up Joint Co. and engaged in similar business with Yinju Co., and contacts with Asahi Sailing Commercial Firm on business. For related judicial interpretation rules, if the customer, based on the reliance of employees individual, makes market dealing and worker's unit, after the employee leaves office, it can prove that customer voluntarily chooses to make market trading with his or his new unit, which shall be deemed as that no unfair means is taken, except otherwise agreed by the worker and the original unit. However, Li Mou and Yinju Co. sign confidentiality agreement, and its business contacts with Asahi Sailing Commercial Firm, is not for the customer's own will. From the evidence provided by Yinju Co. A series of identity disclosure marks, such as mails used in contacting Li Mou and Asahi Sailing Commercial Firm, will still bring misjudgment to the other side contacting with Yinju Co., which functions as misguidance. Therefore, the act constitutes the behavior of infringing business secret.

In this case, the defendant's act mainly involves the requirements of in violation ofagreement, obligee's commercial secrets, disclosing, using or allowing others to use their mastery of the commercial secrets. After affirming that defendant act constitutes a violation of commercial secrets in this case, it also involves the liability for compensation. In this case, the plaintiff Yinju Co. requests the defendant to pay compensation of RMB 1, but fails to provide the relevant evidence to support its litigant claim, the court's decision reason doesn't explains this problem. Relevant judicial interpretation rules that, damage compensation infringing the commercial secret can refer to the method determining damage compensation of patent infringement; Business secret caused by infringement act, which has been known to the public, should determine the damages based on the business value of commercial secrets. Business value of commercial secrets, can be determined based on its research and development costs, benefits, available profits, time keeping the competitive advantage to implement the business secret. So in this case, the compensation for infringement of trade secret remains open to question.

Finally, when commercial secret infringement judgment stops the civil liability of infringement, the time stopping the infringement, generally lasts until commercial secret is known to the public, but if the time ruling to stop the infringement is obviously unreasonable, under the condition of protecting the obligee's commercial secret competitive advantage, the obligee can be ruled to stop using the commercial secrets within a certain time limit or scope. Customer information involved in the case, is mainly specific way, transaction content, and trading habits contact with the customer, etc., commercial secrets of this type are not like technical commercial secrets, as long as science and technology steps forward, some technology as commercial secret could be open, unless commercial secrets of customer information exists intentional leaks, otherwise it will not be easily referred by the public. In addition, like Li Mou, as personnel getting and maintaining related customer information of original company, trading content and trading habits of these customer information more or less have the habit of the participants like Li Mou. Assuming demanders in the field of assuming are less, and suppliers' customers requirements are almost the same, just contact way of corresponding demand for each supplier is different, trading habits are different, so the time deciding stopping the infringement generally lasts until the commercial secret has been known to the public, which is obviously unreasonable, so it is suggested that to stop the infringement practices will be subjected to the non-competition period in this cases. But in this case, as the demander in the market is more, and customer information involved in the case refers to a company only, so it should be ruled that the defendant stop the infringement of business secret until the commercial secret has been known to the public.

B. Does defendant Li Mou, Chen Moumou violate any competitive restriction?

Competitive restriction, also known as competition prohibition, refers to prohibition on specific competition acts the person has certain relationship with obligee, namely the obligee has the right to demand a particular person which has specific civil legal relationship with it, is not the competitive behavior for it. The object prohibited by competitive restriction is specific behavior, namely the behavior forming competitive trade with the obligee; The prohibited subject is limited to specific person, that is, the obligor who has specific civil legal relationship with obligee. In legal relationship of competitive restriction, the obligee enjoys the right of claim, can requests the obligor uncompetitive behavior; Taxpayers bear a kind of inactive duty. According to the source of its legal effect, competitive restriction can be divided into statutory competitive restriction and agreed competitive restriction. The former refers to that, specific person's obligation of prohibiting improper competition comes directly from the law prohibited provisions; The latter comes from agreement between the parties. According to the principle of freedom of contract, the parties are free to make a non-compete agreement, make one or both parties bear or exempt from non-compete obligation. According to its obligatory subject, competitive restriction can be divided into competitive restriction of on-the-job employees and former employees. The competitive restriction of on-the-job employees, is mainly statutory competitive restriction, employers may also agree on non-competitive obligation of on-the-job employees by agreement way. Former employees' competitive restriction belongs to agreed competitive restriction, namely, former employees should bear a kind of ostensive non-compete obligation, and its basis should be lawful and valid non-compete agreement, and non-competitive regulations unilaterally made by the employer cannot be the basis for leaving staff's ostensive or implied obligations for competitive restriction.

About regulations on statutory competitive restriction, our legislation is not regulated intensively, but scatters in a variety of legislation. For example, Article 148 of Company Law regulates, directors and senior management personnel shall not, without the consent of the shareholder meeting or general meeting of stockholders, use convenience of position, to seek for business opportunities for themselves or others belonging to the company, to manage himself or manage the same kind of business with the company where he works; Article 32 of Partnership Enterprise Law stipulates, a partner may not manage himself or cooperate and manage business competing with the partnership enterprise; Article 37 of Implementation Regulations of Sino-foreign Joint Venture Lnterprise Law, general manager or deputy general managers shall not concurrently work as general manager or deputy general manager of other economic organizations, shall not participate in business competition from other economic organizations to the enterprise, and so on. The scholar thinks the workers or employees knowing or aware of commercial secrets in office should be force forcibly imposed a non-compete obligation, arguing that workers or employees owe duty of loyalty to the company, same as managers and directors. If the laborers are allowed to engage in competitive activities, they are easy to consciously or unconsciously disclose or use business secrets of employer's unit in competitive activities, weaken their competitive advantage, damage the interests of its economy, causing unfair competition, so as to obtain illegitimate interests. Although there is legal protection on trade secrets, those means exist very adverse factors to the obligee, and therefore, it can't deny the laborer mastery of commercial secrets bear non-compete obligation due to independent legal protection for business secret.❶ The author doesn't agree with this view, workers' business secrets competitive problems known and learned in office, not

---

❶ Gui Juping, "On Legal issues of Competition Prohibition Agreement", in Legal and Business Research 2001 (1).

only can be uses business secrets method to solve, also can use breach of contract to solve. General employing units can agree on employers' on-job-competitive problems in the labour contract, if the worker breaches of contract, he will bear corresponding liability for breach of contract. The two means are enough to protect the interests of employing unit, so it's not necessary to include it into the statutory competitive restriction.

Competition prohibition stipulated in Labor Contract Law only refers to departing employees' competition prohibition, namely contractual prohibition of business strife, referring to that after workers dissolve or terminate labor contract with employing unit, they shall not work in other employing unit which produces similar products, or engages in similar business with this unit, or produce themselves or operate similar products, and engage in the same business. First of all, the subject of competition prohibition is limited to the employing unit's senior management staff, senior technicians and other personnel with a confidentiality obligation, in addition to that, the company's general staff shall not apply the non-compete clause. Secondly, competition prohibition's scope, region, period is agreed by employing unit and laborer, competition prohibition agreement shall not violate the provisions of laws and regulations. Again, employing unit should provide laborers with economic compensations every month in the non-competition period, if laborer violates non-compete agreement, they should pay liquidated damages to the employing unit in accordance with the contract. The *Explanations on Several Applicable Law Issues on on Trial of Labor Lispute Cases* (*IV*) issued by Supreme People's Court has more detailed provisions: firstly, lift non-compete agreement, for employing unit, within the non-competition period, non-competition agreement can be requested to terminate at any time, in this case, laborers have the right to request employing unit to pay laborers additional non-compete economic compensation for three months; For workers, only in the case of employing unit's serious breach of contract, competitive restriction agreement can be relieved; Secondly, about the liability for breach of contract, for employing unit, if in the party agrees on competitive restriction and economic compensation in labor contract or confidentiality agreement, after the labor contract is relieved or terminated, 3 months' economic compensation caused by employing unit isn't paid, laborer can request to terminate the non-competition agreement; For workers, once violating non-compete agreement, after paying the liquidated damages to the employing unit, if employing unit continues to perform the non-compete obligations in accordance with the contract, workers shall continue to perform; Thirdly, Calculation problem on agreeing on economic compensation, in case of disagreed prohibition of business strife compensation, laborers perform the non-compete obligations, they can require employing unit should pay monthly economic compensation at 30% of average wages in the 12 months before relieving or terminating the labor contract, if 30% of the average wage is lower than minimum wage standard of labor contract performance, pay in accordance with minimum wage standard of labor contract. Finally, the duration of the non-competition shall not exceed two years.

Specific to this case, Yinju Co. 's business scope includs: geographic information system engineering, global positioning system construction; digital spatial information processing, data processing and production, digital city construction; computer software development and sales; computer network engineering construction; document scanning processing, digital processing, data file scanning; software exports and data service outsourcing; selling (excluding market retail and supermarket retail) household appliances, computers and spare parts, communications equipment, basic software, application software. Joint Co. 's business scope includs: the computer network engineering, intelligent systems engineering design and construction, computer software and hardware development and sales, operating goods and technology import and export, etc. Both of the two companies' business scope are partly overlapping, so there is competition between them. Chen Moumou and Yinju Co. signed "employment contract" with deadline from 1 August 2008 to 1 August 2011, acting as the director of Yinju Co., and departed on 7 September 2010. Li Mou and Yinju Co. signed "employment contract" with deadline from 1 May 2010 to 1 May 2012, acting as deputy general manager of Yinju Co., and departed on 16 July 2010. On June 8, 2010, Joint Co. was founded, Chen Moumou acted as company's legal representative, Li Mou, acted as chairman and general manager, at this time, two people hadn't departed from the original company. Li Mou, as former executives, violated the provisions of Article 148 of Company Law, namely, the statutory competitive restriction, so revenue obtained by Joint Co. from 8 June 2010 to 16 July 2010, should be delivered to Yinju Co.. And the labor contract signed by Li Mou, Chen Moumou and Yinju Co., also stipulated competitive restriction during the service, two people's behavior violated the contract, so they should bear the liability for breach of contract. Labor Contract Law and Explanations on several applicable law issues on Supreme People's Court on trial of labor dispute cases (IV) stipulated the parties' competitive restriction in the labor contract or confidentiality agreement, after removing or terminating the labor contract, laborers must be provided with economic compensations, so workers bear non-compete obligations. After they both depart, Li Mou as the company's executives, Chen Moumou, as personnel with a confidentiality obligation, both comply with the main requirements to bear obligation of non-competition, and engage in work having competitive relationship with the original company, constituting competitive acts. Competitive subsidies agreed by Chen Moumou and the original company, are included in the remuneration, and this convention is not in conformity with the law, non-compete agreement after Li Mou's departure also did not stipulate the economic compensation. Chen Moumou and Li Mou can perform the non-compete agreement to the court till they fail to get economic compensation paid by Yinju Co. in three months after departure, before that, they still should perform the non-compete agreement. If Yinju Co. pays economic compensation, two people can be asked to continue performing the non-compete obligations. In the case, the plaintiffs Yinju Co., also fails to put forward litigation claim related to competitive restriction.

V. Significance of this Case

Enterprise customer information is the important resource for the survival of the enterprise resources, since some companies confidential consciousness is weak, fails to sign a confidentiality agreement with employees, also take appropriate security measures for customer information, after job-hopping, a lot of foreign trade and technical staff easily use the customer information of original unit to make unfair competition and draw in business. Malicious competition, that is, involves in company executives' job-hopping to set up a company, using the original customer resources to carry out the business, finally the court rules the case constitutes unfair competition.

The case has warning significances for current common employee to breach non-compete obligation and violate "the original owner".

(Li Yuanyuan & Li Yaguang)

Study on Wang Moumou vs. Amoy Municipal Administration for Industry and Commerce & Yudian Co. Administrative Penalty Dispute

I. Case Brief

The plaintiff Wang Moumou, and the third party Amoy Yudian Automation Technology Co., Ltd. (hereafter "Yudian Co.") sign the labor contract, and the two sides agree to hire Wang Moumou job as an assistant to the general manager, with labor contract deadline from 1 November 2007 to 30 November 2010. On 10 December 2007, the two sides signed Agreement on Protecting the Commercial Secrets, agreeing on that, during the working period in Yudian Co., Wang Moumou shall not disclose Yudian Co. 's any internal "scientific data, production technical information, customer information, supplier information, and new product information of enterprises, development plan" to outside, and Yudian Co. will add 10% of basic salary per month to Wang Moumou as confidential subsidy. On 16 September 2010, the two sides signed written Agreement on Labor Contract Termination, to terminate the labor relationship between both parties, and agreed that, "No matter in-service or departure, the plaintiff Wang Moumou shall not disclose Yudian Co. 's any internal research materials, production technology information, customer information, supplier information, and enterprise development planning to outside, and offenders should compensate Yudian Co. 's all the losses incurred from it". On 21 September 2010, the plaintiff Wang Moumou departed from

Yudian Co.

Amoy Automatic Techonolgy Co., Ltd. (hereafter "Eckert Co."), was founded in on 16 May 2011, whose legal representative was Wang Moumou. On 8 May 2012, the third party Yudian Co., reported to the defendant Amoy Municipal Administration for Industry and Commerce (hereafter "MAIC"), Eckert Co., Wang Moumou, Zhang Moumou, Lin Moumou were suspected of infringing application software, supplier information, customer information and other business secrets of Yudian Co. and AI products. According to electronic data expert opinion of Fujian Zhongzheng Judicial Expertise Center [2012] SJZi No. 10, submitted main control chip machine code of artificial intelligence temperature controller/regulator between Yudian Co. and Eckert Co. is consistent, and the collection code after the collection is also consistent, both has the same source. The experts group does not recognize Wang Moumou's proposition to break main chip and memory chips of Yudian Co. through reverse engineering, also denies Wang Moumou's presentation of calibration process. The defendant, Municipal industrial and commercial bureau, based on it, makes a decision of administrative penalty of MAIC [2012] No. 151, cognizes Wang Moumou's agreed requirements for violation of the provisions of the commercial secrets with Yudian Co., allows Eckert company to use its mastery of business secret of Yudian Co., which constitutes the illegal facts of infringement of trade secrets of others. Order the parties Wang Moumou to stop the infringing act, with a fine of RMB 150 000.

The plaintiff Wang Moumou defies the administrative punishment decision on defendant municipal industrial and commercial bureau, institutes an administrative lawsuit to Siming District People's Court, then the court notifies Yudian Co. according to law, as the third person to participate in the litigation.

II. Desisions

After hearing, Siming People's Court rules that based on trial, Yudian Co. has taken the corresponding security measures for its important technical information. After identification, Eckert Co. products and Yudian Co. products constitute a "same nature". The plaintiff Wang Moumou, prior to resignation, acts as assistant to general manager of the third party of Yudian Co., with convenient condition for "contacting" technical information of Yudian Co. Plaintiffs claim themselves to get products involved in the case through reverse engineering, but according to the plaintiff's statement, entrust them to crack chip program involved in the case, and get it by purchasing after covering the cost. The plaintiff's called "purchasing" chip program behavior, does not belong to "reverse engineering" stipulated by law, and the plaintiff has no sufficient evidence to prove that its source of getting chips is real, effective and legal purchase behavior. In addition, the panel also denies the correction process called by Wang Moumou. Finally, court rules the defendant to make administrative penalties on Wang Moumou, firmly believes the facts clear, evidence sufficient, the applicable law correct, procedure legitimate, and rejects the plaintiff's claims.

III. Key Issues

The key issues of this case are as follows:

Firstly, does the chip program of AI series' intelligent instrument belong to business secrets?

Secondly, does Wang Moumou misappropriate third party's business secret?

IV. Analysis

A. Does the chip program of AI series' intelligent instrument belong to business secrets?

According to the provisions of Clause 3 of Article 10 in Anti-unfair Competition Law, business secret refers to "Technical information and business information, unknown to the public, which can bring economic benefits to the obligee, with practical applicability, and take security measures by the holder." Therefore, to recognize whether the chip program of AI series intelligent instrument of the third party Yudian Co. belongs to business secret, should start from the following several aspects:

a. Unknown to the public

According to Article 9 (1) of the *Interpratation on Certain Applicable Law Questions about the Trial of Unfair Competition Civil Cases* by Supreme People's Court, interpret "unknown to public" as "the relevant information is not commonly known and easily got by the related personnel of its field". Confidentiality is the most notable feature commercial secret differing from the patented technology, and known technology. Because trade secrets maintain its economic value in secret state, once disclosed, its economic value will be fully or partially lost. Looking from TRIPs, determine the general standards of secrecy, usually unknown to the public or never entering to opening field. Commercial secret is not known by the public, because it has the content differing from known knowledge and information, technically speaking, due to considerable personal effort of inventors and discoverers, not easy to master by the public, with uniqueness. ❶

Siming People's Court rules that, the plaintiff Wang Moumou submits evidence to the court at litigation phase, to explain some publicly known technologies, such as "precision grade, programming input technology, modular technology, AIBUS communication protocol, improved PID regulation algorithm independent control technology, three-phase three-wire trigger", so as to prove that Yudian Co. 's technology involved in the case has been known to public. But these evidences are not proposed by the plaintiff in the process of the defendant's implementing in administrative behavior, so they cannot serve as evidence in the process of administrative law enforcement. And in the process of litigation, in addition to the notarial deed, other evidences are copies or network printing in the form, so they are not in conformity with the statutory form, what's more important is, the above evidence is not directly associated with "openness" of core chip pro-

---

❶ (2009) Zhe Yong Zhi Zhong No. 3.

cedure of the AI series intelligent instrument products involved in the case. Professor Luo Moumou, also points out in the opening of the hearing, these data are only general technology principle and general guidance, not involving the specific technical parameters and other core technology. In conclusion, the plaintiff Wang Moumou, proposes the evidence proving AI series intelligent instrument products chip program open to the public is insufficient.

The above analysis on Siming District People's Court, fully considers the difference between "general technical principle and general guiding narration" and "specific technical parameters", thereby correctly identifies "unknown to the public aware" features of core chip program of AI series intelligent instrument products in this case, worthy of affirmation. In the case between Dongguan Hongbao Precision Machinery Factory and Yang Jun's infringement of trade secret dispute, Guangdong People's High Court also rules that while analyzing whether technical drawings information involved in the case is "unknown to public", "Although the products involved in the technical drawings have entered the public markets and Hongbao factory has carries on the related propaganda, but for the technical drawings information involved in the case, to enter the public market is just plain, external characteristics description of technical drawings' corresponding appearance of the product, overall size, the whole machine functions, characteristics, rather than specific technical parts' design requirements and technical parameters. Technical chart involved in the case includes many product varieties, and the technology involved in each product is not generally known and easily obtained for its relevant personnel in the field, have the features of commercial secrets unknown to the public."❶ Therefore, in future, in considering the elements "unknown to the public" court should closely examine the relationship between "general" (overall) and "details" (specific).

b. Bring economic benefits and have practicability

It is generally accepted that, business secrets' commercial value refers to e-

---

❶ (2011) Yue Gaofa Minsan Zhong No. 228.

conomic benefits to the obligee or competitive advantage. According to Article 10 of the *Interpratation on Certain Applicable Law Questions about the Trial of Unfair Competition Civil Cases* by Supreme People's Court, relevant information has actual or potential commercial value, can bring competitive advantage, which should be identified as "bring economic benefits, to obligee with practicality", stipulated in Article 10 (3) of Anti – Unfair Competition Law. The Supreme People's Court announces also made clear in appeal cases between Quzhou Wanlian Network Technology Co., Ltd. and Zhou Moumou in violation of business secrets dispute of 10 innovative cases in Chinese courts intellectual property judicial protection in 2012, commercial secrets practicality requires business secret must be transformed into concrete and implemented scheme or form.[1] A kind of information to get the protection of the law, must be translated into specific and implemented scheme or pattern, and the law does not protect the pure idea, general principle and abstract concepts. Based on it, if certain information is still in discovery, not specific or prior to practical application, it still can't be identified as trade secrets. The value of the business secret requires use of the business secrets can bring economic benefits to the obligee, and enhance competitive advantage. The benefits include the real economic interests, also include the potential economic value, specific performance is able to improve technology, improve labor productivity and product quality, can help to improve the enterprise management, reduce costs and expenses.

In this case, the AI series intelligent instrument products are Yudian Co.'s core products, bringing significant economic benefits for the company, As the chip program of product's core technology (including procedures chip and correction chip), it clearly belongs to important production technical data. As you see, its economic benefit is considerable, has stronger practicability.

c. Obligee takes security measures

According to Article 11 (3) stipulated in the *Interpretation on Certain Appli-*

---

[1] (2011) Hu Gao Minsan (Zhi) Zhong No. 100.

cable Law Questions about the Trial of Unfair Competition Civil Cases by Supreme People's Court, "confidentiality agreement" belongs to a confidential measures taken by the holder of the commercial secret. As if confidentiality measures taken by commercial secrets are reasonable, they are sufficient to constitute confidentiality requested by law, to require obligee to take confidentiality measures is not realistic, will lead to huge social cost, also too harsh. The United States E. I. Du Pont Co. 's appealing case for Christopher well illustrates it.

"Keep business secret agreement", "labor contract" "written agreement on labor contract termination" signed between the plaintiff, Wang Moumou, in this case, and the third party Yudian Co., expressly agree upon that the plaintiff Wang Moumou shall not disclose Yudian Co. 's internal "scientific data, production technical data" and other commercial secrets obligation and responsibility. Wage acceptance form also reflects the plaintiff Wang Moumou can receive confidential subsidies during the work in Yudian Co. every month. It's visible that, the third person can bring important technical information of economic benefit, and has taken corresponding security measures.

In conclusion, the defendant rules chip program of the AI series intelligent instrument products involved in the case as Yudian Co. 's trade secrets in administrative penalty decision is proper.

B. Does Wang Moumou misappropriate third party's business secret?

Anti-Unfair Competition Law stipulates in Article 10, an operator shall not take the following means to infringe trade secret by stealing, luring, coercion or other improper means to obtain the trade secret of obligee; by disclosing, using or allowing others to use the preceding means to obtain the obligee's business secrets; by breaching the contract, or in violation of the obligee's requirements for commercial secrets, disclose, use or allow others to use its mastery of commercial secrets.

The third party knows or should know the illegal acts listed in the preceding paragraph, acquire, use or disclose the trade secrets of others, as a violation of commercial secrets. So, in this case, does Wang Moumou's behavior constitute an act of infringing business secret? Siming People's Court adopts "substantial similarity + contact" rules, starting from the constitutive elements of commercial secret, around the two pieces of information of "substantial similarity" characteristics, recognizes that the plaintiff Wang Moumou has "illegal contact" factually, including obtaining trade secret of obligee; And there is no evidence to prove the fact of "legitimate sources", including the goodwill use or disclosure, its own research and development, the reverse engineering as well as other reasonable ways to obtain the same commercial secrets, eventually determine Wang Moumou behavior constitutes an act of infringing business secret.

So-called "substantial similarity + contact" rules, refers to the court in the trial of infringing commercial secrets cases, if the commercial information (including technical information and business information) used by defendant and the commercial secrets of obligee is same or substantially similar, at the same time, the obligee also has evidence to prove defendant has mastered the conditions of the commercial secret before, then it must be used by the defendant to prove the legal source of business information, otherwise it shall bear tort compensation liability. Although "Substantial similarity + contact" rule in Chinese intellectual property legal source, has been simply stipulated in "Several provisions on the ban on commercial secrets infringement" issued by state administration for industry and commerce in 1998, it's widely used in the trial practice of commercial secrets infringement cases in China.

a. Contact

The key to apply "material similarity + contact" rule is the understanding of "contact", is also the core of the profound connotation of evidence rules. In this case, in November 2007, the plaintiff Wang Moumou entered into Yudian Co., working as the assistant to general manager, second only to general manager, can directly obtain commercial secrets from the obligee as the employee of former obligee in infringement of trade secret law relations. Based on its special status, the contact behavior is self-evident, and the law has removed the obligee's proving responsibly for it. Sign "Keep business secrets agreement" and Yudian Co., receive confidential subsidies a month, because the plaintiff Wang Moumou has direct relationship with the obligee, so it's obvious for him to get the business secrets contacted by him from the obligee, therefore he should be very clear for commercial secrets' affiliation holder. Therefore the plaintiff Wang Moumou "contact" Yudian Co. 's technical information has high probability on legal level.

b. Substantially the Same

Business secret is a kind of undisclosed technical information or operating information to maintain rights and interests by obligee through security measures. In commercial secrets' infringement cases, the obligee should and can provide the proof for only controlled rights facts, such as secrecy, confidentiality, the possibility of the other party to obtain commercial secrets, etc., but the way and methods to get the same commercial secret for the other party tend to have difficulty of proof. This is because the business secret is not exclusive with absolute sense, the same secret information may be owned by multiple main body, the way to its legitimate access is also not the same, such as conception, acquisition in good faith, reverse engineering, etc. Therefore, many scholars and judges claim to adopt the method of getting technical secret means on the defendant, to presume fault liability. ❶

In the trade secret infringement lawsuit, the plaintiff, namely the obligee, bears proof responsibility for "substantial similarity", namely to prove "information used by the applicants and their business secret has consistency or identity", the protected secret information and the information accused of infringing use is the same information. The defendant, namely alleged infringer, provides proving for "legitimate sources" elements, namely rationality of the use of commercial secrets, which is the inverted burden of proof on the program.

---

❶ See He Zhonglin, "Hot Issues of Evidences in Intellectual Property Cases", in Guidance and Reference of Intellectual Property Trial (Vol. 1), Law Press, 2007, p. 87.

In this case, Eckert Co. 's products appearance, circuit board, the use of raw materials, components layout, has basic same function and basically identical purpose with Yudian Co. products. Based on electronic data expert opinion on *Fujian Zhongzheng Judicial Authentication Center* 〔2012〕SJZi No. 10, it can be seen that, submitted machine code of main control chip of artificial intelligence temperature controller/regulator between Yudian Co. and Eckert Co. is consistent, and the collection code after the anti-collection is consistent, both has the same source, and constitute "same substantiality".

c. Legitimate Source

In "contact + substatianlly the same" case, the plaintiff needs to prove that only technical information involved in the case legal sources, then he can exempt from tort liability. The plaintiffs claim to get products involved in the case by reverse engineering, according to statement of the plaintiff Wang Moumou, which is entrusted to crack chip program involved in the case, get it after paying it, however, Wang Moumou himself did not crack the chip program. Siming People's Court ruled that "reverse engineering" referred in Anti-Unfair Competition Law, refers to relevant technical information to obtain the product through technical means from the open channel to remove, survey and map, and analyze. "Purchase" chip program behavior referred by Wang Moumou, does not belong to "reverse engineering" stipulated by law. Wang Moumou proposes the saying to get chip program by reverse engineering has no legal basis.

The case in fact belongs to the "afterwards reverse engineering defense". In the process of reverse engineering, whenever contacting others secret information, the existence of the legitimate reverse engineering will be denied. In practice, to implement reverse engineering, and at the same time, the case contacting secret information is universal. Before the start of the reverse engineering, reverse engineering's implementing people contact the confidential information, and thus looking for considerable information in the public domain, coupled with the product to formulate process of reverse engineering. Whatever contact information way, as long as it's contacted, legitimate reverse engineering will be overturned. Law in every country has specific provision, after one party obtains others' business secrets by unfair means, get legality of the behavior for proposition with reverse engineering, which will not be supported. In this case, the reverse engineering implementation person, after the plaintiff Wang Moumou contacts secret information, it can be illegal behavior of reverse engineering only.

The Article 12 (2) of *Explanations to Several Applicable Law Issues on Cases of Trial of Unfair Civil Competition* of Supreme People's Court has specifically provided: it's not supported for the parties to know others' business secrets by unfair means, claim to get legal acts for reverse engineering. In addition, as a reference, Article 16 of "Opinions on several issues on trial of commercial secrets cases of Jiangsu Supreme People's Court" stipulates: to obtain commercial secrets through reverse engineering, does not constitute a violation of trade secrets. But in addition to the product is get by unfair means. To obtain others' commercial secrets through improper means, to defend for reasons of obtaining afterwards through reverse engineering, should not be supported.

All of thses logics can be suported by comparative study. For example, American Illinois court's judgement: when the defendant uses the plaintiff's secret information, the defendant has reverse engineering ability for publicly available products and cannot deter assuming trade secret theft responsibility. ❶Delaware court's judgement: if others take unfair means to get litigation products, the possibility of legitimate reverse engineering cannot stop the court to award the plaintiff's requests for pre-pleading prohibitions.❷ Ohio court's judgement: even if the plaintiff's business secrets, can be found independently or acquired by reverse engineering, but the court forbids the defendant to use business secrets obtained by

---

❶ ILG Industries, Inc. v. Scott, 273 N. E. 2d 393 (Il. 1971).

❷ Technicon Data Systems Corp v. Curtis 1000, Inc., 224 U. S. P. Q. 286, p. 291 (Del. Chan. Ct. 1984).

breach of confidentiality relationship. ❶

So, does "to buy the cracked chip from others" referred by Wang Moumou belong to "legitimate sources" as the law stipulates? The plaintiff Wang Moumou provides QQ chating records, Everbright Bank account details inquiry and and remittance voucher, to prove its involved chip process has a legitimate source. But Wang Moumou's QQ chatting records are unilateral printout, form of evidence is not in conformity with the statutory requirements. And in content, QQ chat records, Everbright bank account details inquiry and remittance voucher cannot prove that the relationship between true identity of someone cracking so-called chip, and payee's true identity, the specific information of the decoding chip, etc. So these evidence are unable to form fully effective chain of evidence, to prove Wang Moumou's source of the chip is real, effective and legitimate purchase behavior. In addition, the plaintiff Wang Moumou claims to be unable to get "correction chip program" of Yudian Co. 's chip program involved in case, and the precision of correction instrument is got in the way by reading "deviation data" in the memory chip of Yudian Co., and save the application in the plaintiff products. But after reviewing the related inspection report and discussing, the panel also denies correction process Wang Moumou referred to.

In conclusion, the defendant's determination of the plaintiff Wang Moumou's infringement of commercial secrets of the third person, has clear facts, sufficient evidences, so the court hereby supports it. In addition, as Wang Moumou has no legal sources to get involved technology information, whether the field-installed instrument is verified qualified, which will not affect the establishment of the infringement.

V. Significance of this Case

This case is a representative intellectual property administrative cases, invol-

---

❶ Valco Cincinnati, Inc. v. N & D Machining Service, Inc., 492 N. E. 2d 814 (Oh. 1986).

ving trade secret infringement disputes between the plaintiff and the third person civil subject, administrative litigation dispute between administrative counterpart and administrative subject composed of plaintiff and the defendant. In court hearing, all experts and experts appear in court and participate in litigation, so court trial procedure has representativeness. The focus of the case is whether the plaintiff infringes commercial secrets of the third person. Under the premise of "same essence + contact", the court makes legitimacy analysis on how plaintiff get the source of the technology involved in the case, affirms that the plaintiff claims to buy involved "chip technology" from others which is not "reverse engineering" as the law stipulates in our country, finally confirms the municipal administration of industry and commerce's administrative punishment on plaintiff's infringement of the third party's commercial secrets that, has clear facts and sufficient evidence. The judgement has certain reference value.

(Zeng Zhengzhi & Liu Yu)

Study on Xiao Moumou Crime of Counterfeiting Registered Trademark

I. Case Brief

During the period from the year 2010 to 2012, the first defendant, Xiao Moumou produced counterfeiting "SUSHOUWANHUA" Brown Sugar Lollipops in a house located in Shantou, and sold them in Amoy. The registered trademark holder of "SUSHOUWANHUA" is Huang Moumou, who does not authorize Xiao Moumou to use the trademark. The lollipops were tested to be products counterfeiting the registered trademark. Another test run by the Amoy Product Quality Supervision and Inspection Institute indicated the lollipops were in compliance with the hygienic standard for candy. During the period from year 2011 to 2012, the second defendant, Chen Moumou bought 155 bales of the counterfeiting "SUSHOUWANHUA" lollipops from Xiao Moumou, and sold these products.

In August 2012, Xiao Moumou was detained on the charge of selling merchandise under a counterfeited registered trademark, and later on 14 September arrested on the charge of counterfeiting registered trademarks; Chen Moumou was also detained on the charge of selling merchandise under a counterfeited registered trademark and later arrested on the same charge, on the same day of Xiao Moumou's arrest. Therefore, the amount that the Procuratorate raised was exorbitant.

II. Decisions

After Hearing, Siming District People's Court ruled that Xiao Moumou's amount of illegal business operation precedes RMB 1 170 000, which is of particular seriousness, and therefore committed the crime of counterfeiting registered trademarks. The Court sentenced Xiao Moumou a fixed-term of imprisonment of 4 years and 6 months. Chen Moumou, knowingly sold the counterfeiting registered trademarks products, and the sales was over RMB 60 000, which is a relatively large value. The Court sentenced Chen Moumou a fixed-term imprisonment of 6 months, and a fine of RMB 40 000.

III. Key Issues

The key issues of this case are as follows:

Firstly, how to determine the amount of illegal business operation proceeds under the crime of counterfeiting registered trademarks?

Secondly, the relationship between the crimes of counterfeiting registered trademarks and other offenses.

IV. Analysis

A. How to determine the amount of illegal business operation proceeds under the crime of counterfeiting registered trademarks?

According to Article 213 of Criminal Law, punishments vary with the seriousness of circumstances. However, CriminalLaw keeps quiet about how to distinguish "serious circumstances" from "particularly serious circumstances".

The *Interpretation Concerning Some Issues on the Specific Application of Law for Handling Criminal Cases of Infringement upon Intellectual Property Rights* (hereafter "the Interpretation") issued in 2004 by the Supreme People's Court and the Supreme People's Procuratorate offers guidance to that question. According to this interpretation, "serious circumstance" refers to the amount of illegal business operation proceeds is no less than RMB 50 000 or the amount of illegal proceeds is no less than RMB 30 000 , or he/she counterfeits two or more registered trademarks, with the amount of proceeds arising from illegal business operation to be no less than RMB 30 000 or the amount of illegal proceeds to be no less than RMB 20 000 , and "particularly serious circumstance" refers to the amount of illegal business operation proceeds is no less than RMB 250 000 or the amount of illegal proceeds is no less than RMB 150 000 , or he/she counterfeits two or more registered trademarks, with amount of proceeds arising from illegal business operation to be no less than RMB 150 000 or the amount of illegal proceeds to be no less than RMB 100 000 . Accordingly, it's very important to define "proceeds arising from illegal business operation" and "illegal proceeds".

a. The connotation of "proceeds arising from illegal business operation"

There is a process of development in the determination of "proceeds arising from illegal business operation". In the April of 1990, Trademark Office of the State Administration for Industry and Commerce stated its opinion in the reply to the Administration for Industry and Commerce of Fujian Province that the calculation of the amount of proceeds arising from illegal business operation should be divided into three kinds: firstly, if all goods are sold, the sales amount shall be the proceeds arising from illegal business operation; secondly, if the goods are not sold, the total loans purchased the goods shall be the proceeds arising from illegal business operation; thirdly, if the goods are partly sold, the total sold amount plus the loans purchased the unsold goods shall be the proceeds arising from illegal business operation.[1] In 1994, the State Administration for Industry and Commerce issued a notice on the implementation of the Trademark Law. In this notice, the State Administration for Industry and Commerce firstly made it clear that all the goods infringing the trademark shall be included in the determination of the pro-

---

[1] Official Reply of the Trademark Office of the State Administration for Industry and Commerce on the amount of illegal business in trademark infringement cases, in April 12, 1990, the commercial and industrial standard [1990] 7th.

ceeds arising from illegal business operation. Secondly, such calculation shall be the income plus the inventory.❶ Article 12 of the Interpretation includes the value of products manufactured, stored, transported and sold in the actions that infringe intellectual property rights in the connotation of the proceeds arising from illegal business operation.

Opinions also vary among scholars. Some believe that, generally speaking, "all infringing goods operated by the perpetrator, including the sold ones and unsold ones, shall be calculated into the proceeds arising from illegal business operation. For those manufacture and process the infringing goods, the proceeds arising from illegal business operation shall be the sales income plus the actual cost of the inventory; if the actual cost is hard to determine, it shall be calculated by the number of the goods multiplied by the unit sales price; if there is no such unit sales price, the actual cost shall be calculated by the number of the goods and the unit sales price of the same kind of goods."❷ While others hold the view that to treat the business operation as a whole, it is a process of profiting, and thus the proceeds arising from such operation shall be the whole amount invested and gained from a particular operation out of the purpose to make profit. Therefore, proceeds arising from illegal business operation almost equal to sales amount, and strictly speaking it's broader than sales amount.

Based on the business operation nature of counterfeiting registered trademarks, the definition given by the Interpretation is reasonable, which is to include all value produced in the whole process of manufacture, storage, transport and sale the infringing goods, to determine the seriousness the perpetrator's action. For one thing, relying solely on sales amount to determine the seriousness of the crime is not enough, because the seriousness is not reflected by the profit the perpetrator gains, but the damage caused to the legal interest. Even if the perpetrator

---

❶ Circular of the State Administration for Industry and Commerce on Several Issues Concerning the Implementation of the Trademark Law and its Detailed Rules for Implementation, No. 229, 1994, 22, 1994.

❷ Jiang Wei, ed: "Criminal Protection of Intellectual Property", Law Press, 2004 edition, p. 92.

did not profit any, the damage to the legal interest has come true, and the social harmfulness shall not be denied, and thus it cannot be treated as the sole basis for the determination of the seriousness of the crime. As to act of counterfeiting registered trademarks, which is using the same trademarks of others on one's own products, the perpetrator's intention is to have his own products entered into the market and make profit, but when the crime is exposed, the sales status of the infringing goods is uncertain, which means the products may have been sold or not yet sold. In fact, whether sold or not, the legal interest by setting the counterfeiting registered trademarks crime is already damaged, because the as soon as the action is on, the damage is along, and such damage is reflected in every link of such action. For another thing, Article 12 (1) of the Interpretation includes the whole process in the definition of the "proceeds arising from illegal business operation". Thus, the proceeds arising from illegal business operation is broader than sales amount. To use "proceeds arising from illegal business operation" to determine the seriousness of the crime can better reflect the nature of such crime and more reasonable.

b. The calculation of proceeds arising from illegal business operation

In practice, the calculation method of proceeds arising from illegal business operation encountered some problem. Article 12 of the Interpretation provides, the value of the manufactured, stored, transported or unsold infringing products shall be calculated at the marked price, or at the average actual sales price of the infringing products that has been found out. If no price is marked on the infringing products or the actual sales price is unable to be found out, the value shall be calculated at the average market price of the infringed products. However, this standard has caused trouble in practice, for example, in the 2011 *Li Mou Counterfeiting Registered Trademark Case*, the defendant used the registered without authorization from the trademark holder on sweaters. Although the sweaters were no sold, the first trial court calculated the proceeds arising from illegal business operation to be over RMB 40 000 000 and accordingly fined the defense about

RMB 20 000 000. This case is also called the "whopping fine case". After the Inner Mongolia's High People's Court sent bake to the retrial, the first trial court, Ordos Intermediate People's Court investigated and found that the average sales price of the defendant was RMB 100, and he did not intend to sell those sweaters at the tag price, and accordingly calculated the proceeds arising from illegal business operation to be RMB 3 980 000, and amend the fine to RMB 1 990 000.

This whopping fine case brought a lot of thoughts. Some scholars questioned the standards posed by Article 12 of the Interpretation, and believed such standards are flawed and the perpetrators may use the standard to evade his legal sanctions. For example, if two persons manufacture a same brand of trousers, and the middle market price is RMB 300. One of them marked the price at RMB 30, and the other one did not mark a price and the actual sales price could not be determined. According to the standard in the Interpretation, the proceeds arising from illegal business operation for the first person is RMB 30 multiplied by the number of products, and for the second person is RMB 300 multiplied by the number of products, and the result is the same conduct may lead to different legal sanctions.[1] This is unreasonable. The notion of proceeds arising from illegal operation requires comprehensive understanding.

In this case, the Siming District Court calculated the Defense Xiao's illegal business operation proceeds based on solid evidence to be RMB 1 170 000, and took the unsold amount into consideration to give a heavier punishment. It not only satisfied the need to prosecute the crime, but also protected the interests of the defense.

During the trail, the defense counsel claimed that Xiao's crime did not have adverse effect on the community. Can this kind of plea get lighter punishments? From the perspective of legal interests, this kind of plea cannot be established, because there are two legal interests harmed by the crime of counterfeiting regis-

---

[1] Chen Fang: "Counterfeit Trademark Products Illegally Identified the Amount of Business", in Fujian Quality Management, 2005 (5).

tered trademark. One is the administration system of the State's trademarks, and the other is the exclusive right to use registered trademarks. The crime of counterfeiting registered trademarks has already offended these interests and therefore the plea that the products are not in the market cannot render a lighter punishment.

B. Relationships between the Crime of Counterfeiting Registered Trademarks and Other offenses

a. The crime of counterfeiting registered trademarks and the crime of selling merchandise under a counterfeited registered trademark

In this instance, Xiao Moumou was first detained by the police on the charge of selling merchandise under a counterfeited registered trademark and later arrested on the charge of counterfeiting registered trademarks. The two crimes can reflect different stage of the acts of the defense, so how to determine the crime and number of crimes in this case?

The Criminal Law determines the crime on the basis of the legal interests invaded, following the principles of "comprehensive evaluation" and "no repeated evaluation". "The comprehensive evaluation principle refers to the evaluation of the crime shall include all the legal interests invaded by the act", and "no repeated evaluation principle refers to the prohibition on the repeated evaluation on the same legal interest invaded by the same act." To distinguish whether the legal interests invaded are the same, we should consider not only the classification of the criminal law, but also the carrier is the same. The determination of one offense shall comprehensive from the social perspective. There are three situations can be regarded as one offense, the first is that to invade one legal interest the perpetrator performed several acts in sequence; the second is to carry out a number of acts invading the same legal interest; the last one is that the former act makes the legal interest remain in a status of invading and the latter act does not extend such invasion.[1]

---

[1] Zhuang Jing: *Crime Concurrence: Structure and System of Crime Analysis*, Law Press, 2006, pp. 49-66.

The key to distinguish the crime of counterfeiting registered trademark from the crime of selling merchandise under a counterfeited registered trademark is the legal interest that has been harmed. When evaluate a crime, we shall evaluate it comprehensively and non-repeatedly. If the actor uses the same trademark on the same products without authorization from the trademark holder, and then he/it sells the products, there are two offenses involved, one is the crime of counterfeiting registered trademarks and the other is the crime of selling merchandise under a counterfeited registered trademark. Due to the legislative reasons, the legal evaluation of the crime of counterfeiting registered trademarks includes that of the crime of selling merchandise under a counterfeited registered trademark. The crime of counterfeiting registered trademarks can cover both the manufacturing and selling.

In this case, although Xiao Moumou conducted both the manufacturing and the selling and involved two crimes, the legal interests harmed by the latter crime is within the scope of the former, and therefore, it is sufficient and reasonable to sentence Xiao Moumou to only one crime, namely the crime of counterfeiting registered trademarks.

b. The crime of counterfeiting registered trademark and the crime of production and sale of fake or substandard products

The crime of production and sale of fake or substandard products refers to the crime the producer and the seller of the products produce and sale in violation of quality control regulations, and the amount is relatively large. The major difference between the crime of counterfeiting registered trademarks and the crime of production and sale of fake or substandard products is the objects. The objects of the crime of counterfeiting registered trademarks are two folds but the object of the crime of production and sale of fake or substandard products is simple, just the administration system of the State over the quality of commodities, and the focus of the crime is whether the commodities comply with the quality standard. If the products comply with the quality standard, but the use of the trademark on the same products is without authorization, the crime will only be counterfeiting registered trademarks. If the actor produces and sells the products counterfeiting registered trademarks, the two seemly separated conducts are indeed implicated, the counterfeiting is for production and sale, and the punishment will be the one heavier of the two. It is also regulated in the *Notice of the Supreme People's Court, the Supreme People's Procuratorate and the Ministry of Public Security on Issuing the Opinions on Several Issues concerning the Application of Law in Handling Intellectual Property Right Infringement Criminal Cases* that where an actor committing a crime of infringement upon IPR commits a crime of production or sale of counterfeit and inferior commodities concurrently, he shall be convicted and punished for the crime of infringement upon IPR or the crime of production or sale of counterfeit or inferior commodities, whichever is heavier in punishment. ❶

In this case, the counterfeiting lollipops were in compliance with the hygienic standard for candy. Therefore, it is sufficient to sentence Xiao Moumou to one crime of counterfeiting registered trademarks. If these lollipops were not in compliance with the quality standard, the punishment shall be the heavier between the crime of counterfeiting registered trademark and the crime of production and sale of fake and substandard products.

V. Significance of this Case

The amount of proceeds Xiao Moumou produced and sold the counterfeiting "SUSHOUWANHUA" brown sugar lollipops exceeds RMB 1 000 000 , and the lollipops were sold too many districts in the Country including Amoy, and Chen Moumou is one of Xiao Moumou's wholesalers. The Siming District People's Court also accepted civil infringing litigations against Tianmi Co. that the trademark holder of "SUSHOUWANHUA" Huang brought over his registered trademark,

---

❶ Supreme People's Court, Supreme People's Procuratorate, Ministry of Public Security, *Opinions on Several Issues Concerning the Application of Law in Handling Criminal Cases Involving Intellectual Property Rights*, [2011] No. 3.

and found that the sellers had a connection to Xiao Moumou's counterfeiting products. The case reflects the Siming District People's Court's determination in the fight against intellectual property rights.

More importantly, the litigations concerning the registered trademark "SUSHOUWANHUA" are representatives of the integration of civil, criminal and administrative procedures in IPR litigations, and show the strength of the combined civil and criminal methods in fighting against crimes infringing IPR. These years, IPR related cases continue to increase; the parties involved are of diversity, and the parties have huge difficulties in obtaining evidence. The IPR infringing actions are generally hidden and professional, especially in the case of network and computer infringement, the electronic evidences are hard to obtain and store because they are intangible and fragile. The separated mode of civil, criminal and administrative procedures to protect IPR has its defects, like repeated trial over one case and inconsistency in judgments, and it also brings burden to the litigation parties.

Therefore, there shall be an IPR Division to deal with criminal, civil and administrative cases. To centralize the adjudication power in one division can avoid the dispersion of legal protection, to keep the consistency in each procedures, to reduce the litigation costs, and lower the cost of the parties, to enhance efficiency, and protect the legal rights of the parties; the forth is to maintain the authoritativeness, and promote administration, to fight the crimes infringing IPR and play a better role in the warning of the society; and to improve the competence of the judges and to avoid the situation that lacks criminal and administrative judges when the three procedures are separated.

This case was selected to be the Top 10 Cases in Intellectual Property Rights Protection by Fujian Courts.

(Li Yuanyuan & Wang Lingye)

Study on Zhang Moumou Crime of Counterfeiting Registered Trademark

I. Case Brief

Since February 2012, the defendant Zhang Moumou used a house located in Xiang'an District, Amoy, as a production site, and purchased labels with "Jinmen Gaoliang Liquor" Covers, bottles, cartons, bulk liquor and filling machine, in the production of counterfeit Jinmen Gaoliang Liquor and for sales.

On 17 March 2012, while the defendant Zhang Moumou's workers Zhang Moumou is carrying the liquor box to a small truck outside of mentioned above location, the Amoy Municipal Public Security Bureau of the Dadeng border police station to its search and seized many "Jinmen Gaoliang" filling personally by the defendant Zhang Moumou himself.

Jinmen Gaoliang LiquorCo., Ltd. (hereafter "Jinmen Liquor Co.") indicates that the liquor mentioned above is counterfeit products, which is not produced by their company, Amoy Tongan Price Certification Center issued a "price appraisal conclusion report" indicates the seizure of the black 823 "Jinmen Gaoliang Liquor" 1 200 bottles worth a total of RMB 405 600, red 823 "Jinmen Gaoliang Liquor" 1680 bottles worth RMB 567 840, totally worth RMB 973 440.

II. Desisions

After hearing, Siming District People's Court ruled that the defendant Zhang

Moumou is guilty for counterfeiting registered trademarks, sentenced to two years imprisonment and fined RMB 100 000. The seized 3 262 bottles of counterfeit Jinmen Gaoliang Liquor shall be confiscated. The seized fake liquor production line shall be confiscated.

III. Key Issues

The key issues of this case are as follows:

Firstly, whether "Jinmen Gaoliang" (a Taiwan Originated Trademark) should be protected by Trademark Law?

Secondly, whether the defendant commits the crime of counterfeiting registered trademark?

IV. Analysis

A. Whether "Jinmen Gaoliang" (a Taiwan Originated Trademark) should be protected by Trademark Law?

The "territoriality principle" is one of the important principles of trademark law, which means Trademarks are territorial. Historically, the intellectual property rights were originally imperial privilege concessions by the feudal monarchy, can only be exercise in the territory under the jurisdiction of that monarchy. In that origin, when modern countries establishing the trademark legal system, they abide by the principle of sovereignty and protection of the trademark rights is limited to that domestic legislation only, the facts relating to the trademark in one country is not binding to others, that is, the "territoriality principle" of the trademark. This principle is also adopted by the universally recognized international convention on the protection of intellectual property rights, the Paris Convention for the Protection of Industrial Property (hereafter "Paris Convention").

In China, doctrine of registration is taken; one can only obtain a trademark right by applying for registration and approved by authorities. However, after the registration of the trademark, there is still obligation to maintain actual use and continued use of that trademark, otherwise it will constitute a trademark right to be revoked grounds.

The current situation is that Taiwan and Mainland China practices different trademark law. Since trademarks are territorial and need to be registered and approved under the trademark law, whether the Jinmen Gaoliang Liquor trademark is protected in Mainland China is a question need to be asked.

Jinmen Gaoliang Liquor is a well-known Taiwan liquor brand, produce by JinmenLiquor Co., and preparation in 2000, 2004 officially stationed in the mainland market, trademark registration in succession by many trademarks, "Chinese Famous Brand", in 2013 to further expand the trademark registration, the current effective trademarks and pending a total of 149 trademarks.

Trademarks in this case involving Jinmen Gaoliang Liquor are registered in accordance with the Trademark Law and the Trademark Office of the State Council Administration for Industry and Commerce. The trademark registrant shall enjoy the exclusive right to use the trademark and shall be protected by law.

B. Whether the defendant commits the crime of counterfeiting registered trademark?

According to Article 61 of the TRIPs: "Members shall provide for criminal procedures and penalties to be applied at least in cases of willful trademark counterfeiting or copyright piracy on a commercial scale. Remedies available shall include imprisonment and/or monetary fines sufficient to provide a deterrent, consistently with the level of penalties applied for crimes of a corresponding gravity. In appropriate cases, remedies available shall also include the seizure, forfeiture and destruction of the infringing goods and of any materials and implements the predominant use of which has been in the commission of the offence. Members may provide for criminal procedures and penalties to be applied in other cases of infringement of intellectual property rights, in particular where they are committed willfully and on a commercial scale."

The provisions of TRIPs are mandatory; the internal laws of Members shall be in conformity with the minimum standards stipulated in the treaty. Since China is a member of the WTO, it is obliged to comply with TRIPs. Article 61 of TRIPs does not provide that all acts of trademark infringement must be sanctioned by penalties, the normative acts of which are willful trademark counterfeiting, and objectively in commercial scale. The means of sanctions may be a choice of a free sentence, a fine, or both, the point is to provide a sufficient deterrent, in which shows the general idea of TRIPS criminal sanctions is most likely general precautionary theory.

While the internalization of the treaty to domestic law, the protection of criminal law in Trademark Law, the special penalties for trademark law, there are Article 67 of Trademark Law, and Articles 213 to 215 in Criminal Law. Which counterfeiting a registered trademark in this case is more related to Article 213 of Criminal Law: A registered trademark of the same trademark, if the circumstances are serious, shall be sentenced to fixed-term imprisonment of not more than three years or criminal detention, and shall also be sentenced to a fine or a fine; where the circumstances are especially serious, the trademark shall be sentenced to not less than three years Term imprisonment of not more than seven years and a fine. In Article 213 of Criminal Law, the subjective elements of that crime did not expressly, but reference to the TRIPS agreement legislative requirements, also reference to the criminal law Article 15 of negligent crime. The subjective elements of this article should be intentional elements without negligence to meet the means of principle and the principle of proportionality. The commercial scale requirement of the TRIPs, the objective condition of which is to use the same trademark as the registered trademark in the same kind of goods. The circumstances of the case should be analyzed on the basis of the constitutive requirements.

Back to this case:

First of all, Jinmen Gaoliang Liquor is a well-known brand, had been certificated as a national well-known trademark, and practiced as a trademark for years. The defendant in this case practice this well-known alcohol trademark, it is difficult to imagine the practice is due to negligence and ignorance, which is against common sense. Also the defendant had confessed his subjective intent. Confession should not be the only evidence, but supplemented by other indirect, secondary evidence, supported with social common sense to judge, the subject was informed that the subjective intentional, should be no doubt.

Second, the defendant sold Gaoliang liquor, the same as Jinmen Liquor manufactured sold, which in the same category belong to 3301 alcoholic beverages. In this case, the perpetrator Zhang Moumou began to produce fake Jinmen Gaoliang Liquor and sales in February 2012, In March 17, 2012 case was cracked.

The use of trademarks and Jinmen wineries in existing products are the same trademark. The questions are whether the involved trademark is registered and well protected, and what are the trademarks under counterfeiting in specific? To examine the specific infringement status of the trademark, we search from the State Administration for Industry and Commerce Trademark System.

金門高粱酒

Figure 1

This trademark has been applied in July 2002, registered in October 2005, and then after the renewal, extended the exclusive use period until 2024. In accordance with the opinion of the Supreme People's Court, the Supreme People's Procuratorate, and Article 213 of CriminalLaw, the "identical trade mark" refers to a trademark that is identical with the counterfeited registered trademark or that is visually substantially indistinguishable from the counterfeited registered trademark and is sufficiently misleading to the public. The difference between "梁" and "粱" in this case is virtually indistinguishable, sufficiently to mislead the public.

Third, the influence of this case is huge and the commercial value is high, so it is often become the object of infringement. The protection of well-known trademarks should be greater than the common trademark according to the Paris Convention, furthermore that the TRIPs established a principle, the protection can even expand to different category of goods.

Therefore, to meet the subjective intent, the same kind of goods, practicing the same trademark, the circumstances are serious, the conduct is both illegal and punishable, thus the defendant is for sure commit the crime of counterfeiting registered trademarks.

V. Significance of this Case

Counterfeit liquor has its particularities: alcohol commodity price is expensive, high added value; manufacturing of counterfeit liquor is endangering the health of consumers, leaving huge social costs; and it is difficult for consumers to distinguish the counterfeit goods.

These features make liquor counterfeiting an ideal target to counterfeit. Banning trademark infringement can promote the healthy development of enterprises. To ensure that the competition for the goods or services distinguished by the mark is not squeezed. Trademarks carrying the company's goodwill, often also reflects the value of goodwill. The aims are to reduce infringement motive, at the same time to improve the marginal contribution of the value of goodwill, to provide incentives for the sound development of enterprises and promote economic development. And this is a positive case involved with Taiwan trademark rights, which can reward Taiwan related enterprise to registered.

Jinmen Gaoliang Liquor is a well-known brand in Taiwan, also popular in mainland china, because the liquor industry is the higher value-added industries of intellectual property rights, well-known brands prices are often quite different from general brand, some ill-intentioned make use of the high value-added, easy to imitate, in order to obtain huge profits. Fujian in recent years, have been a considerable number of counterfeit Jinmen Gaoliang Liquor. Fake liquor production conditions are poor, endangering the health of consumers. Continuing to increase the protection of intellectual property rights, and strictly implement the law on counterfeit trademark criminals, through strict probation applies to increase the crackdown, effectively safe guarding the legitimate rights and interests of consumers, regulate the market order.

The case was rated as the High Court of Fujian Province in 2014, the typical case of consumer protection.

(Li Yuanyuan & Cao Yujun)

Study on Lin Moumou et al. Crime of Selling Counterfeit Registered Trademark Goods

I. Case Brief

"CONVERSE" is a world famous brand in the area of sports shoes, owned by a American company. From 2009 to 2010, Lin Moumou, Wang Moumou and other eight defendants worked jointly or separately with Xu Mou and "Xiaoli" in Fuzhou and Amoy, by setting up shops in "taobao. com" to sell counterfeit rubber shoes online which were labeled the mark of "CONVERSE", and they rented warehouses to store such goods in Amoy. On 30 August 2010, the police arrested Liu Moumou, Lin Moumou, Lin Moumou, Yan Mou, Yan Mou, Wang Moumou, and seized counterfeit rubber shoes of 81 000 pairs, the value of which reached up to RMB 18 788 574 yuan, including one part of counterfeit shoes carried price tags amounting to RMB 17 830 180, and the rest without price tags amounting to RMB 958 394. The aforementioned shoes were identified as illegal products because of counterfeiting the registered trademark of "CONVERSE". On 7 December 2010, the public security organ arrested the defendant Lin Moumou. On 5 January 2011, the defendant Wang Moumou surrendered voluntarily to the public security organ.

II. Decisions

After hearing the case, the Siming District People's Court held that Lin Moumou, Wang Moumou and other eight defendants knew that the products were counterfeit products tagged with other's well-known trademark without obtaining permission, still did they sell the products jointly or separately in Fuzhou and Amoy through the network and the amount of the counterfeit products totaled RMB 18 788 574. The court ruled that the defendants' committed the crime of selling commodities carrying a counterfeit registered trademark and they were sentenced to fixed-term imprisonment ranging from two years to six years and to be imposed on fine ranging from RMB 100 000 to RMB 3 000 000.

III. Key Issues

The key issues in this case are as follows:

Firstly, how to calculate the value of counterfeit products that had not yet been sold?

Secondly, whether the "appraisal report" issued by the trademark right holder could be adopted as evidence?

IV. Analysis

A. How to calculate the value of counterfeit products that had not yet been sold?

The crime of sale of counterfeit registered trademark of the goods, refers anyone who sells counterfeit registered trademarks of goods, of which the amount of sales reaching the larger amount. One of the problems that must be dealt with in the practice of solving intellectual property infringement and crime is the determination of the amount of crime. The amount of the sold infringing products can be calculated directly on the basis of the actual sales price. However, there is no such sold price for the unsold counterfeits that we have to consider other factors when determining the amount of crime. In fact, the major controversy in the trial process of this case is how to calculate the total amount of the counterfeit rubber shoes, which had not yet been sold. The prosecutor advocated the price should be calculated in accordance with the price tag marked in the boxes; however, the eight defendants held it should be calculated on the minimum sales price, or on the actual average sales price of the products.

a. The criminal amount in the intellectual property cases

In order to handle the criminal amount properly involved in the intellectual property cases, it should be clearly and accurately understood the legal concepts related to the amount of crime in such cases, such as the sales amount, the value of goods, the amount of illegal business, illegal proceeds of crime, etc. These legal concepts which play an important role in the identification and punishment of intellectual property crimes determine the relationship between crime and non crime, this crime and other crime, how penalty shall be applied and so on. Especially, it is a major difficulty for judicial organs to clarify the fuzzy boundaries between the amount of sales, the value of goods and the amount of illegal business in the course of handling intellectual property crimes.

"Sales amount" as prescribed in Article 214 of Criminal Law shall beinterpreted as all the illicit income which has been or can be obtained from sales of the merchandise under a counterfeit registered trademark in accordance with Article 9 of the *Interpretation Concerning Some Issues on the Specific Application of Law for Handling Criminal Cases of Infringement upon Intellectual Property Rights* promulgated by the Supreme People's Court and the Supreme People's Procuratorate in 2004. The "obtained income" refers to the actually received illegal income from selling commodities carrying a counterfeit registered trademark; and the "deserved income" refers to the payment to be obtained from selling counterfeit goods, which has not yet been received.[1]

"The value of goods" has not been provided in the Chinese criminal law. According to Article 2 of the *Interpretation Concerning Some Issues on the Specific Application of Law for Handling Criminal Cases of Production and Sale of Fake or*

---

[1] Liu Xianquan, "Analysis on the Calculation of Crime Value in Intellectual Property Cases", in Legal Science, 2005 (6).

Substandard Commodities promulgated by the Supreme People's Court and the Supreme People's Procuratorate in 2001, that the value of goods consists of the actual sales amount and the value of unsold products. In judicial practice, the seized counterfeit goods haven't been sold in the majority of such cases, and no evidence about sales prices is available to value the sold products, so the judicial organs usually make conviction and punishment based on the calculation of the amount of the unsold products. The basic spirit of the above judicial interpretation is also of reference value for the determination of the sale of counterfeit trademarks.

"Amount of proceeds arising from illegal business operations" refers to the value of the infringing products that the violator has manufactured, stored, transported or sold pursuant to Article 12 of the *Interpretation Concerning Some Issues on the Specific Application of Law for Handling Criminal Cases of Infringement upon Intellectual Property Rights* promulgated by the Supreme People's Court and the Supreme People's Procuratorate in 2004. From the perspective of literal interpretation, the amount of illegal business is the total value of the infringing products involved in the illegal business activities, that is, the amount of the profits of the infringing products that are illegally manufactured, as well as the infringing products the amount of profits, the amount of illegally stored infringing products and the amount of profit from the sale of infringing products.❶ It can be seen that the scope of "illegal business" covers a much wider range than sales.

In sum, the so-called sales amount refers to the amount that has been or can be obtained after the sale of the product. The value of the goods is generally used to calculate the total amount of some products that have not yet been sold, and the amount of illegal business does not include both of the above and other profits.

In this case, the main concern is the sale of goods "value of the amount of" identified. In judicial practice, local courts often refer to the judicial interpretation

---

❶ Hu Yunteng & Liu Ke, "Some Issues of Judicial Interpretations on Criminal Enforcement of Intellectual Property", in Legal Science of China, 2004 (6).

of the amount of illegal business provisions to calculate the value of the amount. According to Article 12 of the *Interpretation Concerning Some Issues on the Specific Application of Law for Handling Criminal Cases of Infringement upon Intellectual Property Rights* promulgated by the Supreme People's Court and the Supreme People's Procuratorate in 2004, in the crime of selling commodities carrying a counterfeit registered trademark, the value of unsold goods shall be calculated in the following sequence: on the marked price or on the average actual sales price of the infringing products that can be found out; or on the average market price of the illicit products.

b. The application order between the marked price and the average actual sales price of the infringing products

As mentionedabove, the value of the infringing products shall be primarily ascertained on the basis of the marked price, or on the average actual sales price of the infringing products that can be found out. But when both kinds of price aforesaid can be affirmed, any law or judicial interpretation does not clarify which one shall have the priority to be applied to calculate the amount of crime. From the logical relationship in literal meaning, either of them can be chosen as the standard calculation method by judicial authorities. Consequently, the difference, existing in the choice of the judgment standard on the calculation of the value of same amount of goods, overvalues or devalues the actual price of the involved counterfeits, as well as results in a wide gap on the conviction and sentencing made towards the same crime.

In fact, it is difficult and complicated, especially when handling online sales crimes, to investigate and collect evidence for verification of the marked price or the actual sales price, for the offender tends to change the price involved frequently. In such cases, the competent judicial office shall appoint a price appraisal agency to verify the average market price of the infringed products to be adopted as legal evidence. Because each case may be under its own special circumstance, the most desirable method to deal with the crime amount is to select a corresponding calculation method according to the details of its case. For instance, there was a similar case judged by Siming District People's Court ruled that Xiao Moumou and Chen Moumou committed the crime of selling merchandise under a faked registered trademark. Since no marked price in the case could be collected, the value of the unsold goods was verified based on the average actual sales price.❶ On the other hand, the span of sales time was considerably long and the range of sales price was substantially wide, thus it applied the average annual sales price as the calculation basis, which was also in line with the objective situation that case and reflected the flexibility and adaptability of courts' judgment.

In this case, the defenders in this case hereto also held that the actual sales price (ranging from RMB 40 to RMB 80 for each pair of shoes) should be exclusively used for calculation instead of the marked price (ranging from RMB 265 to RMB 295 for each pair of shoes) in the shoes' boxes, as the marked price was not the actual reference price for sales, which were printed in the boxes aimed at mixing the counterfeits with the genuine products. From the point of containment of infringement, increase the protection of intellectual property rights point of view, if the behavior of people to avoid punishment, deliberately counterfeit goods price is very low, and its actual sales price is often higher, according to the price of the crime may be light the price of the act. Calculating the value of the goods at a higher actual selling price reflects the severity of the criminal sanctions and is conducive to counterfeiting. However, the defendants did not provide such actual evidence to prove the specific average sales price of the infringing products involved that the court could not agree their objection and ultimately adopted the marked price for calculation. Calculating the value of the unsold counterfeits based on marked price sets a benchmark and makes a great significance for fighting against such criminal behaviors. Taking the special background and social harm of this case into consideration, such judgment is more rigid in applying the rules.

---

❶ (2013) Si Xingchu No. 766.

c. Conviction and sentencing for the case where the counterfeits are unsold or partly sold

In this case, the offenders, knowingly selling merchandise under a faked trademark with a relatively large sales volume (the value of sold counterfeits was RMB 1 009 079 and the value of sold counterfeits was RMB 18 788 574), constituted an accomplished crime and an attempted crime simultaneously. They shall be sentenced to the severer punishment under an accomplished crime or an attempted crime, as provided in Article 8 of *Opinions on Several Issues concerning the Application of Law in Handling Intellectual Property Right Infringement Criminal Cases* formulated in 2011, that if the sales amount and the value of unsold merchandise fall within different statutory penalty ranges or fall within the same range of statutory penalty, the offenders shall be heavily punished based on the circumstances within the range of the heavier statutory penalty or within the same range of statutory penalty. Therefore, Siming District People's Court made the judgment that the defendants committed the crime of (attempted) sale of merchandise under a counterfeit registered trademark and they were imposed on lenient or mitigated punishment.

B. Whether the appraisal opinion on the authenticity of the goods involved issued by trademark right holder could be adopted as evidence?

It was appraised by the right holder of "CONVERSE" trademark that the rubber shoes involved were counterfeits which carried the registered trademark of "CONVERSE". But the defenders maintained that the "appraisal opinion" aforesaid is a victim statement rather than an expert opinion. Now we have to discuss whether such "appraisal opinion" on the authenticity of the goods involved issued by trademark right holder could be adopted as expert opinion or victim's statement.

a. The evidence attribute of the "appraisal opinion" provided by the involved right holder

Generally speaking, the Appraisal Opinion, also "Expert Opinion" or "Expert Testimony" in judicial proceedings, is raised by judicial appraiser, with the aim of distinguishing and estimating technical problem involved in the specific case by the use of scientific and technical expertise.

As provided in judicial interpretation, when handling intellectual property right infringement criminal cases, public security organs, People's procuratorates and People's Courts shall authorize qualified appraisal institutions recognized by the State to conduct necessary appraisal.❶ The appraisal organization entrusted by the judicial organ is in the neutral status that shall have no interest with the victim or the accused party and its appraisal opinion shall have no subjective bias. However, according to the normative document issued by the Trademark Office, the trademark registrant may also be entrusted to issue the "appraisal opinion" issued, which also may be adopted as evidence.❷

The appraiser in the proceedings shall have no interest to the case involved. Strictly speaking, the "appraisal opinion" issued by the entrusted trademark registrant shall fall into the range of victim statement provided by the criminal victim to Police Department, or People's Procuratorate, or People's Court, detailed on criminal behavior about infringing victim's rights and other circumstances. Victim statement and appraisal opinion belong to verbal evidence, both existing in the form of human statements. The difference between them is mainly three points: first, the victim statement is irreplaceable, but the appraisal opinion can be replaced; second, the victim statement is biased, but the latter is neutral.❸ Besides, in the criminal cases of infringing trademark rights, the trademark right

---

❶ Article 3 of *Opinions on Several Issues concerning the Application of Law in Handling Intellectual Property Right Infringement Criminal Cases* formulated in 2011.

❷ "*The reply on the relevant issues on the identification on the counterfeit registered trademark and logo*" issued by Trademark Office mentioned that in the investigation of trademark violations, the industrial and commercial administrative authorities may entrust the trademark registrant to carry out the appraisal on the counterfeit registered trademark goods and trademark involved. The trademark registrant shall issue a written appraisal opinion, and bear the corresponding legal responsibility. If the appraised party has no contrary evidence to overturn the conclusion of the appraisal, the administrative authority for industry and commerce shall adopt the appraisal conclusion as evidence.

❸ Tang Zhen, "Evidence Attributes and Their Review of the Authenticity of Commodity Authentic", in People's Judicial Practice, 2013 (6).

holder is usually in the victim status and his opinion on the authenticity of counterfeit goods is a victim statement because its issue needs no appraisal qualification.

In practice, it is also opposed by defendant that the trademark right holder does not satisfy the qualification to issue an appraisal opinion because the right holder is on the side of the interested party. There is no doubt that the basis of such defense is an objective reality. However, it cannot exclude the proof effectiveness of the "appraisal opinion". In another word, although the "appraisal opinion" provided by right holder cannot be used as Expert Opinion, it can be adopted as victim statement. For example, in "Gu Mou, Zhang Moumou sale of counterfeit registered trademark of goods crime appeal case", the Shanghai First Intermediate People's Court ruled that the victim's agent Chen Moumou issued by the written "identification of the statement" is not evidence of criminal proceedings in the identification Opinion, its content for the identification of the victim unit, the evidence attributes should be classified in the evidence of criminal proceedings in the victim statement.[1]

b. The proof power of the "appraisal opinion" issued by the involved right holder

As we know above, the "appraisal opinion" issued by the right holder shall have the proof effectiveness, unless the defendant has adverse evidence to overturn it. In order to protect the trademark rights from being infringed, right holders tends to invest large maintenance costs, including technical factors, which merely mastered by themselves. Meanwhile, right holders know more about their goods and they is more sensitive to counterfeit goods, therefore, it is convenient and easy for them to carry out the appraisal activity, and certainly the time and costs of judicial appraisal can be reduced.

However, itcannot be guaranteed that the "appraisal opinion" issued by the trademark owner is neutral and accurate, since the objective existence of his status

---

[1] (2012) Hu Yizhong Xing Zhi Zhong No. 3.

of interested party may have a negative impact on the proof effectiveness. Confronted with such risk, a comprehensive method would be considered without question that the "appraisal opinion" should be combined with other evidence to ascertain relevant facts. Considering of the strained relationship between victim and suspect, the judicial authorities shall combine "appraisal opinion" with other evidence to examine its proof power, and when there is no contradiction or undone questions between all the relevant evidence to clarify the case fact, can it be used as a legal testimony for deciding the case involved.

In this case, except the "appraisal opinion" issued by the trademark rights holder, there were other expert opinions (such as The Judicial Appraisal and Inspection Report produced by Fujian Center for Forensic Expertise, Special Auditing Report issued by an accounting firm, Inspection Report provided by Products Quality Supervision and Inspection Institute of Amoy City), other documentary evidence, material evidence, witness testimony and so on. After comprehensive analysis, the People's Court found that the contents of all the evidence point to the same fact that the defendants in this case did sell faked goods under the registered trademark of "CONVERSE" and it enhanced the effectiveness of the aforesaid "appraisal opinion".

V. Significance of this Case

Fujian Province is the world's major footwear brand OEM production base, with thousands of shoe-making enterprises; products are sold around the world. However, in recent years, some areas of Fujian imitation of foreign high-end rubber products, frequent cases, damage the legitimate rights and interests of trademark owners, disrupting the market order, but also against the consumer's right to know and fair trade rights. It is a realistic requirement to purify the market environment and demonstrate the strength and determination of intellectual property rights protection in Fujian.

The case is complex, evidence is difficult, and the fight is extremely difficult. On the one hand, the case involved counterfeit "CONVERSE" trademarks fake shoes products are also high imitation shoes, in the trial process by the Amoy City product quality supervision and inspection identified, in line with the standards of qualified products. So the case involved in the illegal behavior is much hidden. On the other hand, the case involves a wide range of regional, involving a large number of people, Fujian Province is by far the largest network sales fake shoes, fake shoes production involving Putian, Wuping and other places, the scope of sales are all over the country.

As to the application of the law, the case reflects the Siming District People's Court to vigorously crack down on the sale of fake goods sales determination. In particular, the handling of the calculation method of the value of the commodity value of the counterfeit registered trademark which has not yet been sold in this case, and the resolution of the authenticity problem in the case of intellectual property crime have a common reference significance to the similar case.

Because of the significant practical significance of this case, the verdict has been selected "Top 10 Cases of Combating with Infringement of Intellectual Property Crimes in 2012" by Supreme People's Procuratorate, with national demonstrative influence.

(Liu Defen & Tian Shuangli)

Study on Ye Mou, Zhang Moumou Crime of Selling Counterfeit Registered Trademark Goods

I. Case Brief

In June 2013, the defendant Zhang Moumou was entrusted by Lin Moumou to purchase a number of Guizhou Maotai Liquors. In order to seek illegal precedes, the defendant Zhang Moumou agreed the idea proposed by Ye Mou that Ye Mou bought the liquors labeled "MOUTAI" logo for 20 pieces containing 240 bottles with the price of RMB 240 per bottle. Then Zhang Moumou resold these liquors to Lin Moumou with the price of RMB 930 per bottle. On 12 June 2013, the police seized the liquors when Ye Mou transported them to the Amoy Gaoqi International Airport. After being identified by the Kweichow Maotai Co., Ltd., the liquors involved were faked goods under the counterfeit registered trademark of "MOUTAI", the market retail price of which was RMB 999 per bottle. On 25 June, the police found Zhang Moumou and Ye Mou in Guiyang of Guizhou Province and they both confessed to their behavior of the sales of the counterfeit Maotai liquors. Upon return to Amoy accompanied with police officers, they were arrested on 28 June 2013. After identification, the liquors involved satisfied the national food hygiene standards.

II. Decisions

After hearing, Siming District People's Court held that the defendants Ye

Mou, Zhang Moumou knew that the liquors were counterfeits tagged with other's well-known trademark without obtaining permission, still did they sell the products and the sales amount reached up to RMB 223 200, thus they constituted the crime of selling commodities bearing a counterfeit registered trademark. The defendant Ye Mou was the crime intent author and the organizer of supplying the liquors. Meanwhile, the defendant Zhang Moumou knew the products involved were counterfeits; still did he actively contact and negotiate with the buyer about the sales price. Therefore, the two defendants played the equivalent function in this joint crime. The crime did not succeed for the causes beyond their will, so the two defendants were given a lighter or mitigated punishment according to the provisions of the law on attempted crime. Given that the two defendants truthfully confessed their crime and voluntarily pleaded guilty upon appearance in court, and the faked products hadn't been poured into society but all been seized, lenient punishment may be casted to the defendants. In summary, the court decided to punish the two defendants leniently. The defendant Ye Mou was sentenced to a fixed-term imprisonment of one year and four months, and is fined RMB 100 000. The defendant Zhang Moumou was sentenced to a fixed-term imprisonment of one year and two months, and be fined RMB 8 000. The counterfeit liquors labeled "MOUTAI" trademark were confiscated and destroyed.

III. Key Issues

The key issues in this case are as follows:

Firstly, which of crime did the defendants' behavior commit?

Secondly, whether the defendants constituted an accomplished crime or an attempted crime?

IV. Analysis

A. Which of crime did the defendants' behavior commit?

The packaging, anti-counterfeit marking, bottle appearance and even the taste of these highly counterfeited Maotai liquors were almost the same as authentic Maotai goods. The defendants bought these counterfeits with low price and sold them with high price. The key issue is whether there behaviors constituted the crime of manufacturing or selling fake and substandard products, or the crime of selling commodities under a counterfeit registered trademark?

Any producer or seller, who mixes up or adulterates products, passes fake imitations for genuine, sells seconds at best quality price, or passes unqualified products as qualified ones, with a sale amount of not less than RMB 50,000 violating state laws and regulations concerning supervision and administration for products quality and safety, commits the crime of manufacturing or selling fake and substandard products. Knowingly selling merchandise under a faked trademark with a relatively large sales volume violating trademark management laws and regulations also constitutes a crime.

From a conceptual point of view, the connotation and extension of the above-mentioned two crimes seem to be far from each other. However, in the judicial practice, the two crimes tend to exist in the same case under a form of cross competition, and confuse courts to make different judgments. In view of this situation, to clarify the boundaries of the two crimes is of great importance in theory and in practice.

a. The distinction between the two crimes

There is a clear distinction between the two crimes in their composition.

Firstly, they impair different legal interests. The crime of selling goods under a counterfeit registered trademark breaks the trademark management system of the State and damages the exclusive rights of the trademark owner, as well as infringes the legitimate interests of the consumers, and rights of the trademark owner are particularly protected according to the jurisprudential base of this crime. Yet the offense of production and sales of fake and substandard products disorders the national product quality supervision and management system as well as impairs the legitimate rights and interests of consumers.

Secondly, their harmful behaviors are different. The offense of selling commodities under a counterfeit registered trademark is the crime by which the offender knowingly sells fake goods under other's registered trademark without obtaining permission. But the crime of production and sales of fake and substandard products mainly regulates the situation that the quality of goods does not meet the original product standards or industry standards, and it is not necessary to counterfeit other's trademark.

b. Overlapping and competing of the two crimes

Specifically, the goods counterfeiting a registered trademark can be divided into two types: counterfeit but not substandard, counterfeit and substandard. The substandard products also may be divided into two kinds: substandard but not counterfeit; counterfeit and substandard. "Counterfeit but not substandard" refers to the fake products sold under a counterfeit registered trademark satisfy the requirements for performance and quality, therefore, if selling aforesaid products constitutes a crime, the perpetrator merely shall be judged to commit the crime of selling goods under a counterfeit registered trademark. "Substandard but not counterfeit" means the goods are unqualified but they do not impersonate other's registered trademark rights, and if the amount of sales of such goods reaches the statutory criterion of crime, the offender shall be identified to constitute the crime of selling fake and substandard products. However, if the products sold by the perpetrator are "counterfeit and substandard", in other words, the goods not only counterfeit other's registered trademark, but also they are fake and substandard products, in which case it would fall into the situation of overlapping and competing between the two crimes.

Theoretical circles have two views on the relationship of these two crimes.

Some scholars believe that there is an inherent legal relationship between the crime of selling goods under a counterfeit registered trademark and the crime of producing and selling fake and substandard commodities, which calls "the overlapping of law articles". To be more specific, no matter whether a case occurs or not, the actual existence of the coincidence of the legal provisions on different crimes can be ascertained based on law articles.❶ That is to say, even if there is no crime, according to Criminal Law, the behavior of producing and selling counterfeit goods may also infringes other's registered trademark simultaneously, and conversely, the goods sold under a counterfeit registered trademark may also be fake and substandard products. As a result, the same act can be evaluated by two articles of law complying with the constituent elements of the two crimes. To handle this coincidence, it should apply the principle that severe law is prior to the light law.

Meanwhile, other scholars hold that the relationship of the two crimes shall apply the theory of "imaginative jointer of offenses", and the sales of "fake and substandard" goods is an act violating two crimes, which shall be punished based on the principle of "severe law is prior to light law". There is no necessary overlap or cross-correlation between the two articles about the two crimes hereto, because the counterfeit goods sold under others registered trademark may or may not be substandard; the production and sale of fake and substandard goods may or may not impersonate another person's registered trademark. However, the sales of "fake and substandard" products is in line with the theory of "imaginative jointer of offenses", that is, it is the occurrence of the unlawful act rather than the internal link between the law articles that is the premise of the connection between the two crimes.

In reality, it is even thought that it is not necessary to strictly distinguish the two theories "the overlapping of law articles" and "imaginative jointer of offenses".❷ If we take the purpose of criminal conviction and sentencing into account first, to give a comprehensive assessment of illegal facts, a corresponding responsibility and a suiting punishment to a crime, the complex and fuzzy relationship

---

❶ Gao Mingxuan ed., *Issues on Criminal Law*, High Education Press, 2006 ed., p. 384.

❷ Chen Hongbing, "Unnecessary of Disguising the Overlapping of Articles from Imaginative Jointer", in Tsinghua Legal Science, 2012 (6).

between the two theories or crimes does not make it difficult for courts to handle cases, because both theories eventually apply the principle of "severe law is prior to light law" to deal with cases. Besides, it is provided in judicial interpretation that, committing the crime of producing and selling fake and substandard commodities, simultaneously constituting the crime of infringement of intellectual property rights, or the crime of illegal business operation or others, shall be convicted and punished based on the heavier one in accordance with Article 2 of the *Interpretation Concerning Some Issues on the Specific Application of Law for Handling Criminal Cases of Production and Sale of Fake or Substandard Commodities* promulgated by of the Supreme People's Court and the Supreme People's Procuratorate in 2001. As we can see, the interpretation does not specify the theory it applies admittedly, but it can solve practical problems without violating the basic principles of criminal law.

Back to this case, the defendants sold the counterfeit liquors and infringed the exclusive right of other's registered trademark. And the liquors involved satisfied the national food hygiene standards, so it is appropriate that the Procuratorate and the Court identified the defendants' behavior as the crime of selling goods under a counterfeit registered trademark.

B. Whether thedefendants constituted an accomplished crime or an attempted crime?

In the preparation process for delivery, all the liquors involvedwere seized by the police officers when being transported through Amoy Gaoqi International Airport. It followed another issue involved in this case that whether the defendants' conducts constituted a completed crime or an attempted crime.

Amount-related Offense refers to that the statutory amount shallbe the quantitative criteria of a constituent element of a crime. The crime of selling goods under a counterfeit registered trademark is a typical amount-related offense, and the degree of harmfulness incurred by the crime to society depends on the amount of the crime. At present, there is an argument about whether the amount-related offense may be under the circumstance of being attempted. It is of great importance to handle this issue.

a. Whether the amount-related offense may be under the circumstance of being attempted

There are several theories on this question.

The first kind of view is the theory of "negativism", that is, there exists no status of being attempted in the amount-related offense. The theoretical basis of this view is that the constitutive elements stipulated in the sub-rules of criminal law are the conditions for the establishment of crime, not the accomplishment of crime. Therefore, if the harmful consequence as one of the constitutive element of a crime provided in the sub-rules of criminal law doesn't occur in the case related to, the suspect (s) involved shall not be deemed to commit a crime, of course, not to mention constituting an attempted crime.[1] For example, in the case of the crime of selling goods under a counterfeited registered trademark with a relatively large sales volume, scholars, who support the theory of "negativism", believe that the sales amount only exists in the circumstances where the fake products have already been sold. If the relevant commodities have not been sold or the sales amount has not reached the legal amount standard, this situation is not a crime, of course, not an attempted crime. However, this view cannot distinguish the amount-related offense focusing on the behavior from the amount-related offense focusing on the consequence, and it thought that the statutory amount as the constituent element of the amount-related offense merely refers to the requirement for the amount-related offense focusing on the consequence, excluding the amount-related offense focusing on the behavior. However, in the case of selling goods under a counterfeit registered trademark, for instance, although the counterfeit goods have not been successfully sold and thus there is no actual sales amount, we could not ignore the infringement on social interests incurred by the preparation act.

---

[1] Zhang Wei, "Research on Amount Crime", in Journal of Criminal Law Study in China, 2010 (3).

Another view is the theory of "affirmation", that is, the amount-related offense may be under the circumstance of being attempted. This view is based on our traditional criminal law theory that the constitutive elements stipulated in the sub-rules of criminal law are the conditions for the accomplishment of crime. The actual occurrence of the statutory amount is one of the constituent elements of crime and it means the completion of crime, but if the amount of crime does not satisfy the statutory criteria, it constitutes the attempted crime. Nevertheless, "affirmation" theory enlarges the scope of attempted crime and confuses the two concepts of "attempted conduct" and "attempted crime", because the social harms incurred by the amount involved in some cases have not yet reached the degree to be punished criminally.

It is also maintained that the theory of "eclecticism" shall be the most reasonable viewpoint. This theory has the same foundation with the "negativism" that the sub-rules of criminal law are stipulated based on the completion of crime. The amount-related offense can be divided into two types: focusing on the crime consequence and focusing on the crime behavior. First, the amount-related offense focusing on the crime consequence shall be satisfied with the constituent element that the value of the products involved reaches the statutory criterion, and if there are enough amounts involved, it constitutes a completed crime; if not, it is not a completed or an attempted crime. The amount of the actual loss and the amount of illicit income are two typical requirements for the amount-related offense focusing on the crime consequence. For example, the crime of sell pirated goods refers to an offender knowingly sells the duplicate works for the purpose of reaping profits, and thus gains a huge amount of illicit income. Second, the amount-related offense focusing on the crime behavior exist both completed and attempted status. If the illegal act has resulted in the basic harmful consequence as provided in criminal law, it constitutes the accomplishment of a crime, however, if the basic harmful consequence does not occur due to the reasons beyond the offender's will but the amount involved reaches the red line to be convicted, it shall be identified as an attempted crime.❶ Compared the illicit income in the crime of selling pirated goods with the sales amount in the crime of selling products under a counterfeit registered trademark, the former shall target to the total amount gained by the offender, but the latter shall focus on the total amount of goods which have been sold or are to be sold and the amount thereof includes the parts which have been gained and can be obtained. So, based on the theory of "eclecticism", the amount-related offense exist attempted status.

b. The amount criterion of being attempted status in the crime of selling products under a counterfeit registered trademark

In general, the amount criterion of conviction in the amount-related offense focusing on the behavior should be applied either to accomplished crime or attempted crime. In other words, regardless of whether the criminal act is completed or just attempted, as long as the crime amount involved satisfies the statutory criterion of conviction, the perpetrator (s) shall be investigated for criminal responsibility. Certainly, there should be difference in the treatment of penalty between the completed crime and attempted crime, that is, an offender who attempts to commit a crime may, in comparison with one who completed the same crime, be given a lighter or mitigated punishment.

However, not all attempted acts should be punished, since the establishment of crime must meet the condition that the illegal act leads to serious social harm. Chinese criminal law upholds the tradition that "to punish the completed crime is a principle and to punish the attempted crime is an exception", so the attempted act shall only be punished criminally in exceptional circumstances. Otherwise, it is understood that the penalty imposed on the attempted crime is lighter, in consideration of the penalty configuration of the amount-related offense in our criminal law. The penalty on amount-related offense is mostly not more than three years of fixed-term imprisonment, and the maximum statutory sentence less than

---

❶ Liu Zhixiong, "A New Probe into Some Problems of Amount Crime", in Legal and Business Research, 2005 (6).

three years imprisonment is usually considered as a misdemeanor. As the social harm incurred by the misdemeanor is relatively minor, it should be under control to push the attempted state of misdemeanor into the scope of being penalty. If neither does the amount of crime under attempted state reach a large criterion nor doer it pose a threat to legitimate rights and interests within the meaning of criminal law, it shall apply the provision of Article 13 of the Criminal Law that if the circumstances are clearly minor and the harm is not heavy, it could not be deemed as crime and shall be regulated by administrative measures.

It is provided in *Opinions on Several Issues concerning the Application of Law in Handling Intellectual Property Right Infringement Criminal Cases* (hereafter "*Opinions*") promulgated in 2011 that whoever knowingly sells merchandise with counterfeit registered trademarks and falls under any of the following circumstances shall be convicted of and punished for the crime of (attempted) sale of merchandise with counterfeit registered trademarks:

1) Merchandise with counterfeit registered trademarks has not been sold, with a value of RMB 150 000 or more; or

2) Merchandise with counterfeit registered trademarks has been partly sold, with sales amount of less thanRMB 50 000, but the total value of the sold and unsold merchandise with counterfeit registered trademarks is RMB 150 000 or more.

As we can see, on the one hand, it is affirmed in the *Opinions* that the crime of selling goods under a counterfeit registered trademark can be under attempted state, not violating the general provisions on the attempted crime and the spirit of strictness. On the other hand, in order to limit the scope of crime, the amount criterion set on the attempted crime is raised from the standard of RMB 50 000 (it is also the amount criterion of the accomplished crime) to RMB 150 000, which reflects the spirit of leniency and the restraining principle of criminal law.[1]

c. The determination of "sale" in the crime of selling commodities with a

---

[1] Li Xiaojun, "An Analysis of the Disputes over the Attempts of the Crime of Selling Fake Registered Trademarks", in Intellectual Property, 2014 (11).

counterfeit registered trademark

When affirming the discontinuation of crime, we should firstly make it clear that whether the perpetrator had commenced implementing a crime, and then discuss the amount of crime involved. If the perpetrator commenced and completed the act of selling, with sales amount reaching RMB 50 000, he shall be deemed to commit a completed crime; if the perpetrator commenced selling counterfeit commodities but did not complete the sales for the reasons beyond his will, with the value of illicit goods reaching RMB 150 000, he shall be deemed to commit an attempted crime. The main objective performance of this crime is selling counterfeit commodities, and only after clarifying the behavior of selling can we accurately find whether the perpetrator commenced implementing the crime involved in specific cases.

Sales in the meaning of this crime is that the ownership of the products under a counterfeit registered trademark are transferred with payment, including the procedure of buying and selling in the form of wholesale, retail, sales agency and so on. Some people believe that specific buyer and seller simultaneously participating in a transaction is a prerequisite for illicit sale. For the reason that the behavior of selling counterfeit goods is particularly emphasized and punished by the criminal law and the behavior of simply purchase of the counterfeit goods which have not yet been sold shall merely be regulated byadministrative sanction, any activity performed by the seller before the appearance of a buyer in order to achieve the sale of the goods can only be deemed as preparatory steps for the sale. It is only when the seller finds purchasers can the commencement of the crime being determined. However, other people hold that the sale in the meaning of this crime covers the whole process from buying to selling counterfeit goods. That is to say, the purchase of infringing goods for the purpose of selling and reaping profits is the commencement of crime, and the completion of the delivery of goods means the accomplishment of crime.

It is debatable to insist that when the offender finds a buyer the crime begins.

According to this article, when the offender knowingly buys the infringing goods the crime begins. Although the goods aforesaid have not yet been sold in time, we cannot ignore the social harm incurred by the offender's act, indulging the illicit behavior of buying counterfeit products with the intention of selling and reaping profits. Meanwhile, in order to avoid enlarging the control scope of criminal law, if the amount of the unsold goods has not reached the criminal statutory standard, it can be regulated by administrative means; if the amount reaches the criminal standard, which may result in social harm, it shall be sanctioned by criminal law. This viewpoint is in line with Chinese criminal judicial interpretation. It is provided that although the counterfeit goods have not yet been sold, as long as the value thereof reaches up to RMB 150 000, the offender shall be deemed to commit an attempted crime.

As to the completion of the sales behavior in this crime, it is generally believed that when the counterfeit commodities have been sold and the ownership thereof has been delivered, as well as the actual sales amount meets the statutory criterion, the crime finishes. On the contrary, where the goods have not yet been delivered and ownership thereof has not yet been transferred, the counterfeits being unsold, it shall be identified as an attempted crime.

In this case, although after buying infringing goods the defendants concluded a purchase agreement upon sales price and transport means of the counterfeit Maotai Liquor with a specific buyer, neither the payment nor the delivery of the goods has been accomplished. What's more, the public security organ had seized all the infringing goods. The sale had not been completed and legal interests related thereto had not been actually or substantially prejudiced, so the court made a judgment that the defendants committed the attempted crime of selling commodities under a counterfeit registered trademark.

V. Significance of this Case

In judicial practice, the crime of selling goods under a counterfeit registered trademark accounts for roughly half of the total number of intellectual property crimes, and manufacturing and selling counterfeit wine is one of the important disaster area.

The vulnerable trademarks on wine aredomestic well – know brands like "Maotai", "Wuliangye", as well as some imported wine brands such as Martell, Blue Ribbon and so on. Manufacturing and selling counterfeit wines even have become a hidden rule in food and drink industry, which are endangering consumers' health tremendously. The trial of this case is of great significance to combat such criminal activities and to protect the legitimate rights and interests of trademark right holders and consumers.

In this case, Siming People's Court not only properly clears up the confusion on the constitution and distinction between accomplished crime and attempted crime of selling goods under a counterfeit registered trademark, but also helps to unify the judgment standard and provide some instructions to similar cases. This case was elected as a classic judiciad case of consumer protection in Fujian Province in 2016.

(Lin Hong & Tian Shuangli)